WILLIAM CARLOS WILLIAMS
AND JAMES LAUGHLIN

William Carlos Williams

A N D

James Laughlin

/·/

SELECTED LETTERS

EDITED BY HUGH WITEMEYER

W · W · N O R T O N & C O M P A N Y

N E W Y O R K   L O N D O N

Copyright © 1989 by James Laughlin
Copyright © 1989 by the Estate of William Carlos Williams
All rights reserved.
Published simultaneously in Canada
by Penguin Books Canada Ltd.,
2801 John Street, Markham, Ontario L3R 1B4.
Printed in the United States of America.
The text of this book is composed in
11.5/13 Bembo (Linotron 202),
with display type set in ITC Garamond Book Condensed.
Composition and manufacturing by The Maple-Vail Book
Manufacturing Group.
Book design by Margaret M. Wagner.
Ornament by Deborah Pease.

First Edition

Library of Congress Cataloging-in-Publication Data

Williams, William Carlos, 1883–1963.
William Carlos Williams and James Laughlin :
selected letters /
edited by Hugh Witemeyer. —1st ed.
p.   cm.
Includes index.
1. Williams, William Carlos, 1883–1963—Correspondence.
2. Laughlin, James, 1914–   —Correspondence.
3. Poets, American—20th century—Correspondence.
4. Publishers and
publishing—United States—Correspondence.
I. Laughlin, James,
1914–   . II. Witemeyer, Hugh.   III. Title.
PS3545.I544Z485   1989
811'.52—dc19
[B]   88–39376

ISBN 0-393-02682-5

W. W. Norton & Company, Inc.
500 Fifth Avenue, New York, N.Y. 10110
W. W. Norton & Company, Ltd.
37 Great Russell Street, London WC1B 3NU
1 2 3 4 5 6 7 8 9 0

CONTENTS

INTRODUCTION

The correspondence of William Carlos Williams (1883–1963) and James Laughlin (1914–) began in December 1933. Laughlin, then in his second year at Harvard University, had been elected to the editorial board of the student literary magazine, the *Advocate*. In this capacity, he wrote to ask Williams for a contribution and for advice about other outlets for new writing. Already a devotee of modern literature and an aspiring free-verse poet, Laughlin had been introduced to the work of Ezra Pound (1885–1972) and his peers by the poet and translator Dudley Fitts, a master from 1927 to 1941 at the Choate School, in Wallingford, Connecticut. When Laughlin visited Pound in Rapallo, Italy, in the last week of August 1933, he was encouraged to contact Pound's longtime friend, "Doc" Williams of 9 Ridge Road, Rutherford, New Jersey. Williams took a month to answer the young man's letter (now lost) and then persisted in misspelling the surname of his correspondent as "Loughlin." More auspiciously, he sent an essay that appeared in the *Advocate* for February 1934. Thus began the relationship between an author and a publisher whose places in American literary history are assured.

In February 1934 Laughlin took a leave of absence from Harvard. Reacting against the business orientation of his prominent family, partners since 1856 in the Jones and Laughlin Steel Corporation of Pittsburgh, Pennsylvania, the restless nineteen-year-old set off for Europe at the beginning of July. After visiting England, Germany, Austria, and Switzerland, he traveled in August to Bilignin near Belley in France, where he stayed with Gertrude Stein and Alice B. Toklas and wrote press releases for Stein's impending American tour. Following a sojourn in Paris, Laughlin went in November to Rapallo, where for six or seven weeks he attended the "Ezuversity," a sort of informal seminar that had gathered around Pound. The young poet showed his work to the master, who, after due consideration, suggested that he could best serve the cause of literature by becoming a publisher.

Upon returning to the United States, Laughlin paid his first visit to Williams in September 1935. They got along well, and Williams gave his caller a short story entitled "A Face of Stone" for the December issue of the *Harvard Advocate*. At Pound's instigation, Laughlin had also been invited to edit a literary page for *New Democracy,* a Social Credit magazine founded by Gorham Munson and others and published in New York. Williams, an ardent convert to Social Credit during the Depression (as was Laughlin), had already contributed several items to Munson's journal. He gave Laughlin a book review and two poems for the literary page, which was called "New Directions."

That name carried over to the small publishing company which Laughlin started in 1936. His aunt and father generously backed the enterprise. Mrs. Leila Carlisle housed it in an outbuilding on her country estate near Norfolk, Connecticut; and Henry

Hughart Laughlin capitalized it with frequent loans and gifts. The first book to carry the imprint of the fledgling company was *New Directions in Prose and Poetry 1936,* an anthology of experimental writing which contained a poem, a short story, and an essay by Williams. Laughlin's long-range strategy was to build his list upon a foundation of works by Williams and Pound, adding new titles and authors as they came on the scene. To that end, he asked Williams for his novel *White Mule,* chapters of which had been appearing in little magazines since 1930.

The offer came at an opportune moment for Williams, whose literary career had slumped along with the world's economy. The Macaulay Company, which had published his novel *A Voyage to Pagany* in 1928 and his translation of Philippe Soupault's *Last Nights of Paris* in 1929, had gone out of business. For several years thereafter, new books by Williams appeared only in small editions issued by short-lived publishers. For example, in 1934 the Objectivist Press published 500 copies of his *Collected Poems 1921–1931.* And in 1935–36 the Alcestis Press printed two volumes of more recent poems in limited editions of 165 and 167 copies, respectively. Most of Williams's earlier books were out of print. After more than twenty years of steady production, he still had no regular publisher.

White Mule was accepted in October 1936. Within two years, New Directions had published that novel (2,100 copies), a collection of short stories entitled *Life Along the Passaic River* (1,000 copies), and *The Complete Collected Poems of William Carlos Williams 1906–1938* (1,500 copies). A second impression of *In the American Grain* (1925) was issued in 1939, a sequel to *White Mule* entitled *In the Money* appeared in 1940, and a pamphlet of new poems called *The Broken Span* followed in 1941. Moreover, Williams figured regularly in the prestigious annual anthologies of *New Directions in Prose and Poetry*. As Laughlin later stated in his autobiographical short story "A Visit," New Directions put the work of Williams "back into active circulation."

In addition to their professional association, author and publisher enjoyed a friendship. Williams could not but appreciate the younger man's admiration and enthusiasm, while Laughlin venerated the senior poet as a literary father and a stylist to be emulated. The writers exchanged poems, short stories, statements of poetic principle, family news, pet peeves, and literary gossip as well as business communications. Laughlin frequently visited Williams in Rutherford or met him in New York, while Williams went at least twice to Norfolk. On the first occasion, in July 1937, he made the acquaintance of Laughlin's father, whose sudden death the following January prompted a letter of sincere condolence to the son. On the second occasion, in August 1938, Williams and his wife, Floss (1890–1976), spent a memorable vacation in a hilltop cottage on Mrs. Carlisle's estate. As a result of these interchanges, the overall tone of the early correspondence is one of camaraderie and affection, evident in such details as Williams's signature to a letter of 1945: "love / Dad."

This is not to say, however, that the relationship was invariably harmonious. Certain tensions existed from the start. In particular, Williams often felt that New Directions was not aggressive or efficient enough in marketing his books. When *White Mule* was published in June 1937, for example, 500 copies of the first impression sold out quickly. An additional 600 copies had been printed but not bound. Laughlin, meanwhile, had gone to New Zealand with a ski team. Williams went to Norfolk in person but discovered that nothing could be done before September. It was not the last time Williams felt frustrated by the absence of his peripatetic publisher. Tied to an unremunerative practice in a small New Jersey town, the workaholic doctor sometimes envied and resented the globe-trotting ski jaunts and bachelor freedoms of his wealthy young friend.

This restiveness intensified in 1943, when Williams assembled enough poems for a new volume but Laughlin turned it down because his paper supply was limited by War Production Board rationing. *The Wedge* was consequently published by the Cummington Press in a limited edition of 380 copies. From 1942 to 1945, New Directions published no new book by Williams. He said little at the time but cited this rejection more than once during his estrangement from New Directions in the 1950s.

The war brought a more immediate problem in its wake: namely, the case of Ezra Pound. Williams and Laughlin had last seen him in the spring of 1939, when Pound visited the United States to lobby members of Congress and the Roosevelt administration on behalf of world peace and monetary reform. Since then, Pound had made more than one hundred propaganda broadcasts over Rome Radio, many of them against the Allied war effort, and had been indicted for treason by the U.S. Department of Justice. He was apprehended in Rapallo in May 1945 and was incarcerated for six months in the U.S. Army's Disciplinary Training Center near Pisa. He was then flown to Washington, D.C., where a federal court declared him mentally incompetent to stand trial. From December 1945 to May 1958, he was incarcerated in St. Elizabeths Hospital, a federal institution for the criminally insane in Washington. In 1949 the award to him of the Bollingen Prize in poetry created a national furor. These events bore directly upon Williams and Laughlin, who remained

loyal to Pound and his poetry despite their disap-
proval of many of his beliefs, writings, and actions.
Their letters to one another about Pound reflect both
their concern and their ambivalence. Williams in
particular developed the mixed evaluation of Pound
which was one of his habitual methods of assessing
his own life and work.

Similarly, he measured himself against T. S. Eliot
(1888–1965), whose allegiance to European literary
and cultural traditions seemed to Williams antitheti-
cal to his own quest for a distinctively American
poetic idiom. Yet his outspoken animosity toward
Eliot abated somewhat at the time of the Bollingen
controversy, when Eliot stood up for Pound and was
in turn criticized as an expatriate and obscurantist.
Laughlin, meanwhile, kept his own counsel about
Eliot, whom he admired as a writer and a friend.

The letters afford lively glimpses of many other
writers as well. Some were New Directions authors,
while others aspired to that status, warmly commend-
ed by Williams to his publisher. A number of contemporary French, Hispanic, and Japanese literary
figures were brought to Williams's attention by New
Directions translations sent to him by Laughlin. In
effect, their correspondence presents a cross section
of artistic America in the mid-twentieth century—not
only of writers but also of painters, musicians,
dancers, theater and film people, editors, translators,
publishers, agents, scholars, and booksellers.

As the war neared its end, Williams began to make
good progress on his long poem *Paterson,* which had
occupied him off and on since 1926. At the same
time, Laughlin cleared the decks for a new wave of
books by his senior authors. Part 1 of *Paterson*
appeared in 1946, followed by the next three installments in 1948, 1949, and 1951. A volume entitled
Selected Poems (1949) prepared the way for Wil-

liams's *Collected Later Poems* (1950) and *Collected Earlier Poems* (1951). A reissue of *In the American Grain* appeared in 1948, as did a paperbound edition of Williams's new play *A Dream of Love*. In the same year, Pound's *Pisan Cantos* and the first collected edition of Cantos 1–84 came out. Pound's translations of Confucius reached bookstores in 1947, and his *Selected Poems* followed in 1949. Under the circumstances, it was an impressive sequence of publications by the little company Pound liked to call "Nude Erections." Some of the best letters Williams ever wrote to Laughlin concern the projects of 1946–51.

The burst of new books brought new honors to Williams. Although the Pulitzer Prize continued to elude him, he received the Russell Loines Award for poetry from the National Institute of Arts and Letters in 1948 and the National Book Award for poetry in 1950. He was invited to become consultant in poetry at the Library of Congress in 1949. Honorary degrees were bestowed upon him by the University of Buffalo in 1946 and by Rutgers University and Bard College in 1950. Invitations to read and record his work arrived regularly, and after 1947 he was a featured speaker at writers' conferences and workshops throughout the country. At last he was enjoying some of the wider recognition he had always craved.

His career had reached a major juncture. His health began to give way in 1948, his sixty-fifth year, when he suffered a mild heart attack. Thereafter he began gradually to turn his medical practice over to his elder son. Having saved few of his earnings, however, Williams was worried about retirement income. He relished the prospect of more time in which to write, but he also realized that writing would soon become his principal means of support. He therefore decided in 1950, when his reputation was bullish, to seek a publisher who would assure him wider sales and greater earnings than he was accustomed to receiving from New Directions. He also decided to put his literary business affairs into the hands of a lawyer, James F. Murray of New York.

He chose Random House as his new publisher, largely because David McDowell was an editor there. McDowell, a former employee of New Directions, had impressed Williams in 1949 by his energetic efforts to publicize Book 3 of *Paterson*. McDowell arranged for Random House to pay Williams an advance of $5,000 on three books of prose: a collected edition of his short stories entitled *Make Light of It* (1950), his *Autobiography* (1951), and the third novel in his Stecher trilogy, *The Build-Up* (1952). Williams told Laughlin that Random House would handle only his new prose works, while New Directions would continue to publish his volumes of poetry. Later, however, he gave Random House both *The Desert Music* (1954) and *Journey to Love* (1955).

Laughlin countered the Random House offer, but Williams, after some vacillation, accepted it. Laughlin felt hurt and betrayed, and said so. As their previous relationship had been both professional and personal, so now was their estrangement. They continued to conduct some business and to encounter each other at New York social gatherings; but their conversations were civil rather than cordial, and their correspondence grew sparse in quantity and constrained in tone. Relations reached an ebb in 1954–55, after *The Desert Music* went to Random House. In later years, Laughlin referred to the troubled hiatus of the 1950s simply as "the break."

This awkward and painful period was further complicated by the strokes which Williams suffered in 1951 and 1952 and by a dispute with the Library of Congress in 1952–53. The consultantship in poetry, which Williams had declined in 1948 because of poor health, was offered to him again in 1952. By this time, however, Senator Joseph McCarthy's influence in Washington was strong, so the appointment entailed a loyalty investigation by the FBI and other governmental agencies. When Williams objected vigorously to this investigation, the library attempted to withdraw its offer. The affair ended inconclusively, after dragging on so long that the one-year term of office had nearly expired. Distanced from Williams, Laughlin played no role in these events; but he knew of them and offered the poet both sympathy and assistance.

Slowly, the break began to mend. Williams made an overture early in 1956, when he offered Laughlin a cluster of uncollected early poems for the *New Directions* anthology. Later that year, Laughlin brought out the first paperback edition of *In the American Grain*. In 1957 Williams finished Book 5 of *Paterson,* which Laughlin received enthusiastically and published in September 1958. He gave a party to celebrate the birthdays of both poem and poet, who turned seventy-five on September 17. A few weeks later, Williams survived another major stroke.

Little by little, he gravitated back to New Directions. In 1957, David McDowell left Random House to form his own publishing company with Ivan Obolensky. Williams followed his editor and gave the new firm both his *Selected Letters* (1957) and a biography of his mother entitled *Yes, Mrs. Williams* (1959). McDowell, Obolensky stayed in business only until April 1960, however. By then, Williams was ready to terminate his relations with other publishers, dismiss his lawyer, and place his future literary business entirely in the hands of Laughlin and New Directions. Laughlin subsequently republished all eight of the books that McDowell had handled.

Determined to show the prodigal father that he was welcome, Laughlin moved swiftly to produce collected editions of Williams's short stories and plays. *The Farmers' Daughters* and *Many Loves and Other Plays* both appeared in 1961. Laughlin spent many hours helping Williams revise and edit the text of the plays, a difficult task for the partially paralyzed author. They also assembled a book entitled *Pictures from Brueghel and Other Poems* (1962). This contained new poems as well as all of those which had appeared in *The Desert Music* and *Journey to Love*. *Pictures from Brueghel* won the Pulitzer Prize in 1963, after Williams's death.

The friendship of author and publisher also resumed. Laughlin again called upon Williams at home and made from one such occasion a short story that expressed his feelings about their reconciliation. ("A Visit" is reprinted as an appendix to the present volume.) Laughlin and Mrs. Williams gradually took over the burden of Williams's business correspondence, as writing itself became more and more difficult for him. The letters of his late years are comparatively brief and infrequent, but they testify eloquently to his courageous struggle against dissolution, depression, and impending death. His final letter to Laughlin is dated November 11, 1962. He died on March 4, 1963.

New Directions continues to publish the work of Williams. Since 1963, out-of-print items have been reissued (*A Voyage to Pagany* and *Imaginations,* both 1970), new thematic gatherings have been made (*A Recognizable Image,* 1978; *The Doctor Stories,* 1984; *Something to Say,* 1985), and previously unpublished work has been recovered from manuscript (*The Embodiment of Knowledge,* 1974). Most recently, a new, two-volume edition of *Collected Poems* (1986–88) with previously uncollected texts and revised chronology has kept the poet's achievement before the public.

NOTES ON THE TEXT

The correspondence of William Carlos Williams and James Laughlin is preserved in several locations. The New Directions Archive at Mr. Laughlin's home in Norfolk, Connecticut, contains approximately 660 items addressed to him or to New Directions by Williams or Mrs. Williams. This correspondence will eventually be deposited in the Houghton Library at Harvard University. Photocopies of this material have already been placed in the Beinecke Rare Book and Manuscript Library at Yale University (catalog designation Za/Williams/295) and in the Van Pelt Library at the University of Pennsylvania. The photocopies at the Beinecke Library constitute the principal copy-text of the present edition. The Harry Ransom Humanities Research Center of the University of Texas at Austin has one letter from Williams to Laughlin (item 90 in the present edition). The copy-text of Williams's short story "Long Island Sound" (item 140 in the present edition) is the photocopy of the signed typescript in the Beinecke collection.

From the other side of the correspondence, the Beinecke Library has originals or copies of approximately 285 items written by Laughlin or New Directions to Williams and/or Mrs. Williams (cata-

log designation Za/Williams/Corresp.). Forty-six
such items are housed in the Poetry/Rare Books
Collection of the State University of New York at
Buffalo. Furthermore, the New Directions Archive
in Norfolk contains copies of some letters from
Laughlin to Williams that are not now in the collec-
tions of Yale or Buffalo. These copies will eventually be deposited in the Houghton Library at Harvard.
All of these sources have provided copy-texts for the
present edition. Laughlin's short story "A Visit,"
reprinted here as an appendix, exists in typescript at
the Beinecke Library (catalog designation Za/Wil-
liams/296). The copy-text used here, however, is the
version published in the *William Carlos Williams
Newsletter* 4, no. 1 (Spring 1978): 1–9, with several
typographical errors silently corrected. Because it was
revised by Laughlin before its appearance in the
Newsletter, this version embodies the author's final
intentions.

From these sources I have selected 149 items for
the present edition—123 by Williams or Mrs. Williams and 26 by Laughlin or his colleagues at New
Directions. I have tried to choose correspondence that
contains important information about (1) the genesis, authorial intention, and publication history of
Williams's writings; (2) his personal and professional
relationship with his publisher; (3) his health and other
aspects of his personal life; (4) his artistic principles
and his evaluations of fellow artists and their works;
and (5) the early history of New Directions and the
aims of its founder. "A Visit" is appended because
it expresses Laughlin's mature view of Williams and
of their relationship.

In preparing the letters for publication, I have
employed the following guidelines. Every letter in
the selection but one is reproduced in its entirety,
without editorial abridgment. The deletion of one

sentence is indicated by ellipses within editorial brackets. Every letter is preceded by a headnote which gives its number in the present edition, its form, and the number of its pages. To designate epistolary forms, I have used the following abbreviations: TLS (typed letter signed), TL (typed letter unsigned), ALS (autograph letter signed), AL (autograph letter unsigned), TCS (typed card signed), and ACS (autograph card signed). Nearly all of the letters emanated from Williams's home in Rutherford, New Jersey; Laughlin's home in Norfolk, Connecticut; or the New York City office of New Directions. Letterheads and inside addresses are therefore reproduced *only* in letters *not* sent from one of those locations.

Some standardizations have been applied to the texts of the letters. The positions of dates, salutations, closings, and signatures have been regularized. Salutations and signatures are printed in small capitals. Typists' initials have been omitted (letters 87, 89, 91, 99, 114, 124, 134, and 135 were typed by New Directions secretaries), and so have typed signatures which follow autograph signatures. Writers' typed or autograph corrections have been silently incorporated, whereas significant typed or autograph insertions are designated by angled brackets. The titles of literary works have been punctuated conventionally: italics are used for the titles of books, plays, magazines, and long poems; whereas quotation marks designate the titles of shorter poems, essays, and short stories. Spacing between sentences and between the final words of sentences and their terminal punctuation has been regularized. Dashes have been standardized to a one-em rule. Typographical errors and misspellings, including those of proper names, have been silently corrected unless they seem intended or are acknowledged by the writer as questionable. One letter (item 148) has been left uncorrected, however, to illustrate the painful difficulties that typing posed for Williams after the strokes of his later years. Likewise uncorrected (except in titles) are the grammar, punctuation, and capitalization of Williams's letters. Because their irregularities often create expressive effects, they have not been altered in the present edition.

Editorial insertions into the text of the letters appear within square brackets. Some indicate missing words, whereas others provide additional information such as dates and proper names. Where abbreviations of proper names have been supplemented by fully spelled names in brackets, periods following the abbreviations have been omitted (e.g., F.B.I.). Further information is given in the editorial notes which follow each letter. Each note is keyed to the text of its letter by the repetition in italics of a word or phrase from the letter. The following abbreviations are used in the notes for the three names which occur most frequently: WCW (William Carlos Williams), FW (Florence H., or "Floss," Williams), and JL (James Laughlin). If a name is not identified in the editorial notes on a given page, the index at the end of the book may provide a cross-reference to another page where information about the name can be found. The index lists proper names (persons, places, titles of works) which appear in the letters and in the editorial introduction and notes.

Some of the items in the present edition have already been published. John C. Thirlwall's edition of *The Selected Letters of William Carlos Williams* (New York: McDowell, Obolensky, 1957) contains complete versions of letters 2, 23, 24, 28, 30, 43, 52, and 57. Abridged versions of letters 31 and 50 appear in Thirlwall's "Four Unpublished Letters by William Carlos Williams," *Massachusetts Review* 3, no. 2

(Winter 1962): 292–96. Short excerpts from many of the letters are quoted by Richard Ziegfeld in "Dear God/Dear Bill: The William Carlos Williams–James Laughlin Correspondence," *William Carlos Williams Newsletter* 5, no. 2 (Fall 1979): 5–20. The texts of 28 letters from the present edition appear in the *Paris Review* 30, no. 106 (Spring 1988): 157–92; however, I neither wrote nor approved the introduction to that selection. Finally, Mr. Laughlin himself has recently published several memoirs which reproduce passages from the correspondence. One of these, "Gists and Piths: From the Letters of Pound and Williams," *Poetry* 139 (January 1982): 229–43, appears also in *Ezra Pound & William Carlos Williams: The University of Pennsylvania Conference Papers,* ed. Daniel Hoffman (Philadelphia: University of Pennsylvania Press, 1983), pp. 197–209, and in *Helix* (Melbourne, Australia), 13–14 (1983): 97–108. Related pieces include "William Carlos Williams and the Making of *Paterson:* A Memoir," *Yale Review* 71 (1982): 185–98; "A World of Books Gone Flat," *Grand Street* 3, no. 2 (Winter 1984): 103–9; and *Pound as Wuz: Essays and Lectures on Ezra Pound* (St. Paul, Minn.: Graywolf Press, 1987), pp. 116–18. Item 140 was published in emended form by Theodora R. Graham in "A New Williams Short Story: 'Long Island Sound' (1961)," *William Carlos Williams Review* 7, no. 2 (Fall 1981): 1–2.

In preparing the introduction and notes for the present edition, I have benefited from the work of other scholars. Richard Ziegfeld's essay, mentioned above, has been very helpful, as has Emily Mitchell Wallace's "Musing in the Highlands and Valleys: The Poetry of Gratwick Farm," *William Carlos Williams Review* 8, no. 1 (Spring 1982): 8–41. Wallace's handwritten, chronological checklist of most of the letters sent by the Williamses to Laughlin has been of great assistance in the tentative dating of undated and partially dated items. Mary Barnard's *Assault on Mount Helicon: A Literary Memoir* (Berkeley: University of California Press, 1984) has also been useful. Above all, I am indebted to two indispensable sources of information about the life and works of Williams, Emily Mitchell Wallace's *A Bibliography of William Carlos Williams* (Middletown, Conn.: Wesleyan University Press, 1968) and Paul Mariani's *William Carlos Williams: A New World Naked* (New York: McGraw-Hill, 1981). These books have been my constant and congenial companions for many months.

I have received valuable assistance from other quarters as well. My principal obligation is to Mr. and Mrs. James Laughlin, whose encouragement, cooperation, and hospitality have sustained the project from its inception. Mr. Laughlin's letters and his story "A Visit" appear by his permission. The letters of William Carlos Williams and Florence H. Williams and the short story "Long Island Sound" are published by permission of William Eric Williams and Paul H. Williams. The following libraries and librarians have provided copies of the correspondence and permission to reproduce them: the Beinecke Rare Book and Manuscript Library, Yale University (Ms. Patricia C. Willis and Ms. Marcia Bickoff); the Poetry/Rare Books Collection, State University of New York at Buffalo (Mr. Robert Bertholf); and the Harry Ransom Humanities Research Center, University of Texas at Austin (Ms. Cathy Henderson). The Research Allocations Committee of the University of New Mexico provided funds for photocopying, and the Inter-Library Loan Department of the same university (Ms. Dorothy Wonsmos) has also rendered essential service. Eva Hesse has kindly allowed the reproduction in letter 131 of a passage written by her. The *William Carlos*

Williams Review and its editors Theodora R. Graham
and Peter Schmidt have permitted the reprinting of
"A Visit" from the issue of Spring 1978 and of "Long
Island Sound" from the issue of Fall 1981.

In addition, the following persons have graciously
provided information, advice, and material assis-
tance: George Arms, George Bornstein, Jerome
Brooks, Barbara Busenburg, Joseph Byrne, Mary de
Rachewiltz, Alan Filreis, Peggy L. Fox, David Gordon, Linda Hamalian, Anne Hammond, Wendell
Harris, Eva Hesse, David R. Jones, James F. Kilroy,
A. Walton Litz, Christopher MacGowan, Paul Mariani, Louis Martz, Jeffrey Meyers, Robbie Miller, José
Morales, Griselda Ohannessian, Marjorie Perloff,
Edouard Roditi, Marvin Spevack, A. Wilber Stevens, John Tritica, Emily Mitchell Wallace, Molly
Watkins, Mike Weaver, and Margaret Wimsatt. All
of these friends and colleagues have helped this book
come into being, but none of them is responsible for
its errors and omissions. I am grateful to the University of New Mexico for a sabbatical leave in 1987–
88, during which most of the editorial work was
carried out. I would like to dedicate that work to my
wife, Barbara.

LETTERS

1. TLS-1 January 23, 1934

MY DEAR LAUGHLIN:

Damn it, my not answering your letter, though it looks bad, was just one of those things. It came, your letter, before Christmas. I put off replying for minor reasons until I felt that you must be at home for the vacation and then—blank. Please forget it. I don't think I've ever done the like since my teens. Must be second childhood.

For a fact though, I've been drowned out with a— or by a mass of living details which have me groggy. We've been trying to swing the Objectivist Press into action, for one thing. I'm writing (when I have a moment to myself) the libretto for an opera—with the composer on my tail every minute. Had to have the finished 1st. Act ready by Jan. 1st. etc etc. To say nothing of my practice—a son at Williams [College], a kid finishing high school, etc. etc. And that human dynamo, Fred Miller, of *Blast,* wanting a short story of the sort he wants for each new issue.

Write me again. What plans have you. Where may I fit into them. Any advice I can give I'll shower on you ad lib. if there's anything you can use.

The only random tip I can give today is send stuff to *The Magazine,* Calif. Bank Bldg., Beverly Hills, Calif. Fred Kuhlman (for the mag.) They pay. Want new stuff. Especially with a view to getting back to some kind of life, something livable—or that represents the facts. Anyhow, it's worth looking into; best luck.

Yours sincerely
W. C. WILLIAMS

/ · /

Objectivist Press: A small New York press founded by the Objectivists, a group of young American writers who included George Oppen, Carl Rakoski, Charles Reznikoff, and Louis Zukofsky. Three days before WCW wrote this letter, the Objectivist Press published its first book, his *Collected Poems 1921–1931.*

an opera: For several years beginning in 1933, WCW and the Hungarian composer Tibor Serly (1901–1978) tried to write an opera based upon the life of George Washington. Although *The First President* was never completed, WCW's libretto was published in 1936; see letter 3 below.

Fred Miller: Unemployed tool designer and writer, whose proletarian magazine *Blast* (1933–34) carried a short story by WCW in each of its five issues.

The Magazine: In 1934–35, WCW contributed one short story and nine chapters of *White Mule* to *The Magazine.*

2. TLS-1   20/9/35

DEAR DR WILLIAMS:

I want to thank you and your wife for a very interesting and enjoyable visit. You are just as I hoped you would be, saying what you mean, like your writing.

I mailed yesterday four copies of the *Magazine;* there were two of each number in that set you gave

me. What I have read of *White Mule* I like enormously; it's the goods, moeurs contemporaines, as
Ezra always likes to say, without any molassis ⟨sp?⟩
or fixins. I wish you could get it published. Have
you shown it to the Caxton Printers, those people
out in the west who do "daring" & "difficult" books.
They have some guts I think. Ask your Chambrun
if he sent it to them and if he didn't make him do it.
The other firm I would suggest is

ARROW EDITIONS

444 Madison Avenue

this a young firm with lots of taste. They have done
Cummings' ballet and they're going to do my book
on Stein when I have it ready. Have Chambrun work
on them if Caxton doesn't bite.

And could you give me the address of that party
that's doing your new book of poems so that I can
write in for a review copy for the *Advocate*.

By the way, it looks as though I may soon be doing
a literary column for Munson in the *New Democracy*.
It was Ezra's idea and Munson seems to approve of
it and want it. It would be half & half, a couple of
good poems by decent poets one issue, a critical
broadside the next. Munson wants it to center on
New Forms, the idea being that Social Credit is the
partial manifestation of a renaissance of all creative
thought. That's a bit thick for me to swallow, but
the kind of stuff I would like to boost is the stuff
that busts away and shimmies, so I guess that will
be OK. If I do that I hope you will give me help—
advice, suggestions, news of lively material to print
and announce, also, of course, some of your poems.
There would be a little money for the poets, out of
my fund, since Munson is broke, not much, but
something.

I think your story about the "Stone Face" is very,
very good. I certainly am glad that you could give

me that. If I can prove to the damnfool editor of the *Advocate* how good it is we certainly will run it. If not, can I show it to Rood of *Manuscript? M* doesn't pay but it circulates on the newsstands.

I'm keeping as well the "How to Write" with a view to the *A[dvocate]*. But the Zukofsky letters wouldn't be suitable. They aren't exciting enough, letters have to be exciting unless they were written by some dead guy with marble whiskers. Then they can be a note to the laundryman about starch on his collars and still rate the first page of *Bitch & Bugle*.

If you find the [Fred] Miller ms. please send it to me at Eliot House E-31, Cambridge, Mass.

servissimus & greetings to Mrs Wms
Laughlin

/ · /

moeurs contemporaines: Ezra Pound adapted the phrase "moeurs contemporaines" or "contemporary manners" from *Le Problème du style* (1902), by the French critic Remy de Gourmont (1858–1915). In the *Little Review* for 1918 Pound published a group of satiric poems under the title "Moeurs contemporaines" and an essay on Henry James in which the phrase is used to mean the "national habit of our time and of the two or three generations preceding us."

Caxton Printers: Located in Caldwell, Idaho, the Caxton Printers published *The Frontier Magazine* and *Northwest Verse*. The libertarian James H. Gipson was head of the firm.

Chambrun: Jacques Chambrun was a New York literary agent.

Arrow Editions: Operated by Florence Codman, Arrow Editions published *Tom,* "a ballet based on *Uncle Tom's Cabin,*" by E. E. Cummings (1894–1962) in 1935. Arrow also announced plans to publish a book by JL entitled *Understanding Gertrude Stein* in the winter of 1936–37, but the project was abandoned.

that party: J. Ronald Lane Latimer, also known as James G. Leippert, was editor of *Alcestis: A Poetry Quarterly* and proprietor of the Alcestis Press. He published WCW's *An Early Martyr and Other Poems* (1935) and *Adam & Eve & The City* (1936) as well as volumes of poetry by Wallace Stevens, Allen Tate, John Peale Bishop, and Robert Penn Warren.

Advocate: In 1933, JL was elected to the editorial board of the *Harvard Advocate,* the student literary magazine of Harvard University. WCW contributed items to the *Advocate* in February 1934 (an essay called "The Element of Time") and December 1935 (a short story called "A Face of Stone").

Munson: Gorham Munson (1896–1969) was a leader of the Social Credit movement in the United States and editor of the Social Credit periodical *New Democracy,* to which both WCW and Ezra Pound contributed frequently between 1932 and 1936. The literary feature which JL edited for *New Democracy* was entitled "New Directions." He retained this name for his publishing company when it began a year later.

Manuscript: This little magazine was published from 1934 to 1936 in Athens, Ohio, and edited by John Rood, Mary Lawhead, and Flola Shepard. *Manuscript* specialized in short stories, but WCW did not contribute to it.

"How to Write": This essay appeared not in the *Harvard Advocate* but in the first *New Directions* anthology; see letter 3 below.

Zukofsky: WCW had known the poet Louis Zukofsky (1904–1978) since 1928. Their correspondence is now housed in the Beinecke Library, Yale University, and the Harry Ransom Humanities Research Center, University of Texas at Austin.

Bitch & Bugle: Irreverent nickname coined by Pound for the prestigious American literary magazine *The Hound and Horn* (1927–34), which took its title from Pound's poem "The White Stag."

3. TLS-1   Oct. 27, 1936

DEAR GOD:

You mention, casually, that you are willing to publish my *White Mule,* that you will pay for it and that we shall then share, if any, the profits! My God! It must be that you are so tall that separate clouds circle around that head giving thoughts of other metal than those the under sides of which we are in the habit of seeing.

Anyhow, nothing could give me greater pleasure than for you to undertake that task. I accept the offer quickly but without any thought of a time limit of any kind. Think the thing over, going at your own pace, and when you are quite ready for the script let me know.

There is one point I have to make. The present script, or, the script as it stands amounts to about 22 chapters, about 300 typed pages. It is the first part only of a much longer book which may or may not someday be written. This book is a unit. It has a beginning and a fairly satisfactory end. It will be called. Book I. It needs touching up toward the end, something I have clearly in mind to do at once. In a month (or less) it will be ready subject to your call.

I'll be looking for the *Advocate* and the anthology. As soon as I can get to it I'll let you have a list of names and addresses—as many as I can think up. I'll try to do it this afternoon. I'm extremely curious about the anthology. Most books of the sort are tooted about so much before they appear that they are stale before the seeing. Best of luck to you in the matter of distribution in which I'll help you all I can.

The New Caravan, 1936, is out this week. I'll send you one as soon as I get my copies.

Mrs. Williams joins me in sending greetings. Where are you week-ends? I suppose here and there. What I have in mind is that if you're in Connecticut as a general thing and can be reached by phone you might like to drop in on Charles Sheeler some Sunday afternoon when we are there. I think you'd enjoy the experience and I'm sure he'd like to meet you.

Sincerely yours
W . C . WILLIAMS

/ · /

White Mule: The first of WCW's Stecher novels, based upon the history of his wife's family, was published by New Directions on June 10, 1937. Although the two sequels had different titles, WCW and JL often referred to the entire series as *White Mule.*

the anthology: New Directions in Prose and Poetry 1936 was the first of the annual anthologies of new writing and graphic work edited and published by JL. It was also the first book published by his new company. It contained a poem ("Perpetuum Mobile: The City") and two prose pieces ("How to Write" and "A Face of Stone") by WCW.

The New Caravan: Edited by Alfred Kreymborg, Lewis Mumford, and Paul Rosenfeld, this anthology contained WCW's libretto for *The First President.*

Charles Sheeler: The American painter Charles Sheeler (1883–1965), whom WCW had known since 1923, lived in Ridgefield, Connecticut.

4. TLS-1 May 31, 1937

DEAR JIM:

A little later: It's a splendid book, excellently presented—but it still seems strange to me. I think you have realized it better than I could do in the slow process of writing it to the accompaniment of discouragement inevitable in view of the small likelihood of any immediate appreciation. You have put a critical estimate upon it which has made it yours somewhat to my amazement. This is the rare collaboration between writer and publisher which is almost unheard of today. I feel it keenly. You've done a fine piece of work, of criticism, in focusing the book at the mind as it should be focused.

Could you let me have a list of the reviewers who will get copies. I want to give five or six copies to friends but do not want to duplicate your own plans for distribution. Maybe Gertrude Stein should get one "with the compliments of the publisher or author"; she has always been very kind to me.

Certainly I feel as if I were sitting before a severe jury waiting to be decapitated. It's because this book has been presented better than anything of mine has ever been presented and it has wakened too many nostalgic visions. I'll snap out of it later on. You'll

probably get another letter from me in a few hours
or days. That's it—daze!

With profound thanks and appreciation.

Yours
BILL

/ · /

critical estimate: The first edition of *White Mule* carried a postscript by
JL entitled "White Mule and New Directions." It combines praise for
WCW's "pure" novel with an attack upon publishers who "have made
literature a business." "To the editor of New Directions," the postscript affirms, *"White Mule* is a symbol—a symbol of his whole hope
and will. New Directions exists only to publish books like this one. . . ."
Gertrude Stein: Since 1925, WCW had paid close attention to the work
of the American expatriate writer Gertrude Stein (1874–1946). He met
Stein in Paris in 1927 and published an important essay on her in 1930.

5. TLS-1   Monday, Sept. 13, 1937

DEAR JIM:

As to Salt, No. He isn't ready for you just yet and
has, besides, other means for publication at his disposal. I do regret the McAlmon incident—especially
after seeing how greatly his script had been altered
after my view of it. I was, in that case, moved by
sentiment. It's a danger which if we fear it too much
may lead us to slight those we should most foster.
What the hell. No Salt.

I've had a lady getting my *Life Along the Passaic
River* ready for you all summer. She's about through
with the copying now. But, it will not be all short
stories. I have a wad of stuff big enough to choke an
ox but the short stories are no more than a quarter
of it. What I'll do is, make a book up after my own
taste and ship you the carbons—meanwhile going
on cutting and rearranging. Then you give your say

so and we'll do a final shuffling before proceeding.

There will also be something for the anthology when you need it—a poem, if it comes out all right. No prose, nothing new. I've been vague and indifferent. I don't precisely know why. The wars in Europe and elsewhere, everything together, age, decay—I don't know what the hell. Floss says I look fine. Maybe I'm resting—like a worm in silk. Anyhow I haven't a thing in prose to offer, just the poem. It will be sufficient—if I can do it.

And welcome home. I knew it would hit somewhere near your neck and fully expected to have them send you home in two pieces. Take it easy! I've forgotten what part of the Bible that is quoted from but it's somewhere in the Old Testament, I think.

Best luck.

Sincerely yours
BILL

/ · /

Salt: Sydney (or Sidney) Salt was editor of *Caravel* (Majorca) and author of *Christopher Columbus and Other Poems,* for which WCW wrote an introduction (Boston: Bruce Humphries, 1937).

6. TLS-2   Nov. 8, 1937

DEAR JIM:

The sample page is splendid, it looks as though we are going to have another good looking book and I am glad that you have decided to adopt my dollar and a half suggestion.

Today, though, I was overcome by a sudden funk. I was reading the proofs, which I have been slow to get at because of other work, when I realized that there is material there which might possibly be considered libellous. Oh it isn't flagrant and I'm fairly certain nobody will say anything but there is the possibility that some smart Kike might make a fifty fifty deal with one of my protagonists on the chance of getting something out of us.

You see, I was taken over by a resident of one of our neighboring burgs some years ago because of a short story I wrote and which the *New Masses* printed without letting me go over the proofs. He sued me for $15,000 because of criminal libel and the case was settled out of court for $5,000 which I had to pay out of my meager savings to that date. It took all I had. In that case, of course, I mentioned specific names—intending to change them later!

In the present case I have been careful not to mention names but my descriptions have been so accurate that as I read the proofs I realized that someone might possibly go with book in hand and look some of these people up. It would not be easy but it could be done. This is especially true of the "Girl With a Pimply Face." In that story I mention that she has been free with various guys as well as the police. That should be cut out as it is definitely criminal libel—or so I believe, names or no names. There may be other spots in the book as damaging though I can't think of any just now.

What I think you should do would be to show the script to a competent lawyer. Let him read it and give us his opinion as to its impunity to a charge of libellousness or otherwise. Let him go over it carefully realizing at the same time that no names are mentioned nor is any place definitely named though it has been in some cases designated rather clearly in the story.

I'd like his opinion also on the efficacy of running a sentence at the beginning of the book stating that the stories are imaginative accounts and in no case do they apply to actual people. Is that sort of statement valid provided no names have been mentioned?

Maybe I'm making a fuss about nothing but it would be impossible for me to exaggerate the importance of money to me in these years. I'm perfectly all right if I can keep on as I'm going, it isn't that but if I were to have an unprotected libel suit slapped on me now I'd be finished. It wouldn't be so good for either of us. It's not going to happen if I can prevent it by proper foresight.

Most of the stories in the book are innocuous enough, in fact the passage I have mentioned may be the only one that is at all questionable but—let's get a legal opinion.

My boys are going on a skiing trip up Mt Mansfield this Christmas vacation in fact a crowd of boys and girls from Cornell Med., Smith College, etc—I don't know where all they are coming from are making up the party.

There are any number of things I could tell you about this that and the other but they can wait till the main issue presented here is settled. The proofs go forward tomorrow morning I imagine—I'm doing my best—in the midst of interruptions.

Sincerely yours
BILL

⟨I'll mark the spots I think should be studied.⟩

/ · /

good looking book: Life Along the Passaic River was published by New Directions in February 1938 at a price of $1.75.

short story: "The Five Dollar Guy," *New Masses* 1, no. 1 (May 1926): 19, 29. For an account of the lawsuit, see Paul Mariani, *William Carlos*

Williams: A New World Naked (New York: McGraw-Hill, 1981), pp. 254–55.

7. TLS-1   Nov. 19, 1937

DEAR JIM:

Suits me. February would be the better time besides. I don't know that you do but if, by any chance, you should find that you want to add two more stories to the list it would give me time to finish them. I'm not suggesting a thing, the book is plenty long enough. I'm only saying that if you want the two new stories this would make it possible for me to get them ready. Please don't even mention this unless you yourself of yourself feel that the book should be bulkier.

I can't quite get the picture of the Dr. Jekyll, Mr. Hyde which you present; some day, under whatever disguise you adopt for it, you'll let us have it. I suppose it disturbs you to some extent. If so, I'm sorry. Are you quitting school for good in February? I presume that's what you mean.

Many unusual advances are being made to me these days though most of them are sterile enough; *White Mule* did get my name around. I am told that I should go on at once with volume two but that is impossible for the moment. I must now finish the book on my mother while she is still alive. It's going pretty well just now. It'll be a rather big book—but we'll talk of that later. Tentatively I've been thinking that it might be wisest to approach a regular commercial publisher concerning it when it is ready. Harcourt, Brace once smiled at me and Simon and Schuster grinned broadly. I'm just talking along. Let it go in one ear and out of the other—a figure of speech from happier times than ours. We know now that it comes out of the nose. I won't make a move without a talk with you. Get to work boy, and forget me entirely for the moment.

Best luck.

Sincerely yours
BILL

/ · /

the book on my mother: Yes, Mrs. *Williams* was published in 1959 by McDowell, Obolensky.

8. TLS-3   November 29, 1937

DEAR BILL:

I have been a long time answering your last letter because every time I think about the subject such a flood of emotion starts rolling around in my head that I can't make any sense.

Your thinking that you want somebody else is a crisis in my life. I had thought I was doing all right in what I had taken up, in what was probably to be my life work, and now, if you doubt me, I don't know.

You are the cornerstone of New Directions and if you left me I think I wouldn't be able to go on with it. I have built my plans around you. You are my symbol of everything that is good in writing, and if you go over to the enemy I just won't know where the hell I'm at.

Because they are the enemy. Look what they've done to our kind. Look what they've done to you yourself. Would they take the *Mule?*

Now that you have made a success they want you, they think they can exploit you.

It isn't a case of publishers. It is a case of life and death, of right and wrong, of good writers starving and lousy writers going to Palm Beach.

Of course, I see the other side. I see that you need money. Well, if you will trust me for a little while, I'll see that you get that.

Am I being selfish? I don't think so. If I thought it were best for you to go to them I think I have the guts to tell you to go. But it isn't. I honestly believe and know that I can do more for you than they can.

Because you are different from their trade. You are literature and not merchandise. They cannot fake you. Perhaps they could sell a few more books for you than I can because they have a machine, but then look at other things.

Suppose your next book is too good and doesn't pay its share in their overhead. Those fairweather friends will kick you right downstairs.

They don't understand you. They don't know what it's all about. They just want to exploit your success.

And another thing. Will they publish [Robert] McAlmon if you tell them to? Or [Louis] Zukofsky? Will they do anything at all except try to tell you what you should write?

But you are free. You must do what you want to do.

But look into the facts before you decide. Let me tell you some facts that I learned the other day from young Harcourt. It is the case of Kay Boyle.

Now Kay Boyle is a pretty good writer, but what can they with all their advertising do for her—Harcourt tells me the last one did 2600. Well, you say, that is twice what we did with the *Mule*. But now look at the other side: Boyle writes a book of poems—

poems that are difficult. Will Harcourt do it? Not on
your life! She writes a novelette that she wants published by itself. Will Harcourt do that? Hell no; nov-
elettes don't sell.

It's like that. They want merchandise. They don't
care about writing. They don't even know writing
until somebody tells them.

What can I do for you? I can push you steadily
with the kind of people who are your proper audience. I can put out good books for you irrespective
of whether they pay their way. In New Directions
you will be the head man. The thing will build up
to you. And if you think you are losing money with
me I'll see that you get that. What are Simon &
Schuster offering you? I'll meet anything they put
up.

Why do I care? Because I know that I need you in
order to do anything for the young ones coming on.
I can print their books for them. But unless the name
New Directions stands for something they'll have a
hell of a row to hoe. With you, New Directions does
stand for something and the people it prints will get
a start and a break. This is not just a monkeyshine.
It's the way the thing works.

If you stick with me and Ezra perhaps comes in
we'll be able to make a machine that can fight the
New York machine. You see it takes more than cash
to do it. It takes a *White Mule* and a *Cantos*.

But, in my distress, I am wandering round and
round. Perhaps this is all just a ghost. Perhaps you
didn't really mean what you said.

To be concrete; this is what I want to do. Bring
out the *Passaic* in February, with the two additional
stories. Print a thousand more *Mules* now before we
chuck the type so that they'll be on hand when
needed.

Do the book on your mother next. Then reprint

the *American Grain* in a dollar edition. Do that before the other if it takes longer than a year.

Then have a good book about you, either by one guy or by a dozen—a symposium. Then Part II of *White Mule*. Then a volume of essays.

In other words a steady barrage of Williams, that will be backed by articles and reviews and word-of-mouth advertising. Also regular advertising where it is likely to do good. Thus, in the present *N[ew] D[irections]* you have a double page spread and we are sending along return cards with it.

I don't mean to slight the poetry. I would like to do that too, but I don't want to swipe anything from Latimer. With certain limitations I think he does a good job.

But I would like to see another collected edition of the poems as I understand the Objectivist one is out of print. Get that and the *Grain* out at a dollar.

But again, you are absolutely free, and you must do what you want. You mustn't think of me. But I think you should think of the other writers whom New Directions, made strong by you, could put on their feet.

Well, think it all over a while and let me know.

Send along the two new stories when you can and tell me whether or not to print more *Mules*.

best
JIM

/ · /

Kay Boyle: Kay Boyle (1902 or 1903–) was a regular contributor to the early *New Directions* anthologies. Harcourt, Brace published her novel *Death of a Man* and *The White Horses of Vienna and Other Stories* in 1936. New Directions published her book of poems *A Glad Day* in 1937.

double page spread: New Directions in Prose and Poetry 1937 carried full-page advertisements for both *White Mule* and *Life Along the Passaic River.*

9. **TLS-2**   Dec. 4, 1937

DEAR JIM:

So be it. My chief reason for speaking of a publisher other than New Directions was that I didn't think you wanted to handle a book as bulky as the biography is likely to be. As it turns out it won't be as large a book as I had at first thought it might be. There is no hurry about it at that save that I shouldn't like to have to wait too long—and I frankly didn't think you were interested. Now it's different. We'll go ahead together not any faster than is reasonable but just as far and as persistently as we are able.

It isn't that I need money now, that's not the point. My sole thought was that sometime or other in the near future I ought to try to make some sort of connection which would enable me to get some sort of returns for my writing. I agree that my chances were slim but I felt that I had to try. I am convinced that my best chances now lie with you, looked at quite coldly. Nor do I expect the impossible. It was impossible for me to know before this last letter what your plans could be.

The McAlmon incident doesn't please me any too well. The book as it finally appeared wasn't as good as the script I saw. The Spanish stuff at the end (completely unknown to me) was rrrrotten and the parts that were left out (about Carnevali) though somewhat outdated did round the book out into a whole of a sort. There were too many typographical errors uncorrected in the book besides to give it any authority. That whole business was a mistake but the lesson has been learned and should not have to be repeated.

Zukofsky's *A* is another matter. It can't sell but

may bring the press a certain distinction. Besides it needs doing for there are moments in it of distinction unique in modern writing. I won't back water on this but, again, no insistence.

Forget the two new short stories. They aren't very good and I need them to keep a couple of customers satisfied. The book is all right without extension. You'll see the stories some time. you ain't missin' anything.

There is one practical point in our arrangements though that needs immediate attention. The biography is now blocked out in very rough form as notes taken during the last ten years of my mother's conversation. There are 179 double spaced typed pages of it. Nothing has been connected up, one inventory follows the other haphazard. Now, there is to be a new quarterly, an art quarterly edited by Dorothy Norman assisted by Edward Dahlberg and financed by Mrs. Norman. The activities of this new group will center around the Stieglitz gallery, An American Place. Mrs. N. whom I met when the Stieglitz tribute was brought out is putting up the cash. She wanted me to be in on the advisory board of editors (unless I am mistaken) but I haven't the time for that. Recently she has been pushing me a little for a major contribution to the first issue and I have consented to send her something.

Just before this last letter of yours I told her that I had the notes of which I have spoken above. She said, fine! She'd print them as they stand. It's lucky you wrote when you did.

Shall I let her print the notes? *White Mule* came out that way. I could say definitely that they are "Material for three chapters" of a book, *Your Grandmother, my Son,* to be brought out in the fall of 1938 (?) by J[ames] L[aughlin] IV of New Directions. Or would this be inadvisable? I'd see to it that the copyright would be in my name. Let me know what you think. I can always find something else for her if I must but it might be very good advertising for us if she makes a splurge. The final book will be much different.

It's noon now and I have to eat. Let's have your reaction.

Sincerely yours
W. C. WILLIAMS

⟨The collected poems are very important to me, of course. Let me play with them on the outside, at least for a year or two. I'm not too sure about Latimer. More of this particular phase another time. W.⟩

⟨It should pay, from past experience with the *Am[erican] Grain,* to have an extra 1000 of *Mule* in the hole.

BILL⟩

/ · /

McAlmon: On December 16, 1936, WCW sent JL a group of poems by Robert McAlmon (1896–1956), a close friend of WCW's since 1920 and publisher of Contact Editions in Paris during the early 1920s. New Directions published the poems in 1937 under the title *Not Alone Lost: Poems.*

Zukofsky's A: For Louis Zukofsky, see letter 2 above. WCW first mentioned Zukofsky's long poem *A* to JL in a letter of March 4, 1937. *New Directions in Prose and Poetry 1938* printed " 'A'-8" and announced plans to publish the entire poem upon its completion. It was eventually published by the University of California Press in 1978.

a new quarterly: Twice a Year: A Semi-Annual Publication Attempting a Clarification of Values first appeared in fall 1938. It featured excerpts entitled "From the Writings and Conversation of Alfred Stieglitz" and reproductions of photographs by Stieglitz (1864–1946). An American Place was Stieglitz's gallery on Madison Avenue in New York; he once told WCW that the name was inspired by *In the American Grain.* After protracted negotiations with Mrs. Norman, WCW's biographical article "Raquel Hélène Rose" finally appeared in *Twice a Year,* nos. 5–6 (1940–41): 402–12. Meanwhile, he contributed an essay entitled "Against the Weather: A Study of the Artist" to the second number of the magazine (Spring–Summer 1939): 53–78. WCW's late poem "The Stone Crock" recalls both Stieglitz and Norman.

the Stieglitz tribute: America and Alfred Stieglitz: A Collective Portrait, ed. Waldo Frank, Lewis Mumford, Dorothy Norman, Paul Rosenfeld, and Harold Rugg (New York: Literary Guild, 1934), contained an essay by WCW entitled "The American Background."

10. TLS-1   Dec. 9, 1937

DEAR JIM:

After all, I couldn't know your intentions relative to the publication of my works until you had told me. Certainly I hadn't the least inkling that you were interested in the collected poems. Why you practically told me to let Latimer do them. But I didn't want Latimer, for one reason and another, so I was about ready to go afield and look for someone else. If you want them, they're yours. That makes it complete. I agree with you, the poems are likely to prove one of the best bets of the lot. But you're taking something on, man, with all this program! We'll do it and make it pay too, I hope.

It's all right about the financial arrangements, at least for the moment. I'm leaving that to you. Later on, if things pick up, we'll talk more about that. I greatly appreciate the retroactive clause. I can use the cash.

To go back to the poems: Latimer holds a few copyrights I suppose though most of the poems in the two small books he printed appeared in magazines—not all though. Since we have talked of a possible collected edition at some time he may feel a little hurt by my turning to you. I hope not but I mention the fact as possible. I shall tell him I prefer it this way. The copyrights, though, may be a slight stumbling block. Maybe not. Those few poems aside I could have the collected poems ready for you almost any time at all. The ones printed years ago by the successors to Four Seas Publishing Co can be used without question since those bastards broke their contract years ago. That's a sore point with me. They haven't made a report on sales or paid me a cent of royalty in ten years.

I'll go ahead with Mrs. Norman. I'm glad you will write to her.

So there we are. I can't tell you how much I appreciate your undertaking this heavy program of printing my stuff on your shoulders. I hope the benefits may prove to be in some degree at least mutual. I notice what you say about reprinting the older work other than the poetry but for the moment it might be best to put that aside. That would be too much though it has always been close to my heart. One book especially, *Spring and All, The Great American Novel and a Novelette*—as one book would give me the thrill of a lifetime.

More later and a thousand thanks. You're much more likely to break your neck than I am!

Sincerely yours
BILL

/ · /

Four Seas Publishing Co: Located in Boston, Four Seas published WCW's *Al Que Quiere!* (1917), *Kora in Hell: Improvisations* (1920), and *Sour Grapes* (1921).

one book: Spring and All and *The Great American Novel* were first published in 1923. *A Novelette and Other Prose 1921–1931* appeared in 1932. WCW's dream of reprinting all three as a single volume was not realized during his lifetime, but in 1970 they were republished with *Kora in Hell* and *The Descent of Winter* (1928) in a New Directions volume entitled *Imaginations*, ed. Webster Schott.

11. TLS-1   December 13, 1937

DEAR BILL:

   That is fine news about the collected poems. We
can make quite a book out of that. I have it in my
mind's eye already—a solid piece of book, about six
by nine, very simply laid out, just black on white,
and plenty of room to walk around in.

   I should think next winter would be the time for
it. It would take a while to put it together likely. As
to the exact date, I'll go into that matter of the Pulitzer
thing more carefully. I think there is a real chance of
that. If not, I despair finally of this flea-bitten country.

   I suggest that you explain your decision to Latimer. If I did it, it might look as though I were steal-
ing you. I hope he doesn't make any difficulties for
us.

   As to the matter of taking on a big program; well
I'm getting along and feel about up to doing something. What am I to do with my life anyway if not
publish people like you? I want to write myself, but
not for a good many years. I don't want to go writing half-assed novels before I know what it's all about.
There is plenty of time. In the meantime I'll get a
writers' press started that will be a force able to fight
the New York bastards. I don't ever mean to let it
turn into another hairoil business. Better death than
dishonour, as they say.

   Maybe I'll get down to see you soon to plan the
poems. Hope so.

                                                    JIM

                          / · /

collected poems: New Directions published *The Complete Collected Poems
of William Carlos Williams 1906–1938* in November 1938. JL entered the

book for the Pulitzer Prize in poetry, but to no avail. At one stage, the Alcestis Press of J. Ronald Lane Latimer (see letter 2 above) planned to bring out a limited edition of the *Poems* along with the New Directions trade edition. This joint project was abandoned, however, when JL told Latimer that Alcestis would have to provide $800 toward the publishing costs.

12. TLS-1   January 21, 1938

DEAR BILL:

Thank you for your message about Father. He was very taken with you and I wish he could have lived so that you could have been friends.

Well this business of the *Collected Poems* is getting thick as hell isn't it?

I imagine that the Oxford offer puts Latimer into the shade, doesn't it?

I think it would be fine for them to do a trade edition. I say this with a pull at my heart, because I want to do it, but I guess that they could do a little better for you than I could, though I'm not so damned sure. I have more money now at my disposal and I'm beginning to feel strong as hell.

But, as I say, I think it would be fine to have them do a trade edition, provided that the copyright rested with you or me. My reason for this is this: I want to start the "New Classics Series"—dollar books like the Modern Library, of which you and Ezra will be the backbones. Naturally, we'll want the C[ollected] P[oems] free to go into that after the trade edition has run its course.

I am suggesting to Oxford that they issue a trade edition, we a small signed edition in conjunction with it. We will guarantee not to issue the dollar edition for, say, three years, and promise, if they wish, to buy up their stock of the trade, when we do.

That seems to me a very good arrangement all round. What do you think of it? I told them that you would insist on no editorial tinkering.

It seems to me that you are coming into your own, and that is a great day for any man, and I hope you enjoy it to the full. You've worked for it!

JIM

/ · /

the Oxford offer: The New York branch of the Oxford University Press included eleven poems by WCW in *The Oxford Anthology of American Verse,* ed. William Rose Benét and Norman Holmes Pearson (1938). Their interest in publishing more of WCW's work proved transitory, however.

13. TLS-2   January 23, 1938

DEAR JIM:

It isn't time for congratulations just yet, I suspect there'll be a catch somewhere before they crown me but thanks anyway. I'm sorry you felt the pang you did at sacrificing the collected poems but at the same time I'm proud to be its object. There's plenty of work for both of us ahead. I'd say to hell with the Oxford edition if I didn't believe that in the end it will be most beneficial to both of us. Those poems are old stuff now, most of them, official recognition has been due them for a long time. Such recognition cannot but further the fortunes of the new work which you and I have most concern with. But, if there is the faintest sign of wobbling on their part in the matter of inclusions, any attempt of the faintest sort toward "editing", you'll have me on your neck so fast it will take your breath away.

Come what may Latimer will not do the collected
poems. He went into his De Luxe editions with the
clearly stated intention to sell at a profit. He asked if
he might use my work and I gave it to him without
question. He wanted then to go on with a collected
poems but I refused. I did later play around with the
idea that he do the collected poems after all but each
time I thought of the thing something stopped me.
He had no reason in the world, apart from vague
discussions of the possibility of the thing, to believe
that he would get the collected poems in the end. I
am sorry but no matter what happens he is not to do
them, even if they are never done.

I didn't answer your question about *New Directions,* the weather got too hot just at that time. It
isn't quite as new as it should be. Merrill Moore's
sonnets are, to me, magnificent. I have for years been
stating that the sonnet is an outmoded form that can
no longer be written. He has given me the lie. And
best of all he has convinced me of something
extremely important. The sonnet, I see now, is not
a form at all but a state of mind. It is the extremely
familiar dialogue upon which much writing is
founded: a statement then a rejoinder of a sort, perhaps a reply, perhaps a variant of the original—but
a comeback of one sort or another. What this man
has done is more or less what we have all been doing
since Whitman's famous "me, myself". He has broken through the binding, stupid formality of the
sonnet and preserved the true sonnet, rescued it Per-
seus like from its barren rock. I am impressed and
delighted. I never had the intelligence to realize that
it wasn't the sonnet that was at fault but the bad
artists who wrote in the form that were the calam-
ity. The imagination rescues us all but how difficult
to realize the simplest formulations until someone,

some ONE, liberates us. Now sonnets can be written again. In fact the new blood from Moore's work, so fundamental to all our poetry, should penetrate far.

Thus, in that case, *New Directions* was real and active in effect but there was too much *Transition* like random shooting—perhaps that's the way it should be, loose, unconfined. But in that case it should have been newer—I'm speaking from the heart. I'd like to see more of "you" in the book, both your own work and your appraisals. Not that you didn't lash out beautifully and not that that hasn't been effective but I want more. What is new? Answer that next time. What is new this year? Answer that. Point out what *you* see and why. Shoot it, you can do it. Otherwise the effect is too loose. We are fed up on Williams, [Gertrude] Stein, e. e. cummings who are not advancing? ? ? etc, you see what I mean. Pick their work with more discretion. Make it hot for them too.

I like Miller and the Cocteau though that is not new. I can't tell you and you don't expect me to tell you but new is new. It's a well gotten up book but NOT sufficiently exciting—as yet. A young work by the young J[ames] L[aughlin]. Shoot me if you want to but keep at it. I look forward to it every year—in its present spirit but gayer, madder.

Be seeing you soon.

Yours
BILL

/ · /

Merrill Moore's sonnets: New Directions in Prose and Poetry 1937 contained "Six Sonnets" by the poet and psychiatrist Merrill Moore (1903–1957). Upon reading this letter, JL invited WCW to contribute a foreword to Moore's *Sonnets from New Directions* (1938), the second of the "New Directions Pamphlets" published by JL. The foreword also appeared in Moore's *The Noise That Time Makes* (1938), *M: One Thousand Auto-biographical Sonnets* (1938), and *The Dance of Death* (1957).

Transition: An avant-garde literary magazine edited by Eugene Jolas, Elliot Paul, and Robert Sage and published in Paris and The Hague from 1927 to 1938, *transition* carried installments of James Joyce's *Finnegans Wake* and a dozen contributions by WCW. The first volume of *New Directions in Prose and Poetry* is dedicated "To the editors, the contributors & the readers of *transition,* who have begun successfully the revolution of the word."

Miller and the Cocteau: Henry Miller's "Walking Up and Down in China: A Chapter from 'Black Spring' " and Jean Cocteau's "Les Mariés de la Tour Eiffel," trans. Dudley Fitts, appeared in *New Directions 1937.* Miller's novel had been published in Paris in 1936, and Cocteau's play was first performed in 1921. WCW met Miller (1891–1980) in New York in May 1935 and commemorated him in the poem "To the Dean" (1944). Starting in 1939, New Directions published a number of Miller's books.

14. TLS-2   January 29, 1938

DEAR JIM:

Instead of a ten page letter I should write you ten words and say, Go ahead with your plans etc. I can't quite do that feeling as I do.

I confess I feel rather heavy hearted at seeing two chances for publication by standard houses going up in smoke. This last was the hardest to digest. A book of *Collected Poems* by the Oxford University Press would have meant a certain prestige for me which I have wanted, not too seriously, all my life.

But would it have done me any good as a writer? Certainly not. All my life I have opposed just the thing that the Oxford University Press represents— within certain limits. The only good that would have come of that venture as well as the publication by Harcourt, Brace & Co. would have been the publicity and increased sales that would have resulted.

You are young at the game of publishing. That's

the fine thing about you as a business bet. You have no preconceived ideas, you are willing to back your real personal convictions. You have published me. At the same time it was distressing to me to have people asking as they still ask: Where can I get the book? Nobody seems to have heard of it.

I haven't such a hell of a long time to go as a writer. I'd like to see a small return coming in . . I think you're my best bet for such a return during the next five years and you'll do me credit in all the other ways that loyalty and honesty and ability too can do credit. Only I feel rather left floating for the moment.

Maybe we ought to have a more definite statement of our agreement—that I turn over my scripts to you and that you will etc etc But if I didn't believe you would anyway I wouldn't even be writing to you.

So, in the end, make your arrangements for distribution as complete as possible, especially make more detailed arrangements for advertising my stuff than you did with *White Mule.* I think inadequate management of sales cost us plenty that time.

I enclose another letter from Ford, I know you'll love it. Dorothy Norman, unfortunately, has me a bit disgusted for the moment with her hesitations and demands that I run in for this and change that and—fer Chrisake! I hope Ford isn't right. I sent her the best work I had, that I had wrung sweat from my very bones to get to her on time—and all I get is, I wish you'd come in so we can talk it over, we don't want to make any false moves, etc etc. till I want to kick her in the fat ass and tell her to get a policeman. Not even so much as, thank you. I wish I hadn't wasted a minute on her.

Today and yesterday I've been plugging Spanish lit. for the *American Scholar* which has commissioned me to do a 3,500 word article—with especial emphasis upon Lorca. I am dizzy from reading. But the history bears me out in the theory I have had. It is amazing to think a thing then go to the record for confirmation and be confirmed in an opinion which is new and significant—which others have not brought out. The pay is nothing for the hours put in on the thing but I lost myself completely this afternoon for at least three hours. I had not done that for a long time. If I am told it won't do I'll vomit. As I get older I notice more and more accurately what it is that drives me to the wall.

Weeel Jimes, it's up to you to carry Papa across the river. Not that I ever expect to make money off of literature—but once in a while it *do* look marvellous to see what crap gets what cash—There I am again. Forgive me. I don't even mean it. What the hell.

To the future sales! But don't let it slip through your fingers again ⟨—if ever.⟩

Yours
BILL

/ · /

Harcourt, Brace: In letter 7 above, WCW tells JL that "Harcourt, Brace once smiled at me" in connection with the biography of WCW's mother.

Ford: Probably either Ford Madox Ford (see letter 68 below) or Charles Henri Ford (1913–), American surrealist poet and editor of *Blues* and *View,* avant-garde magazines to which WCW contributed.

Spanish lit.: WCW's essay "Federico García Lorca" appeared not in the *American Scholar* but in the *Kenyon Review* 1, no. 2 (Spring 1939): 148–58. Lorca (1899–1936) became a martyr of the Spanish Republican cause after he was assassinated in Granada by opponents of his political views.

15. TLS-2   February 11, 1938

DEAR JIM:

   I haven't written to you for the past week because
of the damned article on Spanish poetry I've been
doing for the Phi Beta Kappa quarterly, *The American Scholar*. I couldn't just slam the words together
in a slip shod fashion, I damn well had to study the
material—and it damn near killed me to do it. Damn
near killed everybody around me too, I guess. Not
quite a divorce but the smells of it maybe. Anyhow,
that's the idea. I finally got the God damned mess
off to the woman who does my typing for me. It's
much too long but, hell, it's at least out of the house
and the dead line isn't until March 1st. I'll cut it
somehow. The subject matter is marvellous. I have
never really had the wit to look into the Spanish
Cancionero. Lorca, the most recent of the tradition
was superb. And to think that he lived all around me
and I never knew a thing about him until too late.
I'll send you a carbon of the thing in its long form.
Maybe you'll want to put it into *New Directions* next
year.
   My talk with Mrs. Norman came off all right. I
couldn't say anything to her. She just didn't want
the type of thing I did for her and I was never able
to talk with her face to face in order to find out what
she did want. Now I know—and she has given me
three months to make up the budget—so to speak. I
think I can run it off some time if I ever get around
to it. Meanwhile you can look at what I did do for
her sometime if you want to. It isn't so hot but it is
at least a bit gay. She is almost funereal in her per-
fectionist gloom. I dunno, I don't think she and I
will mix. . . . The world isn't going to be moved
that way. But maybe I'm wrong, I usually find that

I am—in many things. I wonder if we aren't going to be wrong even about death? I'm betting on it. We can't possibly break the record of our lives and hit that on the nose either.

The poems won't be hard to get together. I want them to come out in subdivisions of the original books as they appeared, chronologically. A very few alterations will have to be made and a few of the poems will need to be omitted for lack of value but the rest had better just follow along as they first appeared. You fix the date of their appearance to suit yourself. I don't give one whoop in hell—so long as you are interested.

As soon as I feel able I want to go on assembling the biography of my mother. It will have quite a general interest I think. Anyhow, that's what I want to do this summer and spring.

You've probably received a letter similar to the one I am enclosing from Henry Miller. I am sending it merely because of the suggestion relative to translations. No need to return it. I am *not* joining the editorial board of his new mag. Nor am I sending him cash. The little cash I have to spare I intend to keep giving to the Spanish Loyalists.

I've just finished reviewing Muriel Rukeysers, *US1*. The gal has good ideas and occasionally hits it off O.K. but in general she attempts too ambitious projects and gets nowhere with them. What the hell. I like her guts but facts is facts. I always try at least to say what I think. I suppose I'll get roasted for not being bowled over by the gal's good intentions. Can't help it. *The New Republic* ast me to do it. Jesus Christ am I sick and God damned tired of all this crappy writing tonight. I'm going to turn down all requests for the stuff from now on until I feel better. I hardly get settled down when something new comes up and I'm floored again. I suppose I ought to be delighted.

But if I get an hour and finally spend three on a few pages with the phone going and tempers rising all around me—Shit with it.

Best luck; nothing much else to say.

Yours
BILL

/ · /

his new mag: The Phoenix: An American Augur, of which Henry Miller was European editor and J. P. Cooney of Woodstock, New York, was founder. Lawrentian in program, the magazine advertised that "as soon as *The Phoenix* has brought together a group of us—no matter how small—we shall go off to Mexico or South America and take up the life-mode which the Aztecs and Incas let fall."
US1: WCW's review of Muriel Rukeyser's book of poems *US1* (New York: Covici, Friede, 1938) appeared in the *New Republic* for March 9, 1938, pp. 141–42.

16. TLS-1   July 20, 1938

DEAR JIM:

Send me a *White Mule* and a *Passaic River,* will you please. I want to give 'em away but I suppose I'd better inscribe them first with a tender greeting of some sort instead of having you mail 'em direct. On the cuff!

Read the enclosed, the last part of it, though it's no news to you. Damn it! ain't there some way so that sort of thing doesn't have to happen?

Inside news, keep it under your hat as a confidence! Constance Rourke, one of the best, has done a noteworthy book on Charles Sheeler, the painter and one of my best friends. It's a pip, text and illustrations combined. Flash! On August 18, *Life* is running six pages of illustrations in color advertising the book. Fer Gawd's sake now don't spill that to *any-body*. The book appears August 11, Harcourt, Brace & Co. It's right down our alley.

Weel, it was a nice meeting last night in Madison Square Garden in support of the Spanish Loyalists. Father O'Flanagan was the most amazingly candid speaker on the relationship between his church and the world that I have ever listened to. He put courage into my guts. There is, yes, sir, there is a world that might be had!

I'm pooping along, like a scow full of sand in the Hudson river against tide. Hi keed?

Yours
BILL

/ · /

the enclosed: To judge from JL's reply of July 23, 1938, the enclosure was a letter to WCW from Constance Rourke, who complained that she had not been able to obtain a copy of WCW's *Life Along the Passaic River* in the New York bookstores of Doubleday and Scribners.

Sheeler: For Charles Sheeler see letter 3 above. *Charles Sheeler: Artist in the American Tradition,* by the biographer and critic Constance Rourke (1885–1941), was published by Harcourt, Brace in 1938. *Life* magazine for August 8 (not 18), 1939, carried a feature on Sheeler's painting and photography under the title "Sheeler Finds Beauty in the Common-place" (pp. 42–45). Two of the article's four pages were in color.

meeting: According to the *New York Times* for July 20, 1938, p. 4, some 20,000 people attended a mass meeting in New York's Madison Square Garden on July 19, the second anniversary of the outbreak of the Spanish civil war. The rally was sponsored by the Medical Bureau and North American Committee to Aid Spanish Democracy, of which WCW was an active member in Bergen County, New Jersey. The Reverend Michael O'Flanagan, an Irish Republican priest, told fellow Catholics in the audience, "[Y]ou are not bound to follow the leadership of your pastor in political affairs. Rather it is your duty to make up your own mind, and pay no more attention to the views of your pastor than you would to the views of any other man of equal political intelligence. I say to every Bishop of the church that if you accept your politics from the Pope you are not worthy of citizenship in any country of the world except Vatican City. And I say to the Pope, 'You are not infallible about anything except religious matters.' "

17. TLS-1   August 1, 1938

DEAR JIM:

The second lot of proofs have been corrected and
are on their way to you. In this lot there are a number of important spots that need touching up. I hope
there won't be any difficulty in this though some
slight expense may be incurred. These are things that
could not very well be foreseen. I ask you not to
veto them. A book like this isn't printed every year.

One thing is the matter of the dates in the "Descent
of Winter" section. The dates as originally printed
in *Exile* went down the page in a straight line and
did not adhere to each poem. Please do this for me.
Fix them up in the original way, I mean.

The spacing of "The Rain," as you will notice is
atrocious. That we shall not have to pay for. The
script is perfect but they did not follow it. Don't let
that get by.

The rest doesn't amount to much other than the
transposition of 2 or 4 poems in the "Spring and All"
section so that the better poem in one case may have
the better presentation and not be cut in half by the
page.

Finally I think it might be a useful thing to place
a date after each of the several subheadings through
the book, such as "The Tempers, 1913" etc etc. What
do you say? That shouldn't be much trouble.

Floss and I have been having an orgy over the
damned thing. It has a decided build up when one
reads it through that is something new to me.

Well, there it is. ⟨The numbering of the subdivisions of the "Primavera" is also important.⟩

Will you supply the skull and cross bones and the
arrows as indicated in the script or shall we leave it
to them. I say let them go ahead. They are merely

the most conventional of symbols. Nothing could be more conventionaler so that their choice could not possibly be anything but perfect.

But don't veto my changes, not this time. Please!

Yours
BILL

/ · /

proofs: The Complete Collected Poems of William Carlos Williams 1906–1938 was printed by Peter Beilenson at the Walpole Printing Office, Mt. Vernon, New York.

Exile: "The Descent of Winter" was originally published in Ezra Pound's magazine *The Exile,* no. 4 (Autumn 1928): 30–69.

transposition: Probably of sections 21 and 22, which are in the reverse order of their appearance in *Spring and All* (1923).

"Primavera": "Della Primavera Trasportata al Morale" has ten numbered subdivisions, of which "Rain" is the eighth. The skull and crossbones and arrows appear in the section entitled "This Is My Platform" (p. 188).

18. TLS-1   March 14, 1939

DEAR JIM:

Floss says no book of poems for me this year. She says it wouldn't be fair to the *Collected Poems.* She says spread the new vein far and wide, get poems into every possible magazine that can be trephined into accepting one. Then, sez she, when you've added a few more and studied them more carefully, then, sez she, mebbe you can have another book.

As a beginning as I think I told you *New Yorker* has accepted and paid for! five and *Poetry* has accepted fourteen while *New Republic* owns one. *Poetry* wants to do two groups, one in July or August and one in the fall. If a book came out before next Christmas these plans would be spoiled. So be it.

Meanwhile *Partisan Review* has accepted the *second* chapter of the new *White Mule,* God damn it. Serves me right for not sending them one chapter at a time. But let it pass. There can be no question as to the justice of their taste, the second chapter is the better of the two first ones in the book.

Jim Higgins has a few really competent poems to show you if he takes my advice. They're really top notch but I advised him to send them first to *Poetry* and not to have you put them into *New Directions.* At least that's the way I feel about it.

My own contribution to *New Directions,* if anybody should ask me to contribute, will be:

THREE LETTERS
from
the collection of
W . C . W .

Boy! and they're *some* letters, every one with a new direction in it. Wait and see. The last one is a promotion scheme invented by John Coffey to further the availability of good but insufficiently known books. It's a pip. I'll send you a copy of that one right away (as soon as it has been typed) I want The Friends of W.C.W. to get busy on that one at once. I think if we gang up and push we'll get somewhere with it. The second is from a gal in Martinique and the first—Geez!—is from a wild man in Paterson, N.J.

Yours
BILL

⟨What the hell is your address, anyway?⟩

/ · /

New Yorker: In a letter of March 20, 1939, WCW told JL that the *New Yorker* had paid $58 for "The Return to Work," "Silence," "Prelude to

Winter," "The Rocking Woman," and "Sparrows among Dry Leaves."
The poems appeared, respectively, in the following issues of volume
15 (1939): April 8 (p. 22), October 7 (p. 66), October 14 (p. 24),
November 11 (p. 21), and November 18 (p. 59). *Poetry* published seven
poems ("Illegitimate Things," "The Poet and His Poems I–II," "Defi-
ance to Cupid," "A Cold Front," "The Forgotten City," and "In
Chains") in September 1939 and seven ("The Observer," "From a
Window," "River Rhyme," "The World Narrowed to a Point," "A
Fond Farewell," "Fertile," and "The Unknown") in November 1940.
The *New Republic* published "The Swaggering Gait" on July 5, 1939.

Partisan Review: "Back to the City," chapter 2 of *In the Money,* appeared
in *Partisan Review* 6, no. 3 (Spring 1939): 92–99.

Jim Higgins: The Irish-American writer Jim Higgins met JL at Harvard
and later became his associate at New Directions. Eight prose sketches
by Higgins appeared in *New Directions in Prose and Poetry 1938,* and the
anthology for 1939 is dedicated "To Jim Higgins / They Also Serve
Who Do the Dirtywork."

THREE LETTERS: JL rejected these letters on March 17, and they
were apparently never published. John Coffey was the young radical
to whom the title poem of WCW's *An Early Martyr and Other Poems*
(1935) was dedicated. During the Depression, Coffey was committed
without trial to a hospital for the criminally insane because he had sto-
len furs from department stores and sold them to feed the poor. The
wild man from Paterson was probably David Lyle; see letter 38 below.

The Friends of W.C.W.: Formed in February 1939 at the instigation of
Ford Madox Ford, Les Amis de William Carlos Williams included
Sherwood Anderson, W. H. Auden, Edward Dahlberg, Waldo Frank,
Marsden Hartley, Christopher Isherwood, Archibald MacLeish,
Marianne Moore, Gorham Munson, Charles Olson, Katherine Anne
Porter, Ezra Pound, Charles Sheeler, Alfred Stieglitz, Allen Tate, and
Louis Zukofsky. The group met five times before disbanding in June
1939.

19. TL-2   March 17, 1939

DEAR BILL:

My address is 229 Perkins St, Jamaica Plain, Mass.,
and the office address is 39 East Springfield St, Boston.

Naturally the manuscript of verse caused a good
deal of excitement. I liked parts of it very much and
didn't like some of it so much. Some poems seem

swell, others seem lacking in your accustomed con-
sequence. My guess is that six months from now a
dozen of them will seem less bright and shiny to
you.

One thing that got me down was the use of rhyme.
I guess I just don't like rhyme. There is something
real about your poetry which just doesn't fit with
rhyme. The poems with those jingles were the ones
that made me the most uncomfortable. I suppose
those were just the ones that the *New Yorker* took.
What do they pay by the way?

I think Floss is right about publication, though I
would be glad to do a book if you wanted. I think
the next thing after the *Collected [Poems]* ought to be
a prose book. Then some verse.

Another thing for you to bear in mind in general
in this. We don't get very far with books done separately. It is for this reason that I plan to do almost
nothing except in the fall. Here's the reason; what
sells books is catalogue, mailing list, salesman's visits, advertising. Now all those things cost so damn
much that we can only afford them by bunching the
books together and splitting the expense. The catalogue runs $700. Salesman runs $400 a trip. Etc. That
is why I don't advise a lone book in the Spring. We
took a licking on *Passaic,* partly because it was cut
off in that way. Fall is the time for books; people are
serious then. In the Spring they're too happy.

The idea of filling the magazines is good. That's
good promotion; if the mags miss any very good
ones they can go into N[ew] D[irections] *39.* I want
something real strong from you for *ND 39.* The letters from your collection sound diverting but do they
pack a big wallop. Lots of wallop wanted. Maybe a
dozen or so of those short sketches you mentioned.

That's tough that P[artisan] R[eview] has taken
Chapter 2. But it won't make much difference if the

whole thing will be out in book form soon. They only need to be in sequence if it is to string along a long way the way they did before.

When will that ole mule be kicking? If we could have her all printed by September we could do better promotion than we did before—advance copies to bookstores and more salesman's pressure, etc. I must confess that first crack was pretty still-born. I didn't know much about the game then. But I do know now. We'll pull the strings this time. Blurbs and a peppy jacket and all that.

Have you heard anything from Roskolenko? I haven't.

[E. E.] Cummings was here Wednesday. Gave a reading at Harvard. Not so hot. He was scared and didn't read his best stuff. I've been trying to get you up here on that program—which pays a hundred bucks or so—but the committee is made up of pricks like Hillyer and Ted Morrison. They got Cummings because he and Hillyer were classmates.

What can you do to your middle finger? A babe gave mine a yank months ago and it still hurts. What would that be?

Did you see Untermeyer's review in *Yale Review?* He says you ought to get the Pulitzer. Well its pricks like him that hand out that gravy. So maybe . . .

Best

Shall I keep that ms. of the poems?

/ · /

My address: JL had returned to Harvard University to complete his bachelor's degree.

the manuscript: WCW had recently sent JL a group of poems labeled "Detail and Parody for the Poem Patterson *[sic]*." Versions of the manuscript are now in the Poetry/Rare Books Collection of the State

University of New York at Buffalo and in the Houghton Library, Harvard University.

Hillyer: At this time, the poet Robert Hillyer (see letter 86 below) was Boylston Professor of Rhetoric and Oratory at Harvard University. The poet and novelist Theodore Morrison (1901–1988) taught at Harvard from 1930 to 1973 and served as Director of the Bread Loaf Writers' Conference from 1932 to 1955. JL had taken a composition course from Morrison at Harvard.

Untermeyer: The writer and editor Louis Untermeyer (1885–1977) reviewed WCW's *Complete Collected Poems* along with four other books in "Experiment and Tradition," *Yale Review* 28, no. 3 (March 1939): 608–13. Untermeyer called the *Poems* "one of the most important books of the year" and "a plausible contender for the Pulitzer Prize."

20. TLS-2   March 26, 1939

DEAR JIM:

Saw Robert Frost today, on his sixty fourth birthday, at the house of a mutual friend in Montclair where he had come for a lecture last night. He's all right, improved with age in spite of what has been said of him. I hope to see him soon again, a more cosmopolitan person than I had been led to believe. He's a good talker, witty, loaded with information and well able to take care of himself anywhere, anytime—unless I'm greatly mistaken. He's going to Harvard next year for a course of lectures.

So long as la grosse Margot can fart and while greasy Joan doth keel the pot I'll drop into rhyme when it pleases me so to do—without injury to anyone and "bow wow!" to [T. S.] Eliot. Eliot is a cultured gentleman and cultured gentlemen are always likely to undersell the market . . I'm glad you like his verse but I'm warning you, the only reason it doesn't smell is that it's synthetic. Maybe I'm wrong but I distrust that bastard more than any writer I know in the world today. He can write. Granted.

But—it's like walking into a church to me. I can't do it without a bad feeling at the pit of my stomach: nothing has been learned there since the simplicities were prevented from becoming multiform by arrest of growth—Birdseye Foods, suddenly frozen at 50 degrees below zero under pressure at perfect maturity, immediately after being picked from the canes. It's pathologic with me perhaps, I hope not but I am infuriated by such things. I am infuriated because the arrest has taken place just at the point of risk, just at the point when the magnificence might (possibly) have happened, just when the danger threatened, just when the transition might, just might have led to the difficult new thing. But the God damned liars prefer Popes, prefer "order", prefer freezing— prefer, if you use the image, the sterilization of the Christ they profess. And the result is canned to make literature, with all the flavor, with all the pomp— while the real thing rots, under their noses and they duck to the other side of the street. I despise and detest them. They are moles on a pig's belly instead of tits—Christ, how I hate their guts. And the more so because Eliot, like his monumental wooden throne on wheels that he carries around with him to worship—Eliot takes the place of the realizable actual which is that much held back from realization by precisely his existence.

Perhaps you're right, I'll sell the introduction if I can, possibly to Mrs. Norman. Under separate cover I'm sending you an undergraduate college paper with two of the short shorts of which there are ten or more unplaced which you may want to select from for *N[ew D[irections] '39.

It's probably wise to plan to print the *American Grain* in the dollar series this fall as I feel sure *Mule* won't be ready the way I'm not writing it these days. The only objection left for me is, mightn't it be wiser to print something else than the *American Grain* as my first in that series? Mightn't it be wiser to print a book the parts of which are even more difficult to find than the original edition of *American Grain* is today? I refer to a book that could be made up as follows—*The Great American Novel, A Novelette* and either the full text of *Spring and All, Kora in Hell* or the long short story "Old Doc Rivers." The last might be the best, in that case: call it, *The Gt American Novel*.

Best luck
BILL

Enclosed a review of Roskolenko's book. In spite of appearances I did not write it with evil intention but after two months of more or less deliberate thought. The review is not to be used—not by us at least. Send it back unless you have other ideas but I see no use in publishing it.

This started out to be a snappy letter telling you that it might be wiser to do a dollar book on my less known prose rather even than *The Am. Grain*—but I was tired and so the clutch started slipping from the first. Christ, I'm tired and so miss the keys, fail to stop when I shd and generally beshit the scene. I'm sorry.

⟨3/27/39 Frost told me yesterday, to go on, that he has been more or less avoiding me for the past 25 years due to the unnecessary insistence of Ezra-the-Pound in London, 1914, that I was the only person in the U[nited] S[tates] that he, Frost, was permitted to associate with, the only one that he could associate with & remain clean. Reverse English, what? W.⟩

/ · /

la grosse Margot: Fat Margot the whore farts in one of the *ballades* in François Villon's *Le Testament* (1456), while greasy Joan doth keel the pot in the rhymed song which ends William Shakespeare's *Love's Labor's Lost* (1598).

Eliot: In a letter of March 24, 1939, JL had suggested that "if you want to see poetry as is poetry—hard as a rock and beautiful as the queen's tit—look at the choruses in Eliot's new play" *[The Family Reunion]*.

short shorts: JL selected four of these prose sketches for *New Directions in Prose and Poetry 1939*. The "Four Pictures," as they were titled, included "The Drill Sergeant," "A Boy in the Family," "The Plumber and the Minister," and "The Official Disclaimer."

American Grain: A second impression of WCW's *In the American Grain* (1925), with an introduction by Horace Gregory, was published in December 1939. It was the first in a New Directions series called "The New Classics," which reprinted important modern works gone out of print or never before translated into English. Each book was priced at $1.00.

a review: WCW sent his review of *Sequence on Violence* (New York: Signal, 1938), by Harry Roskolenko (1907–1980; also spelled Rosko-lenkier), to the *New Republic;* but it was not published until James E. B. Breslin included it in his edition of *Something to Say: William Carlos Williams on Younger Poets* (New York: New Directions, 1985), pp. 101–2.

21. TLS-2   April 5, 1939

DEAR JIM:

Of course I recognize Eliot as a noteworthy artist, and of course I know and recognize the literature that stems from and is parcel of the tradition of literature purely. It may be great and properly directed is great. Perhaps Eliot is great.

On the other hand I say and believe that all that is implied above is secondary to something else, something hot from the blood that, at its best, uses the traditional literary and makes the great masterpieces of the world. It is this latter that is likely to be displaced and forgotten by the former.

My objections to the collegiate sons of bitches to whom Eliot and Pound, at their worst, play the pimp, is that they tend to elevate the first category against the second. The second is trackless and enormously difficult. It is always under the great handicap of monumental invention for its contents and form. But the pimps of literature seize the position due great imagination and all its prerogatives and puff themselves up at the true artist.

This wouldn't be so bad if they did not at the same time actively, very often, drive down the already sufficiently harassed man seeking to rescue and build up a present world in his creations (a Frederick Ives in N.Y. today in music)—a generous world of the spirit which is the great garland of the artist in his supreme unselfishness—when it exists.

The Pounds and the Eliots—Pound less than Eliot—have no eye for the artist in the sense that I outline him above. They do not make themselves, as they should, his abettor. They want to *tell* him, right enough but not to serve him. They place themselves and their kind at the peak displacing their betters—their less skilled betters but their betters.

By this they are actively the enemies of the highest reaches of the artist's imagination and will always be the ones to keep the artist down, seldom to help him up.

———————

I am enthusiastic for the gemischte volume, it's a real idea and one for which I feel indebted to you. We'll say more of that later.

Yes, with Floss' blessing, *In the American Grain* should be the first volume of the dollar series—if you do it. She says it would be dumb to do anything else. So I'm dumb.

Let the Olson bill go. I hear he's broke—Ford said so last night. He's a good guy and probably hasn't the $2.50 handy.

It's different with Roskolenko. He went out

deliberately to rook you and, God damn it, right or left thats wrong still in my eyes.

I haven't heard that Ezra is coming but it looks to me to be one of the surest signs of the approaching war that I have heard of to date. I hope he does keep his trap shut if he's for that murderous gang he says he's for. I can hardly bear the thought of shaking hands with the guy if he does show up here—I'd say the same to my own father under the circumstances.

Yours
BILL

/ · /

Frederick Ives: WCW may have been thinking of the American composer Charles Ives (1874–1954).

Olson: At this time, the poet Charles Olson (1910–1970) was a teacher at Harvard University and a member, with Ford Madox Ford, of Les Amis de William Carlos Williams (see letter 18 above).

Ezra: Pound arrived in the United States from Italy on April 21, 1939, to lobby members of the Roosevelt administration and Congress on behalf of world peace and monetary reform.

22. TCS   [April 24, 1939?]

DEAR BILL:

I am very mightily cheered by your approval of the poems. Nobody here understands what I am after at all. They all claim that a visual form cannot relate itself to the tradition of an oral form in poetry and that the lines should be run out like free verse. I personally get an effect of tension from the war between the strictly artificial visual pattern and the strictly natural spoken rhythms. That is what I have in mind anyway. Also to try to write concretely, using everyday objects for your symbols and allegories, and to avoid poeticisms.

I just got a cryptic card from Ezra. He's in Washington and gives no plans at all.

                                                            Jim

/ · /

the poems: In a letter of April 22, WCW praised two poems, one entitled "Easter in Pittsburgh," which JL had sent him on April 14.

23. TLS-1   April 26, 1939

DEAR JIM:

One of the most difficult and important things, I should say, for a young man to learn would be the limitations of his teachers, at Harvard as elsewhere. It's forbidden ground in most cases, deliberately hidden and desperately defended against attack. The facts of the case aren't desired besides which the natural modesty of youth makes us susceptible to just the sort of deceit that those in positions of authority practice against us—when we are young—to hide from us just that which we should know.

It takes us most of our lives to find out how limited the world is. Very little is understood other than that which has been underscored by authority. Nobody will take the trouble to really get down to work on new proposals. Perhaps the university as such must inevitably place itself as a barrier to the new just by being a defender of the old and the established. I once heard the elderly and intelligent and tolerant Dean Gaucher (is it?) of Princeton (much to my surprise) discourse on that subject. He was overruled later by several of his hirelings.

Aristocrats with their blanket lack of esteem for anyone who is not an aristocrat are often, I suppose, in an advantageous position toward the beginnings of their lives because of that. It is hard otherwise to grasp that we know, that we are able, that others are barriers to our progress right from the beginning. I for one have hung back just from a lack of conviction of the dullness of others. I have said, Why should I presume? when I should have said, For Christ's sake get the hell out of my way and at once! So much time is lost.

Damn the bastards for saying that you can't mix auditory and visual standards in poetry. Who the hell ever invented these two categories but themselves? Those are the questions that set up all academic controversies. The trouble with them is that they aren't real questions at all they are merely evidence of lack of definition in the terms. Define your terms and the question disappears. Philosophy is full of them until someone who knows what he is about shows them up.

What they, the formulators of that particular question do not know, is that an auditory quality, a NEW auditory quality, underlies and determines the visual quality which they object to. Let it pass, Jim, it's one of the limitations of the present grade of teachers. Do your stuff, listen hard and make discoveries. If we're right we'll turn out to be termites in their wooden legs. If we're wrong the birds will eat us.

Yours
BILL

/ · /

Dean Gaucher: Christian Gauss (1878–1951), professor of Romance languages and from 1925 to 1945 dean of the college at Princeton University.

24. TL-2

DEAR JIM:

By all means have Lorca in the 1939 *N[ew] D[irections]*. There's so much of the Spanish stuff that is unknown, old and new. Geez how I'd like you to use some of the novella by Quevedo I've been translating, 1627 stuff, right on the ball. I could give you anywhere from twenty to forty pages or more if you had room for it. Maybe ten pages would be enough— the only difficulty being that unless the whole business is offered it might be too puzzling for the ordinary reader to get the drift of it. I'm using the whole novella as a framework to hang my mother's biography on. Probably best not to fool with it now.

The one to look up in connection with Lorca is Rolfe Humphries who is in Mexico on a Gug[genheim Fellowship] now I think. Maybe you have his address, if not he could be reached through *Kenyon Review*. I'm not familiar with Alberti, don't know him at all.

We had a gay party last night. Too bad you didn't show up, everybody wanted to see the wonder child. There were about twenty here including Higgins and his girl, more of a child than I had suspected—but maybe I'm wrong, I usually am in such matters. Marsden Hartley and my new Scotty pup (6 weeks old or so) were the heroes—he pissed on everything. Hartley was well primed by my Bill and a pal with good Gordon gin so that he positively glowed. Haven't seen him so young and happy in years. But we didn't do any reading, just talked and drank and ate. A marvellous night was accorded to us by God in the matter of the weather, superb. We started it in the back yard among roses and lilies and ended after midnight indoors.

Pound spent the night here Monday [June 5]. He spread himself on the divan all evening and discoursed to the family in his usual indistinct syllables—at that it wasn't bad, if you believed him. I found unfortunately that he has acquired a habit of avoiding the question at issue when he is pressed for a direct answer. Not so good. But he does go, he does see the important faces and he does have some worthwhile thoughts and projects in hand. I like him immensely as always, he is inspiring and has much information to impart but he gets nowhere with it, "a static explosion in a granite quarry" is the way Munson spoke of him. The man is sunk, in my opinion, unless he can shake the fog of Fascism out of his brain during the next few years which I seriously doubt that he can do. The logicality of fascist rationalizations is soon going to kill him. You can't argue away wanton slaughter of innocent women and children by the neo-scholasticism of a controlled economy program. Shit with a Hitler who lauds the work of his airmen in Spain and so shit with Pound too if he can't stand up and face his questioners on the point.

Enclosed is a story that has been batted around everywhere without acceptance. If you care to use it in *N[ew] D[irections] 1939* I'd like to see you do so. I like the thing but because of its length and a slightly diluted quality no one wants it. If you also do not want it, say so. It's about all I have now aside from the Quevedo translation which is probably unsuitable.

Tooraloo, must get at the new *White Mule*. By the way, I've decided on the title for volume two: *A Taste of Fortune*. It has a somewhat musty flavor at that but it goes, I think, with the story. I did think of using, *In the Money*. Like that better? The second is snappier and more up to date. And, my dear publisher, what about the publication of the book? Suppose you go into the plant? How about having somebody like Simon & Schuster or the other bastards buy up the sheets of the original *White Mule* and bind the new volume up with them into one glorious whole. Just an idea. This time it's got to be pushed hard.

I didn't set out to write a letter as long as this. What the hell's the matter with me?

Sincerely yours

/ · /

Lorca: New Directions in Prose and Poetry 1939 carried Gilbert Neiman's English translation of García Lorca's *Bodas de sangre [Blood Wedding]* (1933). The translation appeared separately as New Directions Pamphlet 5 in 1939. New Directions later published other translations of the Spanish poet and playwright (see letters 15 and 16 above). These included *III Tragedies: Blood Wedding, Yerma, Bernarda Alba,* trans. Richard L. O'Connell and James Graham-Luján (1947), and *Selected Poems,* ed. Francisco García Lorca and Donald M. Allen (1955).

novella by Quevedo: Since 1936, WCW and his mother had worked on a translation of *El Perro y la calentura* (1627), by the Madrid satirist Francisco Gomez de Quevedo y Villegas (1580–1645). Their translation was eventually published as *The Dog and the Fever: A Perambulatory Novella* (Hamden, Conn.: Shoe String Press, [1954]).

Rolfe Humphries: The poet and translator Rolfe Humphries (1894–1969) had received a Guggenheim Fellowship to prepare a bilingual edition of *The Poet in New York and Other Poems of Federico García Lorca* (New York: W. W. Norton, 1940). Humphries's translation of Lorca's *Gypsy Ballads* appeared in 1943. He was also coeditor of the anthology . . . *and Spain sings: Fifty Loyalist Ballads* (New York: Vanguard Press, 1937), to which WCW had contributed an adaptation of a ballad by Miguel Hernández entitled "Wind of the Village."

Alberti: The Spanish poet and painter Rafael Alberti (1902–) was a friend of García Lorca and a prominent Communist spokesman during the Spanish civil war. Alberti went into exile in 1939, stopping in the United States before taking up residence in Argentina. New Directions published his *Selected Poems,* trans. Lloyd Mallan, in 1944. Alberti returned to Spain in 1977 to take a seat in the Cortes, or Parliament.

Marsden Hartley: It is not clear just when WCW and the American painter Marsden Hartley (1877–1943) first met, but they almost certainly knew one another by 1919, when they both contributed essays on the poet

Wallace Gould to the *Little Review* and WCW bought a watercolor landscape of New Mexico by Hartley.

Munson: For Gorham Munson, see letter 2 above. WCW had known him since 1916.

a story: "Comedy Entombed" was published in *Trend* 1, no. 4 (April 1942): 4–7, 25, and later reprinted in *New Directions 9* (1946).

In the Money: The second novel of WCW's Stecher trilogy was *In the Money,* published by New Directions on October 29, 1940.

25. TLS-1   February 18, 1940

DEAR JIM:

If you wish to postpone the payment of whatever royalties may be coming to me, as you say, until Spring, it's all right with me. I occasionally think of the matter and wonder where I stand but shall have to continue to leave it in your hands. Do as you think best.

Just pounded out another chapter of the *Mule* this afternoon, the 24th. That leaves only three to go. I have been driven to the wall recently by the influenza cases and other urgent personal matters so that there has been little time for writing. And God only knows what in hell the book's going to be like anyhow. It needs a hell of a lot of touching up and cutting and generally revising. It's a different book from the last, at least I imagine it so. There's more of the business battle in this book. Not that little Flossie doesn't come in all the time but she appears more on the fringes in this book than the last—occasionally filling the eye, of course, but not to such an extent as in the first book.

The thing is I write along and don't seem to be saying a damned thing. It looks stupid as hell to me. Not that it doesn't excite me as I write, it does—but God damned if I know whether it isn't second child-

ishness on my part or what the hell it is. When I read
it later (some of the chapters) I get a somewhat of a
thrill out of it. But why? Damned if I know. It still
seems like crap to me.

Maybe I'm low. I am low.

On the other hand I finished up the collection for
your pamphlet, the thirty pages. It was to be thirty
pages, wasn't it? Thirty printed pages. I made up my
booklet and sent it to be typed, Mrs. Heath has it
now. The old stuff won't bother you. It's a progres-
sion, a poem about every five years. Just five of them.
Then a group. Then a couple of recent shots. That's
all. I'd like to keep the book as it is. It makes a decent
whole.

Yours
BILL

/ · /

your pamphlet: WCW's *The Broken Span,* published on January 2, 1941,
was the first of New Directions's Poet of the Month pamphlets. In a
letter to JL of February 1, 1940, WCW spoke of it by the title *To Continue.*

26. TLS-1   Aug. 23, 1940

DEAR JIM:

Floss is picking up but has lost the hearing of her
left ear. I don't believe we shall have any complica-
tions. She ought to be up and about next week.

Your first paragraph is excellent, your second not
so good though the meat of what you want to say is
there. I have rewritten this second paragraph and
believe that my version has certain advantages over
the other.

I especially dislike "very great" and "poetic".

What about the poetry pamphlet? You saying nothing on that score.

You know, Jim, you once asked me what I thought about Henry Miller. I didn't answer you for the simple reason that I didn't much like what he had written but I suspected my own judgment but something happened yesterday that cast a little more light on that. I read a letter sent to Fred Miller, no acquaintance of Henry's, by a jazzaroo who is down South working his way from hot joint to hot joint trying to pick up a living throwing dice.

Now this alligator is an adventurer, an occasional jazz orchestra player, a writer—anything at all. But his letter makes Fred Miller's stuff look like the anemic ravings of a convent girl. Those joints, those American joints especially in the south are a chapter I have never even dreamed of—where the men piss on the floor under the tables and fuck the girls openly in the booths along the wall. As this man entered this particular joint a girl named Elizabeth zipped open his fly, jerked out his Dick with one deft motion and said, How you doin', boy?

This chap, who has the entrée to these places because of his jazz propensities, says it's impossible to believe. That one letter made my hair (such as it is) stand on end and this was not a letter written for effect but just a simple letter to a friend. He says he like to write a book on it but doesn't believe anyone would think he was telling the truth. He's a pulp writer as is Fred (to make a little cash only) but intelligent. I'd like to get my hands into such a book. I bet that collaborating with him I could make that thing stand up like nobody's business. Well, that's my answer.

Yours
BILL

/ · /

Your first paragraph: Probably a draft by JL of the two-paragraph dust-jacket blurb for WCW's *In the Money.*

Fred Miller's stuff: WCW probably meant to say "Henry Miller's stuff."

27. TLS-1   Sept. 24, 1940

DEAR JIM:

O.K. let the wops play with it, they won't get anywhere, so what's the difference. It makes me smile that the ol' Idaho What's It should even remember me. He's even more of an infant than I believed. In fact that's the answer to all his snot. The only thing is that it's dangerous as hell if taken seriously by thinking people.

It all revealed itself to me yesterday when I was reading his new Canto, Chinese Numbers I calls it. He doesn't know a damned thing about China, the Chinese or the language—that's what makes him an expert; he knows nothing about music, being tone deaf—that's what makes him a musician. He's a misplaced romantic, that's what makes him a historical realist. And he's batty in the head, that's what makes him a philosopher. But in spite of it all he's a good poet. I had to acknowledge it as I read along in that chinese abaca frame of his enumerating verse. It had charm, it had sweep, it had even childish innocence written all over it. He thinks he's being terribly profound, frowningly serious and all he's doing is building blocks and it's lovely. He hasn't the least idea where he hits true and where he falls flat, he wants to be praised for one thing and he contradicts himself upon the same count in the next paragraph. He's got to be loved to be praised, as one loves a Mongoloid idiot, for his sweet character.

I'm wasting my time when I get sore at such a character. Anger simply doesn't apply in his case. As I read I relented, found myself smiling and enjoying. I had to confess I was wrong in trying to treat him as a logical entity, as a poet he is valuable, as a man someone ought to goose him.

All the proofs were sent forward to you last week. I had your card today but shall have to wait until you call on the phone this evening, I suppose, before you can be acquainted with all this. Lousy weather and vile news, no matter who is winning the war it is still vile news.

Yours

BILL

/ · /

Idaho What's It: Because he was born in Hailey, Idaho, Ezra Pound's friends sometimes called him the Idaho Kid.

Chinese Numbers: Cantos LII–LXXI, containing Pound's Chinese-history cantos, was published by New Directions on September 17, 1940. WCW received a copy from JL on September 19.

28. TLS-1   Sept. 25, 1940

It's easy to forget in our dislike for some of the parts Ezra Pound plays and for which there is no excuse that he is a master of language ⟨& makes mistakes too sometimes⟩. That goes far. It might be his only virtue and still be a mark of greatness. It is hard to appraise as it is hard to achieve, hard to isolate for criticism as for the honors earned. It is even possible that Pound himself is self deceived and performs his miracles unconsciously while he frowns over some asininity he proposes and leans upon so heavily. His language represents his last naivety, the childishness of complete sincerity discovered in the child and true poet alike.

All that is necessary to *feel* Pound's excellence in this use of language is to read the work of others—from among whom I particularly and prominently exclude E. E. Cummings. In the use of language Pound and Cummings are beyond doubt the two most distinguished American poets of today. It is the bringing over of the language of the day to the serious purposes of the poet that is the difficult thing. Both these men have evolved that ability to a high degree.

Two faulty alternatives are escaped in the achievement of this distinction. There are plenty who use the language well, fully as well as Pound, but for trivial purposes, either journalism, fiction or even verse, I mean the usual stroking of the material without penetration where anything of momentous significance is instinctively avoided. There are on the other hand poets of considerable seriousness who simply do not know what language is and unconsciously load their compositions with minute anachronisms as many as dead hairs on a mangy dog. These latter are the more pernicious, their methods well accredited by virtue of all academic teaching, simply make their work no good. they would need to go through the crises both Pound and Cummings experienced in ridding themselves of all collegiate taint.

It is impossible to praise Pound's line. The terms for such praise are lacking. There ain't none. You've got to read the line and feel first, then grasp through experience in its full significance HOW the language makes the verse live. It lives; even such unpromising cataloguing as his cantos of the chinese kings, princes and other rulers do live and become affecting under his treatment. It is the language and the language only that makes this true.

P.S. Just had a moment or two waiting for a patient in my office just now, thought it might interest you and perhaps serve in some way. No importance. Chuck it if you want to I'm keeping no copy.

BILL

29. TLS-1   Nov. 24, 1940

DEAR JIM:

I suppose it's too late to make any changes in the pamphlet of my poems you are issuing in January? I've been looking the work over and find that there is more than one spot in which it is weak. If too late, so be it; if not too late, I'd like to drop out one or two poems completely, substituting two later and better ones of about the same length for them. There are a few word changes that might also be made to advantage.

On the other hand don't let yourself feel disturbed about it if the pages are all set up, they'll have to take the good with the bad as they find it.

Such situations as this are bound to occur when work is gathered quickly together. A verse maker should never be in a hurry. The mind is a queer mechanical machine that allows itself to be caught in traps. A rhythmical jig takes hold of us forcing us to follow it, slipping in the words quite against our better judgement sometimes. We grow enamoured of our own put-put and like to see the boat push ahead— even to its destruction sometimes: a heavy figure for a stupid happening.

What I really wanted to say is that to make a good poem it is often necessary to wait until we have forgotten the conditions under which we wrote in the first place. Going back, we see clearly (perhaps) where we have been led astray—there is a free field once more, the defects stick out like boulders. What the hell's the matter with me, why don't I quit this crap? I dunno.

Yrs
BILL

30. TLS-1   Dec. 14, 1940

DEAR JIM:

Before it is too late please send me four (4) copies of *In the Money* to be charged as usual to my account. I want them before Christmas. Many thanks.

Floss is very pleased with her check, it will buy her a good coat with a fur collar! If there's to be more so much the better, good for you too.

The world's nuts, I can't keep up with the mere reading I ought to do touching it. There is so much, so much, so much I might do that I, more than ever in my life before, feel desperately in need of giving all my time to writing (considering reading, serious, persistent reading as merely another phase of that.) How am I to do it? Yet I must do it or confess myself a failure. I planned my life (apart from a ten year lag due to wars, economic catastrophes, etc) to march through a tunnel at the far end of which was sunlight. By that I mean time, TIME to do what I knew I must do to breathe again! If I do not end as a full time writer then I have not succeeded in my plan. Everything depends on that.

Ezra is an important poet, we must forgive him his stupidities, I do, no matter how much he riles me. But I prefer not to have to do with him in any way. He wants to patronize me. Don't tell me this isn't so for I know better. His letters are insults, the mewings of an 8th grade teacher. That's where he thinks I exist in relation to his catastrophic knowledge of affairs, his blinding judgements of contemporary values. In one sense he is quite right to protect himself as he does. But my perceptions overtook him twenty years ago—not however my accomplishments. When I have finished, if I can go on to the finish, there'll be another measuring.

Meanwhile I salute his native sensitiveness which try as he may he cannot quite live down. It makes me laugh to read of his being spoken of as a musician and of a high order. He has a complex ear for metrical sequences, marvellous! And he has a naively just concept of the value of knowledge—in other words he is a poet, a great one, but a musician— never!

What the hell, all I started out to do was to ask you to send me four books.

Yours
BILL

31. TLS-2   January 6, 1941

DEAR JIM:

The enclosed explains itself, do what you think best—perhaps a gift such as that suggested has some slight publicity value.

All right, I'll have a book ready for you next fall. It may or may not be the biography though I think it had better be that, for many reasons, among them the fact that I've put most work into that during the last five years so that it should be about ready for you at the time specified.

But there's also the poem *Paterson* I want to bring finally to a focus and a play in verse with, perhaps, a long dissertation on verse and its modern structure and uses—not for the public particularly but for me—and Ezrachen! I want to have a go at verse again. I haven't written any for years, it seems, and I know I shall never again write as I have written in the past. I want to know what's in there, I'm curious. Something has happened within me, perhaps a final catharsis of the whole material of verse. But if I'm empty at last I want to prove it.

There'll be no story of the courtship of Flossie, not while I'm sane and still undegenerate, I couldn't do that one—though it might be the most interesting episode in the *White Mule* cycle. But that brings up the whole question of how much a writer may tell. Ol' Bill Shakespeare did pretty well without telling anything at all—much. I'll take after him in that respect. His literary judgement probably told him that it wasn't interesting, really, and that will have to be my own excuse, if any is needed.

So we come back to me mither's biography. It can be a good book, it'll be a longer book than any I've done so far. Would you want to put in about half a dozen reproductions of old pictures? They really belong and I have a few beauts. I'll plug away at the thing. Right now I'm trying to date up a stenographer. My pal of the past few years has finally failed to answer my letters. Guess that finishes that. I'd rather have a professional anyway if I don't have to pay too much. It's got to be.

Paul seems to be on his way to the altar (halter) like yourself but I imagine he'll go through with it and you won't! Just a guess.

I'm starting to read Hemingway's novel. I'll bet he got his title out of a book of quotations, damned good lead off what with the quotation from Donne—which in itself is something. The book teaches me one thing: a novel is not only a story but NEWS, the kind of news newspapers can't sell and that you've got to feed 'em the bunk—love and war and all the old fuck stuff. That's what they must have. You can hear the gum snapping in their jaws as they just feel it sinking into them. And I'm not fooling, they all do it from Aeschylus down on through. Perhaps some of us lay too much stress on the value of literature as excellence in itself. You got to have a message, a MESSAGE! You ask ol' Ez, he'll tell you. You got to have something to say, Bill, that's the secret of the thing. You got to have something to say.

In a word you got to go and be where the news is happening and then dish it. But I'm glad it wasn't I whom they blazoned on the pages pheasant shooting with my third wife. That made me a little sick at the stomach. They needed a little touch of John Barrymore to make it convincing. Poor ol' Hem and his guts trying to get under the barbed wire while she held it up for him, so to speak.

Just jealous!

What the hell am I writing all this for? My guts are cockeyed of late, get me all crossed up. Too much work, too little cross country running. Wish I wuz a hero and could get up at dawn as I uster and put in two hours at it before breakfast. I just don't feel like it any more.

No I go me out to see why Mrs. Shugg should choose to get weak and faint after going upstairs and why Mrs. Crippendorf can't crap and Mrs. Crappendorf can't quit. I've done me three short plays in PROSE (God damn it) to make up an evening's entertainment as a piece. Being typed now.

OH YES! Here's one I've forgotten time after time for months: You have a short story of mine I might sell, it's called "Comedy Entombed." I want that thing to move. Do you mind? By the way I haven't received either the new poetry pamphlet or *New Directions 1940* which you said you'd send me for Christmas.

So! I've gossiped enough. Did you hear that Jim Higgins father had died?

I know a nice Norwegian ski professional, plenty good looking too. If you could look her up and be nice to her, casually once or twice it might be a nice boy scout stunt. She lives in Boston, a friend of Paul's, tit for tat. The poor kid seems to be lonesome as hell here. Paul says she's a pip and really can ski. If interested say so, if not that's all I'll say.

Yrs
BILL

/ · /

Paul: WCW's younger son, Paul, had just become engaged to Virginia Carnes; they were married in June 1941.

Hemingway's novel: The title of Ernest Hemingway's *For Whom the Bell Tolls* (New York: Charles Scribner's, 1940) comes from the seventeenth meditation in *Devotions upon Emergent Occasions* (1624), by the English poet and preacher John Donne (1572–1631). The novel is dedicated to Hemingway's third wife, Martha Gellhorn, whom he married in Idaho on November 21, 1940. *Life* magazine for January 6, 1941, carried a three-page photo spread entitled "The Hemingways in Sun Valley: The Novelist Takes a Wife." A photo on p. 50 is captioned "Under a barbed-wire fence go the Hemingways after a covey of pheasant in a pasture." Martha holds up the top strand of wire as Ernest climbs through.

32. TLS-2   June 16, 1941

DEAR JIM:

We'd better be cautious in what we say to each other at the present time or some slip will occur and our very happy writer-publisher relationship—not our friendship—come to grief. It isn't, as you know very well, that I expect to live even for a day from my earnings as a writer—I'd be out of luck if I ever had such expectations—but I do sometimes find it important to sugar my cake thereby and at my own convenience.

At the moment I have very little interest in being published by anyone unless it amuses me or I am well paid. I have practically nothing else to gain from it. What I really want to do right now is to write, without a time schedule. But if I am well paid then it would really help me to move ahead in the craft. That, at least, makes my own attitude clear I think.

You've been of great service to me in the past. I want to be of service to you in the present and as long as we know what we're about. I think, on the old basis, we've about worked out our usefulness to each other. You're established as a publisher and I've cleaned up my portfolio. My suggestion is that I ship off the play to you at once, such as it is, for early publication as you suggest and if, only if, you find it saleable. After that let's bring the knife down until further notice.

When, if ever, I complete another script of whatever sort I'll promise you to give you first crack at it reserving to myself the right to submit it elsewhere as I please and on my own terms. I don't know what's going to happen and I haven't a plan except as stated, nothing whatever under the rose but I do feel now that I want more freedom to go as and where I please.

This play is an experiment in the presentation of verse for the stage. By staggering it with complete prose scenes I get an effect I want in counterpoint and in a certain vividness which I could not get otherwise, also I think the verse can be put over more in a manner to avoid an antagonism to verse natural in a present day audience. And the verse itself is something of great interest to me. I've been tearing my head apart for years to get at a mode of modern verse suitable for a long poem which would be simple as speech itself and subtle as the subtlest brain could desire on the basis of *measure*. That's been the great problem ever since Whitman. No one has approached it as yet. Almost all long poems are crap to me because they are metrically uninteresting, especially Eliot's work which is crafty enough, God knows but not fit otherwise to wipe a good man's bottom.

Hit or miss I think that I am on the trail of such a verse. It's that bottle-neck that has held up the Geo Washington libretto, the long poem *Paterson* and several verse plays I have in mind. And because I've been plugged up to the transverse colon with that I haven't been able to put any enthusiasm into the long prose alternates that should come between the verse studies. That's the way I work. I hope I am loose now, completely loose. I've been hard at it inside for too long a time.

The play as you see it has not been thrashed out in detail as yet. That's important. But there it is. I intend that it shall be acted more than read from a book. It may be a complete failure, that I cannot say until I have seen it on the boards—if it will ever get there even for one rehearsal. But I am sure as I can be of anything that it will *sound* right in the best of the verse parts.

So with them incautious words, more power to you.

Sincerely yours
BILL

/ · /

the play: WCW's *Trial Horse No. 1 (Many Loves): An Entertainment in Three Acts and Six Scenes* appeared in *New Directions: Number Seven 1942.* It was later called simply *Many Loves.*

33. TLS-1   September 3, 1941

DEAR JIM:

You're too busy writing and living to properly look after a publishing business so I have made up my mind to go out after another publisher. Several have offered themselves in the past and may again today. I shouldn't be surprised if your own publishers took me on but that's unimportant. I want to be free to make a better connection. I'm in no hurry. I want someone in New York whom I can approach more conveniently than is possible with you and one who can get me better distribution than you seem to be able to. That sums it up as fully and fairly as I can state it. I hope you won't mind too much.

The play has been finished, copyrighted and is now going the rounds of the producers. If and after they have turned it down I shall give it to an agent, possibly Brandt & Brandt's Play Dep't. We'll see. I had word from The Theatre Guild but they are afraid of it. They wrote very cordially, however, and advised me to try again. That's all right with me. I have joined the Authors' Guild. If I'm going into playwrighting (is that the way to spell it?) seriously, it would be best for me not to have the play published now. If no one takes it I'll do two more, already planned, following out my verse theories, and then, if the plays still remain unproduced, make a book of them with a solid preface.

Floss and I enjoyed Bread Loaf, met the celebrities there, and revelled in the sunlight and cooling breezes. Marvellous location on a fine day but, I imagine, not so good when it rains. And there's no lake there—that I saw. If I can't swim I'm not happy on a vacation. I got to swim. Have had two rather sad letters from Ezra, he seems to be in a state of aphasia, doesn't remember that there's a war going on and can't understand why his newspaper from Tokyo doesn't come through. Is he ripe for an awakening! He is just as alert mentally in some phases as he has always been and just as stupid in others. Can't learn. It's a type. I have lashed out at him to the fullest of my ability, an article to be published in *Decision* in September. A letter of his refuting some of my charges (accidently pat) will be subjoined to my statement. You've got, I suppose, to kick a jackass in the balls sometimes to make him move. I doubt that Ezra'll move, I don't think he has the savvy for it—or is too tied up with local politics to understand what's going on in the world.

Yes, you sent Floss a check for two hundred dollars and that is all.

Yours
BILL

/ · /

your own publishers: Possibly Florence Codman's Arrow Editions (see letter 2 above). In fact, no book by JL had appeared by the time this letter was written.

Bread Loaf: In the fourth week of August 1941, WCW lectured at the
Bread Loaf Writers' Conference in the Green Mountains of Vermont.

an article: WCW's "Ezra Pound: Lord Ga-Ga!" *Decision* 2, no. 3 (September 1941): 16–23, was followed by Pound's "Says Ez," 23–24.

34. TLS-1   January 23, 1942

DEAR JIM:

So be it. If you want to use the play for *N[ew]
D[irections]* in ten months I'll have it ready. It wasn't
ready when you last wanted it, I'm glad I didn't let
it go. I've learned a lot since then and I learned it by
withholding the play and letting it wander about. I
had hardly a contact through it that didn't teach me
something valuable. I'm now ready to rewrite—I only
hope I can make it, this time, the thing it should be,
I'll probably learn still more before it is finally in
shape to be seen. It really should be put on the stage
but I'm afraid the homosexual flavor of the theme
though it has nothing whatever to do with homosexuality as such will scare the piss out of a producer—completely needlessly.

I'm glad dear Ezra had sense enough to stop his
broadcasting after December 7th. He sure can be a
shit when he once gets a clean diaper on.

There seemed to be something else I wanted to
say but it escapes me now. Perhaps it is that Thomas
Eliot will have something "pleasing to you", says
Macdonald to me in a recent letter, in the next *Partisan Review*. I hope he does though I can't believe it.
That's one guy who ought to be saddled and ridden
by somebody who could put him to a good use. Wish
I could do it but I know I ain't the one for it, more's
the pity. He has the habit of spawning the shoddiest
of college professors and such drips as Randall Jarrell

who certainly needs a radical operation on him somewhere to raise his voice a little. I don't think implants, though, would flourish in his meat.

Oh well, Jim . . glad you keep your prod busy. One of them is going to get you someday or maybe not, I love 'em all. I don't know a fruitfuller field to poke around in. It ain't man. At least not for me. Oh a man has some gift often, something very special, some genius he might transmit, witness my early profit from Pound, from Chas. Demuth even from Bob McAlmon. They all had something I lacked and which I envied them. Take any good quarterback on any college team. He's a millionaire in almost any man's eyes. But a woman to me is richer than the sky. One can dig there forever—and maybe never get anything perhaps. But that ain't true. More power to you. I hope one will always be handy for if not youse is likely to run dry. I know it.

BILL

⟨My *Harper's Bazaar* poem will be in March issue. Not Feb.⟩

/ · /

stop his broadcasting: Pound's broadcasts on economic, political, and cultural matters over Rome Radio began in January 1941 but were suspended for several weeks after the Japanese attack on Pearl Harbor on December 7, 1941, when the United States entered World War II. The broadcasts resumed on January 29, 1942.

Macdonald: The essayist and critic Dwight Macdonald (1906–1982) was an influential editor of *Partisan Review* from 1937 to 1943.

Randall Jarrell: The poet, novelist, and critic Randall Jarrell (1914–1965) was teaching at the University of Texas when WCW wrote this letter. WCW had criticized his reviewing in a letter to *Partisan Review* 7, no. 3 (May–June 1940): 247–48.

Chas. Demuth: Born in the same year as WCW (1883), the American painter Charles Demuth met the poet in Philadelphia in 1903. Demuth was then a student at the Pennsylvania Academy of Fine Arts, while

WCW was enrolled in the University of Pennsylvania. They remained friends until Demuth's death, in 1935.

Harper's Bazaar poem: WCW's "War, the Destroyer!" *Harper's Bazaar,* March 1, 1942, p. 49, was dedicated to Martha Graham and published with a photo portraying her as a bomb victim.

35. TLS-1   Feb. 6, 1942

DEAR JIM:

The script of the play will be ready by June, in fact all cuttings, revisions and emendations have been completed—the thing looks like an old woman's mind, all crossed up, and needs now only to be copied out fair to be presented to you in its final state—the picture, perhaps, of an old woman's mind! What an old woman!! Let's hope at least it's that. Damn it, it ought to be acted and would be acted out if they weren't all so afraid of their guts.

But should you be called to the army before that, what then?

The matrimonial bulletin is thrilling as hell, nuf said. More power to you and my congratulations to the lady.

S[imon] & S[chuster] are after me again for the biography—but I can't just write it to please them. The further I go with the damned thing the more complex and fascinating it becomes to me but, at the same time, the more difficult it becomes for me to finish it. I'm not letting it run away with me, it isn't that; to tell the truth the more I write the better formulated the material is becoming. But one vista opens back of another as I go on. That takes time to develop. I'll write a note to Maria Leiper telling her to pull up her drawers. If they get sick of waiting that will be just too bad.

A note from Kay Boyle from Nyack, she's trying

to help Marcel Duchamp to get to America. Something else . . something else . . Oh yes, the new Untermeyer anthology is coming out soon. He's given me an accurate biographical note this time and is using 15 of the poems. He's also doing a new anthology of world poetry, beginning with the Bible I think. In that he's using my "Tract" (the funeral) and one from *The Broken Span,* "The Hounded Lovers." At last it's coming out with one clear loud blast that my maternal grandfather's name was SOLOMON HOHEB! Circumcise that one if you're able to.

Reading *Troilus and Cressede* these days to rinse my mouth of the badly translated *Faust.* Chaucer is a good novelist and even better a poet. If one must rhyme let him rhyme that way—like digging your hand down in a bag of cow-peas and pulling up a few dozen. Good, clean indifference and let 'em fall where they will. He beats poor old literary Shakespeare a mile, just slops 'em in. But you got to have the language for it, a loose jointed varying dialect that takes 'em where it finds 'em—latin, french, german, danish, greek, italian and irish, with a few localisms thrown in.

BILL

/ · /

matrimonial bulletin: In his most recent letter, JL had announced plans to marry Margaret Keyser of Salt Lake City, Utah. The wedding took place in April 1942.

Marcel Duchamp: The French avant-garde artist (1887–1968), whose works and personality impressed WCW during Duchamp's sojourns in the United States between 1915 and 1923. Duchamp returned to New York in June 1942, remaining until 1946.

Untermeyer anthology: Modern American Poetry: A Critical Anthology, ed. Louis Untermeyer, 6th rev. ed. (New York: Harcourt, Brace, 1942), pp. 307–15, contains fifteen poems by WCW. The introductory note explains that WCW's maternal grandfather, "Solomon Hoheb, of Dutch-

Spanish-Jewish descent, was born in St. Thomas" (p. 307). "Tract"
and "The Hounded Lovers" appear in Untermeyer's *A Treasury of Great
Poems* (New York: Simon and Schuster, 1942), pp. 1112–15. For
Untermeyer himself see letter 19 above.

Troilus and Cressede: Narrative poem (ca. 1385) by Geoffrey Chaucer
(ca. 1343–1400), written in stanzas of rhyme royal. In *Paterson 2*, WCW
uses the name "Cress" as a pseudonym for Marcia Nardi.

badly translated Faust: Goethe's Faust, trans. C. F. MacIntyre (Norfolk,
Conn.: New Directions, 1941).

36. TLS-1   June 9, 1942

DEAR JIM:

Just got your letter—speaking of tips, while this
one is hot—and don't think I'm specializing in
women—for the past month or two I've been pon-
dering over some poems by a woman that have got
under my guard. I think they are as close to honest
work as I've seen in a decade and that's not all.

This ain't no ingenue and she ain't dumb. But she's
open and mind and body have formed something
distinguished and low (and high). I wish I could do
something for her, an unknown and unwanted. She
has enough for one of your Poets of the Month series.
I ain't foolin', she'd make a hit. Her name's Marcia
Nardi. Don't write to her as I have all her stuff here
going over it carefully.

She's pint size, bedraggled to the point of a Sal-
vation Army reject but she's got the guts of a Kelly.
I'm afraid the damned thing will die if we don't pick
her up. Take my word for it she's a piece of good
steel.

More on other subjects later but I wanted to keep
this single.

BILL

/ · /

Marcia Nardi: WCW first met the poet Marcia Nardi (1903–) on March 29, 1942. He helped her publish her work not only in *New Directions* but also in *Botteghe Oscure.* Her letters to him figure prominently in the first two books of *Paterson.*

a Kelly: Probably Captain Colin Kelly (1915–1941), first United States air hero of World War II. Having attacked the Japanese cruiser *Ashigara* three days after the battle of Pearl Harbor, Kelly crashed in his B-17 after ordering his crew to bail out of the burning bomber.

37. TLS-1   June 17, 1942

DEAR JIM:

She ain't Auden or Eliot, hasn't any of the smell of such swine—don't forget I live near Secaucus and know what I'm talking about—but don't reject her hastily, especially for that reason. She has something else. May I add that it would give me the greatest pleasure if you could find room for a good selection of the enclosed verses in the next *New Directions.* I am sending what I take to be a fair sample of her work, there is more of it but not much more.

She asked me not to plead for her, wants the verses to speak for themselves. I told her she needed a push, that her work did not appeal at the first glance since its virtue was not on the surface of it—no matter how good a critic might pick it up. The form is nil but there are lines and passages that are worth all the facile metrical arrangements ever invented and these do actually give the verse a form of its own.

She speaks the language, speaks it to a purpose and says more than enough that is worth hearing. The effect is poetry.

That's as strong as I can put it. I wish you'd take my word for it that this is authentic stuff besides which it is a seed that needs planting. Her work would greatly benefit from publication now. Please let me know what you can and will do, at an early opportunity. I'm not personally involved, don't make that mistake. But if the publication of such work as this woman offers isn't the primary purpose of an annual such as *New Directions* then I don't know what it's purpose can be.

I'm having a hell of a time with the Anais Nin thing. I've rewritten it four times and am going into the fifth. It requires as much discretion as insight. At first I was inclined to overpraise. Now I'm at the point where criticism must be somewhat reined in. I hope to hit the proper level of sane judgement somewhere between these two positions shortly. By the way, what is your time limit?

Had a call from *Time* this A. M. asking for news of dear Ezra. The rumor has got about that he is trying to return to [word missing] U.S. and that he is being refused entry. They say he's starving, more or less. Maybe he could subsist on the fat in his head for a while, make him a better man. Anyhow, I hope his misery may be at least a little alleviated. I suppose it's just raw courage that has made him what he is.

BILL

/ · /

She: Marcia Nardi.

Anais Nin: WCW's review of *Winter of Artifice* (Paris: Obelisk Press, 1939), by Anaïs Nin (1903–1977), appeared in *New Directions in Prose and Poetry Number Seven 1942,* pp. 429–36.

38. TLS-1   July 13, 1942

DEAR JIM:

Working like hell on *Paterson,* it's coming too. I'm
limiting myself to an "introduction", a summary of
the whole poem which will in all probability not come
to an end for another twenty years if I live that long.
The Introduction serves all my purposes and will
make a book in itself. I'm getting really excited about
it. Thrilling material I'm digging up every day you
might say. It's a theme for everything I've got and
more. Wish I had more. I'm trying my best to have
[word missing] in shape for this fall, hope you'll be
able to handle it. You'll see. It'll be a book.

Yesterday I went to Paterson for a contact I've
long delayed making, a man I've written to but never
seen, David Lyle. A strange character, fits mar-
vellously into my material both personally and
symbolically (tho I hate that word, it robs all actu-
ality from the meaning). He's a New Englander,
Gloucester was his home, has a grand head filled with
God knows what—but very stirring. I've never
known anyone with such a background of reading
in the fields he affects, with names, page numbers
right there tic tic tic right on the button. Quite a
thrill to find anything like that around these parts.
And he's NOT writing a book, just living and moving among people, organizing groups etc etc. A
wonderful guy, good to look at, six foot three etc
etc Blond. Has read everything on God's earth,
including poetry, Whitehead and so many others I
was dizzy. But I gotta throw him, somehow. I know
how those British generals in Libya must have felt
facing Rommel.

He sez he wrote to New Directions for a copy of
my *Collected Poems* and was told the book is out of

print. How come? No need to answer only don't make it too long a wait. I told him to get in touch with Gotham Book Mart.

Would you mind dropping that Nardi woman a note that you have accepted the six or more of her poems you're using? She has some others you might want to see. Do it, please. Her new address is, Marcia Nardi, 40 Perry St., N.Y.C. AND if you can manage it, will you not send her something in advance? She can use it. I seldom ask, gimme a break this time.

Always glad to hear from you if there is any news. A good bit in the current *Poetry* on writing verse for the stage by one Alan S. Downer. Have you seen the first issue of *VVV*. Look it up.

BILL

/ · /

an "introduction": This introductory summary was published as "Paterson: The Falls," *View* 3, no. 1 (April 1943): 19.

David Lyle: Since 1938, WCW had corresponded with David Lyle, a former radio operator with a photographic memory, who periodically mailed out newsletters containing his digests of huge amounts of information gathered from many different media. At one stage, WCW planned to incorporate some of Lyle's letters into Book 1 of *Paterson,* and the death of Lyle's wife, Mary, on March 20, 1947, inspired a passage in Book 2.

Whitehead: The English philosopher Alfred North Whitehead (1861–1947).

Rommel: In a brilliant campaign during the summer of 1942, the Afrika Korps of the German field marshal Erwin Rommel, the "Desert Fox" (1891–1944), drove British forces out of Libya.

Downer: Alan S. Downer (1912–1970) was director of dramatics at Wells College when he wrote "The New *Theatrum Poetarum*," *Poetry* 60, no. 4 (July 1942): 206–15. He later became professor of English at Princeton University and an authority on American drama.

VVV: New York Surrealist magazine edited by David Hare, whose editorial advisers included André Breton, Marcel Duchamp, and Max Ernst. The first number (June 1942) contained WCW's poem "Catastrophic Birth."

39. TLS-1   July 17, 1942

DEAR JIM:

You're wrong my kind fellow, Lyle showed me
the card or brief note from New Directions (I forget
who signed it) stating specifically that the *Collected
Poems* was out of print but that you would have more
very shortly. I held the letter in my hand and read it
with my own eyes. I'll have him send you the thing
for you to read also. Not that I care too much, in a
sense, but I thought you should know. Maybe there
was a confusion as to titles, can be.

Did you see Randall Jarrell on *New Directions* in
the current *Partisan Review*? An unpleasant case of
bad teeth, someone should get him a new tooth-pick,
his old one is all worn out; better would be to extract
his old stumps and buy him some new dentures, he
can't chew anything. All the reviews (not all) in this
issue of *PR* show the same coloring. Isherwood at
least acknowledges that he has not familiarized himself with his subject. Auden confesses his inadequacy
at the finish. But Jarrell is the worst. They all know
the tricks. They all are conditioned by the same
cerebral inadequacies. They, as a group and a reac-
tionary trend, all pack the same dangerous illegal
punch. Jarrell is the most unashamed. He goes out
to maim and must be watched, he's dangerous. I don't
know anyone I'm more determined to destroy. I
confess he's tough and that I am still studying him,
not able to handle him quite yet. The thing is that it
is the academic mind at its most arrogant and most
fatally deficient stage. The whole Princeton faculty,
as a group, is its prime example in America, worse
by far than Harvard. Harvard at least has produced
a Cummings and the New England background
springs from agnosticism or an agnosticism or con-

stitutes an agnosticism that New Jersey has never suspected. This is deep in my blood. These men are aimed at my guts and I at theirs. Don't let them get away with it if you yourself can do anything about it. What, for instance, does Jarrell say in his attack on your *New Directions* that is worth restudy? Not one thing. He cannot chew it, it nauseates him, he breaks out into a fever and nearly faints. He'd do the same before anything that he cannot put his little two foot measure around. And yet [Dwight] Macdonald permits him to spit up his small stomachful into the pages of *PR*. It wouldn't fill an ordinary rotten tooth. Pick, pick pick. You finally get a chunk of last week's chicken. It's meat all right, but how little and how stale.

I'll be looking for the play proofs. Have a good time in Pittsburgh.

Yours
BILL

⟨Yeah, send Nardi the nine bucks. She cd use even a five spot.⟩

/ · /

Partisan Review: Volume 9, no. 7 (July–August 1942), carried the following reviews: "In All Directions," by Randall Jarrell (pp. 345–47), "An American Life" *[Sherwood Anderson's Memoirs],* by Christopher Isherwood (pp. 341–42), and "The Rewards of Patience" [Louise Bogan's *Poems and New Poems*], by W. H. Auden (pp. 336–40). Jarrell describes *New Directions 1941* as "a reviewer's nightmare . . . a queer mediocre hodge-podge in which a few nice and a good many awful things are smothered."

40. TLS-1   July 21, 1942

DEAR JIM:

   The difficulty encountered in trying to make a
small selection from these poems is twofold. First
there are two classes of poems, the early fairly regular partially rhymed ones and the later freer ones.
The separation is sharp. You shouldn't mix them.
Either the selection should be made from one group
or the other. I chose the second, the later group. But
that isn't quite fair. The second difficulty is that the
poems are chiefly valuable for the excellence of a few
lines here and there, a limited selection doesn't bring
in enough of the total material to give the sense of
the whole which I want.

   If your verdict is inexorable, it must be six poems,
we'll have to do the best we can but I wanted to
print all the poems in this lot or, as I first said, to
give her a small paper book. I think she's good enough
for that. The trouble is, you see, that if you don't do
the right thing by this writer you're going to lose
everything. She has a rare spirit, a very rare spirit in
a woman and she is a woman in a very special and,
I think, valuable sense. I think she's got a very small
percentage of metal in her ore but it is a valuable
metal.

   You see, as you say, it's very difficult to get the
good out of her work. Very few people will stop to
refine, in the judgements, so poor an ore. That has
been her life and it is palpable in everything she does.
The rare is so very diluted but when it comes out it
surpasses in excellence the bales of facile work one
sees everywhere. Besides nobody is going to stop in
a busy life to bother with her. They won't. That's
why it is important for N[ew] D[irections] to give
her a break.

I think the woman is wrapping up in the shoddy of her miserable existence a flash of real merit. If we turn her down then she is lost. Even that isn't what I mean because I'm not sentimental in these things. I mean that if we let her go by the board the very thing we purport to live for, excellence as a writer, is junked. Can't do it, Jim. Give her more space. I've done my best to make a selection of six poems but a few more came over than I intended. Do what you can for the woman. Perhaps something can be extracted from this letter to serve as a note otherwise I'll scribble out a few words later. If you want biographical material she'd have to give that herself.

Best
BILL

/ · /

six poems: In the end, JL accepted eighteen poems by Marcia Nardi, along with an introduction to them by WCW, in *New Directions Number Seven 1942*.

41. TLS-1   Dec. 9, 1942

DEAR JIM:

Hope you've sold enough of the Christmas pamphlets to make them pay but I couldn't see them for my own purposes—not from New Directions. I'd rather put my money into other books of yours which I like better.

As to *Paterson* perhaps I was a bit optimistic in saying I'd have it ready for the Spring List, maybe I will but I'm not so confident as I was a few weeks ago, the pressure is too heavy on me medically these days. I start but get stuck before I can really get up any speed. I'm keeping at it, nine pages of a possible hundred is all I can boast of so far.

Did you read Eliot's essay on "The Music of Poetry" in the current *Partisan Review*? Rather astonishing, isn't it, in view of his indifference for the past twenty or thirty years to the very things he appears there to have so grandly discovered: the inadvisability of persisting in dawdling with past forms, the importance of *place*—the italics are his own etc etc. You'd think a professorial bastard of the sort would make some attempt to give credit where it is due. It's not in them. No matter.

Hope you're keeping up.

Yours
BILL

Wanna do a small book of new poems including those in *Broken Span*—or is that against your principles? I got as many again—dropping a few of those—a little book but with some chesty work to go into it. Think it over. Not that I'm forgetting *Paterson,* no sir. But Fate is heavy over our heads these days and soon the smoke will close down.

/ · /

Christmas pamphlets: A Wreath of Christmas Poems, ed. Albert M. Hayes and James Laughlin (Norfolk, Conn.: New Directions, 1942).

Eliot's essay: T. S. Eliot, "The Music of Poetry," *Partisan Review* 9, no. 6 (November–December 1942): 450–65.

a small book: After being turned down by New Directions, *The Wedge* was published in September 1944 by the Cummington Press, of Cummington, Massachusetts.

42. TLS-1 Wednesday [December 1942]

DEAR BILL—

Your various sendings are being sent out as received. The mails are very slow. Your letter of the 16th just getting up here today. The girl will probably send you invoices on each shipment but you don't need to pay them separately. Let them accumulate for a while.

About this Hermann Broch. I think I have heard of him. Generally speaking I would rather get some promising young native started than put effort on these old Europeans who have already had their careers over there. However, if he is really good we'd be willing to give him a break and certainly am glad to read the ms.

You ought to know a kid named Tennessee Williams, a protégé and I suppose a c[letters omitted]r for Kirstein, who has sent in a really beautiful piece of stage poetry. The kid has it, I think, that beautiful lyric excitement that was in Lorca. Quite a kid. Wears a sweater and pants. Very self-possessed. Has no address etc, but seems to live all right, off K, I suppose. In with the Broadway gang and also the Piscator crowd. Broadway doesn't seem to have spoiled him yet.

I enclose a couple of reviews you may not have seen. Please return them. Nobody yet seems to have seen what I see in the metric of the verse passages. But maybe I am just iggurant.

Best wishes
JIM

/ · /

Hermann Broch: On December 21, 1942, WCW wrote to ask JL whether he would like to see Jean Starr Untermeyer's English versions of the work of the Austrian novelist Hermann Broch (1886–1951), who fled to England in 1938 to escape Hitler and who eventually settled in New York. Untermeyer's translation of Broch's *The Death of Vergil* was published in 1945 by Pantheon Books (New York).

Tennessee Williams: JL published the verse drama "Dos Ranchos or, The Purification," by the American writer Tennessee Williams (1911–1983), in *New Directions in Prose and Poetry Number Eight 1944,* pp. 230–56. New Directions soon became Tennessee Williams's principal publisher.

Kirstein: The versatile Lincoln Kirstein (1907–) was founding editor of *Hound and Horn* from 1927 to 1934, founding director of the School of American Ballet from 1933 to the present, and director of the New York City Ballet Company. He has written fiction, poetry, and books on art and the history of dance. In 1964 New Directions published a volume of war poems by Kirstein entitled *Rhymes of a Pfc.*

Piscator: The influential German theater director Erwin Friedrich Max Piscator (1893–1966) worked in New York from 1939 to 1951. Tennessee Williams was a student in Piscator's Dramatic Workshop.

43. TLS-2   January 24, 1943

DEAR JIM:

Don't fuss about it, the idea of the new book was born in my mind while I was trying to squeeze up enough stuff for a possible new appearance in your poets' series. It came of a difficulty I had to select a small collection of unpublished poems while a whole mass of scattered things, some already published here and there needed assembling.

My plan is to use a few of the very early things that did not get into the *Collected Poems.* From there I'd go to a script you never saw, I believe, called "A Folded Skyscraper." There is a series of improvisations there some of which appeared in *Transition, This Quarter* and *The Little Review.* In this script also several notes, auditory scraps from the language, are piled up. Among these for my plan was not to follow a strict chronological order this time I'd put in various small bits, poems from this or another magazine that have escaped general notice, use at least half the things from *A Broken Span*, the complete short verse scene from the 2nd Act of *Many Loves*, all the worthwhile pieces from the original script from which *The Broken Span* was selected and finally the new things, eight or ten of them to bring me once more up to date. This would be a useful book for anyone interested in me and would at the same time have sufficient bulk of diversified interest for the general reader. It would show in retrospect far better than any chap book of carefully selected new work could possibly manage just what I have always been trying to do.

Paterson, I know, is crying to be written, the time demands it, it has to do just with all the peace movements, the plans for international infiltration into the dry mass of those principles of knowledge and culture which the universities and their cripples have cloistered and made a cult. It is the debaleing, the keg cracking assault upon the cults and the kind of thought that destroyed Pound and made what it has made of Eliot. To let it into "the city", culture, the benefits of culture, into the mass as an "act", as a thing. *Paterson* is coming along—this book is a personal finger-practicing to assist me in that: but that isn't all it is.

If Stevens speaks of "Parts of a World" this is definitely "Parts of a Greater World"—a looser, wider world where "order" is a servant not a master. Order is what is discovered after the fact not a little piss pot for us all to urinate into—and call ourselves satisfied. They don't know what they're talking about.

Would you want me to try the general market? I say this with full knowledge of the consequences. I know any number of reasons you might give for saying you'd rather not have me do this and I know that I don't want to do it. At the same time you've

got to be asked. Maybe no one would have the book.
You'd be in a much stronger position to me then.
And if they accept it I know it will only be to tie me
up with some later work. I'd rather stick to you for
both friendly and also selfish reasons but I myself
feel too cloistered with you. I get restless, I want to
break out and take my beating if I must. I know the
shittiness of the general publisher. In other words I
wish you'd do the book.

After trying you out thus, I'll do just what you
want me to. If this is an impossible time for such a
book to appear I'll be glad to wait for further devel-
opments and your advice. If you are definitely not
interested and want to turn me loose, say the word.
I merely want to get your impression and to talk the
thing over with you in complete confidence.

Sincerely
BILL

/ · /

"*A Folded Skyscraper*": In *The American Caravan,* ed. Van Wyck Brooks
and others (New York: Macaulay, 1927), WCW published two poems
and two prose pieces under the heading "From: A Folded Skyscraper."
The full manuscript as WCW describes it here was never published.

Stevens: Parts of a World (New York: Alfred A. Knopf, 1942) is a book
of poems by Wallace Stevens (1879–1955).

44. TLS-1   January 25 [1943]

DEAR BILL—

Thanks for your candid letter. Here's what I think.
If I had plenty of paper I wouldn't hesitate to ask for
the book of poems you outline. But if I must save
on paper I would rather have it for *Paterson,* which

sounds to me much more exciting, a real new direction and something very important.

Why don't you arrange with someone who isn't hit by the paper edict as I am to do the other book of poems. But please save *Paterson* for me. Don't commit yourself on that. You can offer them your prose book as bait—we agreed on that, you recall, that you were free to take that to a bigger house that could advertise more.

It will give me quite a twinge to see you coming out with anyone else but I do want to save the little paper I have for really exciting things and for new kids. By the way I've located one who really thrills me—a funny lad named Tennessee Williams—really Poetic in the deep-lyric sense—and the damndest subject matter and flashes of insight. I think you'll like him.

Had an idea. We only have about 150 *Mules* bound up, but we have 700 sheets and we have 500 sheets (400 & some copies) of *In the Money*. How's for binding the two books together and selling them for $3 as one? Might liven up things a little. What would you call them together? Like the idea? No rush about it—binderies too busy now to do small jobs—but something for later.

Here's the kid. Getting to be a fat little bugger. Out with his grandma now in Pittsburgh. He's bright as a fox. Knows everything that goes on.

Best,
JIM

/ · /

the paper edict: In a letter of January 22, 1943, JL explained to WCW that "there is a W[ar] P[roduction] B[oard] order limiting publishers' paper to 90% of their 1942 use. This is hitting me very hard because four of my 1942 books were postponed because of manuscript delays."

45. TLS-1   February 21, 1943

DEAR JIM:

The enclosure speaks for itself, it isn't the reason for this letter but might serve as a text for it. I don't think you're publishing the right books.

The thing is, you're trying to make a success of the publishing business and unless I miss my guess, that's the wrong steer. You are a young man making a reputation, my opinion is it's going to cost you plenty. That is, that what you do now is going to be your reputation and you've got to take the rap now in order to come out on top.

You can't make money and make the right sort of reputation as a publisher at the same time. I'm looking at this as a long term investment. You've got to build up your stable on a much broader basis, the serious man, the gifted man—but also the difficult man whose books will not sell BUT who looked back on twenty years from now will be seen to have been the true winner.

Alright, you want me to be specific. I know you've backed some good ones—also some stinkers. I'd say pick fewer and give them a much freer rein. You yourself shouldn't try to pick what they do. You need only

Indiscreet, none of my business, uncalled for: thank you Flossie.

To go on. I was sitting here talking to Zukofsky last evening when he showed me his *A Test of Poetry,* a sort of teaching anthology, one of the most important books I've looked at in years. Yet it's been kicking around the shitty publishing houses for five years and no one has the guts or the insight to print it. Not only that but it has appeal, appeal to a person like Floss, a unique appeal to anyone seriously interested and groping among the poets. So long as that book remains unpublished you can have your Harvard coterie, all of them and some others needless to name.

Well, there it is. I've been thinking all day how pat Zukofsky puts his finger on the correct key and how out of key nine tenths of the published work I look at really is. The test of poetry is—the evidence of a serious adjustment of the faculties to a job. It is nothing else. To salvage this seriousness and not misname it, not try to "claim" it as the possession of any intellectual Elks Club, any bastard church crowd or other condom wearer—it should be the ONLY purpose of a young man, reputed to be rich and wanting to start and make a name for himself as a publisher. Anything else is shit.

Ah weel, ah weel. Life does not last forever. I'd gladly yield any place I have to Zukofsky if I could wake anybody up. And by Christ I'm gonna try.

Yours
BILL

/ · /

teaching anthology: Inspired by Ezra Pound's *ABC of Reading* (1934), Louis Zukofsky's *A Test of Poetry* was published in 1948 by the Objectivist Press, which had been revived in Brooklyn, New York. In a letter of October 11, 1948, WCW told JL that Zukofsky's wife, Celia Thaew, had invested "around $800" in the publication.

46. TLS-2.   [Inside address:] Alta Lodge, Sandy, Utah
March 6 [1943]

DEAR BILL—

If you don't like the books I'm publishing now isn't that partly your fault for not giving me more

advice about manuscripts? You know I always listen
to you. For example, I'd be glad to see this thing of
Zuk's. I don't recall ever seeing any of it. Why not?

As for my trying to make money that is just rub-
bish. I've just figured up the results of last year for
N[ew] D[irections]—a loss of $23,000. Now I don't
call that making money by a long sight.

You can say the money could have been better
spent. Probably. But the only way I can publish better manuscripts is to get ahold of them. I take the
best I can get, though, to be sure I do try to vary the
types so as not to get into a cult rut. And lately this
paper quota business has been a nuisance.

As for Derleth, I promised him two years ago.
That is past history. But I'm still waiting for a decent
manuscript from him. He can write very well but he
writes too much. I'm trying to force out of him a
group of all good poems instead of four bad ones to
every good one. Barnard is a snob. Derleth has written a few poems that are much better than her best.
He has also written a lot of bad ones. Still he's a
poet.

I really think Bill you haven't read most of the
books we have put out lately and so are not in a
position to judge what's up. All of a sudden just
because Zuk turns up with something good—which
I don't recall ever hearing about—you go off half
cocked and tell me I've been slipping. Hell, read a
few of the books. I think you'll find some things
you'll like. . I may misjudge the situation. Maybe
you have been following the books. But your letter
doesn't sound like it.

Well it'll all come out in the wash. And I'm not
looking for reputation either. That is all a lot of hot
balls, part of the big fake front game. What I am
looking for is the little pleasures of life, one here,
one there, something the kid does, or a good page

in a book, or the sun out on the new snow—stuff like that, that adds up to a feeling of general well-being. The hell with reputations, making money, poets' jealousies, ambitions, wars, struggles of all kinds, and mostly anything that impinges on the effect in life of a good art form.

as ever,
JIM

⟨Please return at your leisure.⟩

/ · /

Derleth: In 1944, New Directions published *And You, Thoreau!,* a book of poems by the Wisconsin writer and editor August William Derleth (1909–1971).

Barnard: The poet and translator Mary Barnard (1909–) spent at least a week in Norfolk, Connecticut, in the fall of 1938, addressing publicity catalogs for New Directions. Her poetry appeared in the first two *New Directions* anthologies (1936 and 1937) and in *Five Young American Poets,* published by New Directions in 1940. From 1939 to 1943, she was the first curator of the Poetry Collection at the Lockwood Library of the University of Buffalo. She visited WCW several times to help him prepare donations to the collection. Her impressions of JL are preserved in her memoir, *Assault on Mount Helicon* (1984).

47. TLS-1   Aug. 7, 1943

DEAR JIM:

Enclosed is probably my best recent poem that seems earmarked, because of its length, for you. Use it in the annual.

No *Paterson* for anybody until my present volume of poems is first published and properly published.

Yeah, maybe the Macleod woman did kind of miss up on most of the points in the play.

Ezra is primarily a jackass not a traitor but he's had it in him to be what he's turned out to be from the very beginning. He's been friendly, for instance, toward me and helped me in a gross sort of way but he's never been generous toward me or perceptive in grasping my particular inner value from any really basic viewpoint. Subtly I've always felt a strong barrier between Ezra and myself, a wall in him against everything I really held most valid. Not that he's been precisely patronizing and yet it has been just that, without its being stated.

I didn't mind this because I knew my position to be strong, I knew I could beat him any way he wanted to take me on, either at fencing (where we started) or otherwise—always excepting his genius for words in which I acknowledge him to be a master. He boasted of his mind. To me his mind was fifth rate. He was dull, obtuse toward my reason for being, never got the vaguest glimpse of me, myself. I suspect he's more than a little conscious of this in his limited way and for that reason thought it wise to keep me on his side—in case!

And now the catastrophe has arrived. How shall I act. Shall I still hold him up upon the only ground he has to stand on—his asserted Americanism. He calls himself an American. I suppose I'll have to be generous, as I have always been. But the shits like him are too numerous—[T. S.] Eliot, [Dwight] Macdonald and some others—that I may be too tired to try. I believe the F[ederal] B[ureau of] I[nvestigation] is going to call me in as a witness against Ezra, not from any volunteering on my part. They've warned me. I don't intend to condemn him. For he, like Eliot, could be useful to what I know to be their basis as well as it is mine—even if their brains have to be beaten out in capturing them.

Yours
BILL

/ · /

my best recent poem: "To All Gentleness" appeared in *New Directions 1944.*

the Macleod woman: Vivienne Koch, wife of Norman Macleod; see letter 68 below.

the catastrophe: On July 26, 1943, Ezra Pound was indicted for treason by a federal grand jury in Washington, D.C. In 1941, WCW had been questioned by the FBI after Pound mentioned his "friend Doc Williams of New Jersey" in a Rome Radio broadcast of July 30.

48. TLS-1. [On stationery imprinted:] Alta Lodge, Alta, Utah
[August or September 1943]

DEAR BILL—

Thanks for sending me Delmore's letter. He is sort of hypped on various things, but a good boy in the long pull, I think. He is mad with me because I think his long book stinks pretty bad and made no pains so to say, but I went ahead and published it as many better critics than I thought it was good and I thought it's intent was good.

I must have missed the argument in *P[artisan] R[eview]* that this letter seems to be about.

Hell, I never agreed with you about Old Possum. His poems send me into a blue swoon. I just eat em up, even the late rather sparse religious stuff. The essays are full of trickery but such fun to read—a sort of literary sensuality like banana splits—and no man ever created such architectural opening sentences. Besides which he has always struck me as a wonderful guy, personally. But I suppose in a vague way I sense what you object to in him.

Etc
JAS

/ · /

Delmore's letter: The poet and critic Delmore Schwartz (1913–1966) became an editor of *Partisan Review* in the fall of 1943, after the controversial resignation of Dwight Macdonald. New Directions published a number of Schwartz's works, including *In Dreams Begin Responsibilities* (1938). The "long book" mentioned here was *Genesis: A Story in Prose and Poetry of the Making of an American.*

Old Possum: A nickname for T. S. Eliot, modeled upon those in Joel Chandler Harris's Uncle Remus tales. Eliot used it first in his correspondence with Pound and then in the title of *Old Possum's Book of Practical Cats* (1939).

49. ALS-2. [On stationery imprinted:] Alta Lodge, Alta, Utah.

[September or October 1943]

DEAR BILL—

Cummington is a fine outfit. I'm all for them. Your book will help them & it won't hurt you because the company is right and the formats very fine. I don't know how wide their distribution is yet, but if Gotham gets behind the book it will get around all right. They can use our lists for circulars if they like. Better have it in the contract that they will later release *free* for a *Selected Poems of W.C.W.* I would like to do one like that as soon as paper eases up. About 96 pages—pocket size—sell for a dollar in New Classics size. Part of a big post-war scheme I have been mulling over.

As usual
JIM

/ · /

Gotham: The Gotham Book Mart, a major New York City bookseller founded in 1920 and managed by Frances Steloff.

scheme: For the results of this "scheme," see the introduction, p. xii.

50. TLS-1   Nov. 15, 1943

DEAR JIM:

Ever since I got well into Forster's, *The Longest Journey,* I've been thinking the best things of you, thanking you for reminding me to read the book but being most appreciative of your having brought the book out at all. That's good reading. It's more than good reading it's important work, it tore me apart and I shall never forget it or cease being thankful to you for bringing it to me. I wanted to say this outright for your satisfaction.

The book builds up a modern hell that is convincing to a terrible degree, the hell of failure to remember the gods. The way Forster builds this up, so British in its bones and flesh, is very nearly forbidding. I was in agony those days, the verge of nervous collapse. I felt eyes in the very actual sky looking at me, very nearly eating into me, accusing me of all the cowardices of which I am capable and which I try my best to subdue. The classic hells are mere child's play beside something that can really enter me in the places where I am hiding and drag me into the light. There are hundreds of ways in which the writer, by small truths, word devices, the correct placing of character in certain types, achieves this effect of truth—when it is so rare to find any sort of truth in most writing. Here the truth is everywhere and persistent and never failing. It hurts.

Then it becomes plain (I haven't finished the last 50 pages of the book) why this hell has been built up—in such an outwardly civilized world. When the purpose of the book finally begins to dawn the contrast is so vivid that the journey back to love, the longest journey, is brilliantly illuminated, brought out as though by Klieg lights by the contrast. I wish

I could write with such authority, it is wonderful. Hail Britannia! I didn't know she could produce such sons—or had I not better say, such a son. There can't be many. But the character Mr. Failing, a superb character though he only appears in the background, may be the link to show that, unobserved, England can still make love operative. This would be a triumph anywhere but more than ever so in such an environment.

But this letter is primarily to give you the assurance of my appreciation. You've got to go on. Sometimes I'd gladly castrate you had I the chance and even that would be putting it mildly. But this time you've affected me and I'm grateful. Keep it up.

Nothing else special to say except that Harry Duncan seems to be a good guy by his letters, he says the book of poems should be out by March. Best all around to you, Happy Thanksgiving and all that.

Yrs.

Bill

/ · /

The Longest Journey: In 1943, New Directions republished two novels by E. M. Forster (1879–1970), *The Longest Journey* (1907) and *A Room with a View* (1908).

Harry Duncan: Duncan and Paul Wightman Williams operated the Cummington Press, publisher of WCW's *The Wedge* (September 1944) and *The Clouds, Aigeltinger, Russia, &.* (1948).

51. TLS-1   Dec. 27, 1943

DEAR JIM:

My only objection to the reissue of *The Grain* is irremovable, the smallness of the type. Also the Gregory foreword isn't sufficiently to the point, verbose though full of good feeling.

My one suggestion would be to get and use testimonials from various people as to their indebtedness to the book. Martha Graham, for instance, once wrote me a letter saying she could not, at one time, have gone on without it. I might be able to dig up that letter. I think she'd co-operate. Then we might get the gal responsible for *Oklahoma* to avow her indebtedness to Martha Graham etc etc. There are many others who might come in. Matthew Josephson, Hiler perhaps, Chas. Sheeler and many another if I could find them or what not.

I don't know how it could be managed. I might think of names as time goes on.

Paul at sea on a destroyer. Bill still in the far Pacific. Paul's wife and my grandson here with us looking for apartment.

Cummington Press silent for the moment but probably going ahead with the new book of poems. A long poem, more or less long, by me in January *Poetry*. Univ[ersity] of Kansas City Press bringing out the introduction to the Cummington book with a few as yet unprinted selections in March issue.

That God damned and I mean God damned poem *Paterson* has me down. I am burned up to do it but don't quite know how. I write and destroy, write and destroy. It's all shaped up in outline and intent, the body of the thinking is finished but the technique, the manner and the method are unresolvable to date. I flounder and flunk. The main thing is that

I'm in the war effort to the hilt—actually, physically, and mentally In other words the form of the
poem stems also from that. It is one, inescapable,
intrinsic but—there is not time. I am conscious of
the surrealists, of the back to the home shit-house
mentality, the Church of England apostasy, the
stepped on, dragging his dead latter half Pound
mentality—with the good and the new and the empty
and the false all fighting a battle in my veins: unre-
solved. But it's got to be born, it's got to be pushed
out of me somehow and in some perfect form. But
that form, involving the future and the past is—
to my weak powers almost too much. I won't
acknowledge I haven't the stuff for it though at times
my fears are devastating.

BILL

/ · /

Martha Graham: In 1938 and 1944, WCW attended performances by
the modern dancer and choreographer Martha Graham (1893–).

Matthew Josephson: The writer, journalist, and editor Matthew Josephson (1899–1978) met and interviewed WCW for the Newark *Ledger* in
December 1920. In 1922–24, josephson was associated with *Secession*
and *Broom* magazines, to both of which WCW contributed. Josephson
introduced WCW to the painter Charles Sheeler in 1923 and later helped
to edit *transition*.

Hiler: JL had recently met the painter, writer, and authority on cos-
tume Hilaire Hiler (1898–1966) in California. It was Hiler who introduced WCW to Henry Miller in May 1935. Hiler, Miller, and William
Saroyan were coauthors of *Why Abstract?*, a New Directions book published in 1945.

A long poem: "Burning the Christmas Greens," *Poetry* 63, no. 4 (January 1944): 207–9.

the introduction: WCW's "Introduction" to *The Wedge* was first published in the *University Review* (Kansas City, Mo.), 10, no. 3 (Spring
1944): 198–99.

52. TLS-2   Jan. 14, 1944

DEAR JIM:

Maybe you're right. If you're able to and want to then, do—for the life to come may be an awful bust. And besides, who can say you were not driven to it, of a purpose? Those are things we may not decipher being only one one at a time.

You know what? Poets are being pursued by the philosophers today out of the poverty of philosophy. God damn it, you might think a man had no business to be writing, to be a poet unless some philosophic stinker gave him permission. But, the shabby little stinkers all want to write poetry themselves and try again and again. Let me not mention any names. I shan't quarrel with philosophy as such, let 'em have it. But there is a fallacy in always insisting that poetry shall "mean" what some little stinker thinks it should. Poets are becoming scared to death lest someone put up a little tennis net for them to hop over before being admitted to the game. It runs deep, I'm not stating it half forcibly enough here. But what is sorely needed is poetic construction, ability in among the words, to invent there, to make, to make well and new. When that is done let the scabby philosophers scramble to interpret—which is their field if any. But we're letting ourselves be gelded by them. To hell with them. I'm afraid the Freudian influence has been the trigger to all this. The Surrealists followed him. Everything must be tapped into the subconscious, the unconscious—as if poetry had ever been different. But poetry has also been a construction in the words—very strange news this to the present day. Am I living too long? I wonder.

                                                    BILL?

Do try to have *In the Grain* set up in a type of larger
face this time if that is at all feasible, it will make all
the difference in the world.

Forget the Martha Graham suggestion. No sense to
it. It would be all right if some spontaneous offers
were made but, you're right, we can't drag people
in by the neck and Martha Graham and Matthew
Josephson won't do all by themselves.

53. TLS-1   April 25, 1944

DEAR JIM:

Sent you a letter ordinary mail this morning or
yesterday, I've forgotten which. This morning
(afternoon) of course your letter arrives. I'm sending
this Air Mail to overtake the first.

Best title I can think of for the two bound together
is *Gurlie and Joe* or *Gurlie & Joe*. Sort of Frankie and
Johnnyish. After all it's a reissue, so to speak, of a
work already somewhat known. Best luck and
thanks. How does this affect our contract? Dam 'f I
know.

Another title might be *First Act*. 's up to you. I
still like *Gurlie & Joe*.

It'd be a thrill to have an issue of your mag all to
myself, there'd be enough I think to fill it. Wanna
republish the introduction to the story of me moder
from *Twice a Year?* Not necessary. Yes, I could fill
an issue I think.

I don't think, though, that I ought to let any of
the *Paterson* get away separately just now. It's too
near finished for that—unless you disagree. After all
Joyce did publish practically all of *Ulysses* and *Anna
Livia Plurabelle* as well as much else before the book

containing it came forth. And Eliot had his *Waste Land* in the *Dial*.

There are four parts to *Paterson*. If you think well of it you could have the first part. Might be a good ad for the rest—or a bad one, what the hell.

The *Paterson,* the bits of the biography of Ma, the Quevedo translation. Geezus, so I'm not dead! You're a friend if ever there was one. And the two new poems—at the very least, those two. It'd make an issue. A real issue. I might even drag twenty pages or more from the journal of which I spoke in my last.

You see what you do to me. Ain't got a friend in the world but you, so to speak.

Don't know anyone who would be fit to write an intro for the new multiple birth. I'll do a few words during the next week and let you have it. That might be best, a statement as to plan—perhaps. See what I can do.

Glad to hear of the little open-face, them old stem winders never was much good.

BILL

/ · /

First Act: This title was chosen for the 1945 New Directions reissue of *White Mule* and *In the Money* as a single volume.

your mag: Probably *Pharos,* published from 1945 to 1947 in Murray, Utah, and distributed by New Directions. Each number featured the work of one writer; the double number of spring 1945, for example, contained Tennessee Williams's play *Battle of Angels.* WCW did not publish anything in *Pharos,* but in 1948 he contributed to its successor, *Direction* (see letter 75 below).

Joyce: James Joyce's *Ulysses* (1922) and *Finnegans Wake* (1939) were both serialized in little magazines before their publication as books: the former in the *Little Review,* and the latter in *Transatlantic Review* and *transition.* Moreover, the "Anna Livia Plurabelle" section of *Finnegans Wake* was separately published on several occasions in 1928–32. T. S. Eliot's *The Waste Land* first appeared in the *Dial* 73, no. 5 (November 1922): [473]–85, and in the *Criterion* 1, no. 1 (October 1922): 50–64.

the journal: In a letter to JL of March 22, 1944, WCW wrote, "I have also a journal of which I have never spoken to you, a whole book-length script of my mumblings and maunderings running from about 1920 to 1935, approximately. It may grow into a book if I ever find myself autobiographically minded. . . ." This journal later became WCW's *Autobiography* (1951).

54. TLS-2   Oct. 24, 1944

DEAR JIM:

The enclosed is of course very attractive, a great surprise to me, kindles an almost lost desire to do another book in the series, *Act Two,* which might be an improvement on past performances at least in the matter of the technique of the novel. The war to which I am wholly devoted at the moment has barred me from many pleasures.

In a previous letter you spoke of a new issue of *In the Am. Grain*: I have no desire to see it reissued. I said merely that if it were to be reissued I hoped the old type-face size might be restored. I have made a few inquiries about that. It seems that photo offsets of the original volume could be made much more cheaply than to have the book reset afresh and that it would make a satisfactory page. The cost I was told might be around $500. or so. I know nothing of the matter. I certainly would not want to put any money into it.

As to notebooks, original scripts etc for Harvard—everything I have had has gone to Abbott at Buffalo library, tons of stuff (more or less) letters, old photos etc. It seems to me it would be best to continue to send them whatever I have in order to keep the material as a unit. I have written to Abbott asking him if he is still interested. He hasn't as yet answered.

Did you get my new book, *The Wedge,* from Cummington? I asked them to send you a copy?

Your most recent Poet of the Year, Melville, whom Matthiessen has so brilliantly edited, makes me think what Pound and Eliot failed to do for our world. They were two little ignorants running away from the big job to play in the sand. Nice little men both of them. This Matthiessen bulks larger and larger in my view recently. He's a Harvard proff isn't he? Rather a better specimen of the breed.

T. Weiss of the Chapel Hill crowd strikes me as a first rate critic, a writer I admire. Also (and not because) he is bringing out a fairly large group of my recent verse in his Winter issue of the *Quarterly Review* he edits, he seems pleased with what I sent him and is featuring it—practically a year's work in verse such as I have been able to write of late.

Had a visit from a Cuban poet and editor, Rodríguez Feo of Havana, editor of *Orígenes,* followed you through Choate and Harvard. Attractive mind and mien. We spent a pleasant afternoon discussing everything from Surrealism to the behavior of Hemingway in Cuba—where he is a recluse except for English speaking visitors, preferably of the european elite.

Spent an afternoon at the N.Y. Public Library looking up material for my introduction to the Quevedo translation. Odd that I should find a translation of *The Dog and the Fever* made by an Englishman, John Stevens in 1709. It clears up several points on which I was stuck. But it amused me to notice that when he in his turn was stuck he simply omitted the difficult passage! It's an idea but not a good one. He finally missed the entire point of the whole book, its double-entendre. Not a subtle brother but had a good clear head on various practical renderings. Rodríguez Feo had read the work in Spanish. It fascinates me. With the introduction and the help I expect to get from the Stevens translation the book should be quite attractive when finished.

So it goes.

Yours
BILL

The one thing that seriously bothers me at the moment is my inability to read. Many of the books in your various series as well as certain books, like Matthiessen's (I've even forgot the name) on American characters such as Melville etc Hawthorne etc etc—simply remain closed to me. I do read, in fact I am always reading but it is usually some periodical or other, a scrap here and there and not prolonged enough. That too I can't for the moment remedy.

⟨Books, especially books of verse, magazines, shower in on me from every source. I am drowned in them.⟩

/ · /

Abbott: Charles Abbott (1900–1961) was director of libraries at the University of Buffalo and founder of the Lockwood Library's Poetry Collection. WCW began to deposit manuscripts and other materials there in 1940.

Poet of the Year: In 1944, the New Directions Poet of the Month series became the Poet of the Year series. The selection had always included poets of the past as well as contemporary writers; in this case it featured Herman Melville, *Selected Poems,* ed. F. O. Matthiessen (New York: New Directions, 1944).

Matthiessen: Francis Otto Matthiessen (1902–1950) had recently published *American Renaissance: Art and Expression in the Age of Emerson and Whitman* (New York: Oxford University Press, 1941). A member of the Harvard University Department of English since 1929, Matthiessen was promoted to the rank of professor in 1942.

T. Weiss: In 1943, the poet and critic Theodore Weiss (1916–), together with Warren Carrier, began to edit the *Quarterly Review of Literature.* It has been published in New Haven, Connecticut; Chapel Hill, North Carolina; Annandale-on-Hudson, New York; and Princeton, New Jer-

sey. WCW contributed fifteen poems and two essays to vol. 2, no. 2
([1945]).

Rodríguez Feo: José Rodríguez Feo (1920–) edited *Orígenes: Revista de
arte y literatura* in Havana, Cuba, from 1944 to 1954. The magazine
published work by Wallace Stevens, T. S. Eliot, Albert Camus, W. H.
Auden, Katherine Anne Porter, and many other well-known writers.
WCW's poem "The Bitter World of Spring" appeared in vol. 1, no. 3
(Autumn 1944): 22–23; the facing Spanish translation by Rodríguez
Feo was the first Spanish rendering of any poem by WCW. Rodríguez
Feo's eleven-year correspondence with Wallace Stevens began in
November 1944, and Stevens's poem "A Word with José Rodríguez
Feo" was written in February 1945; see *Secretaries of the Moon: The
Letters of Wallace Stevens and José Rodríguez Feo,* ed. Beverly Coyle and
Alan Filreis (Durham, N.C.: Duke University Press, 1986).

a translation: "The Dog and the Fever" is the fourth of *The Comical
Works of Don Francisco de Quevedo,* trans. John Stevens (1707; 2d ed.,
London: J. Woodward, 1709).

55. TLS-2   11/1/44

OK JIM:

Spent some time on *The Phoenix and the Tortoise*
and find it deficient and marvellous, the most or one
of the only serious poems in our language (you notice,
I hope, that I say *our* language) and most brilliant.

Technically it is—sane, the line not lying or copied,
a difficult development that leaves (as I leave) much
to be desired—though one of the few lines our language has developed following Whitman: not yet as
distinguished as as it does not copy more developed
work in English. It is sound from the view of crafts-
manship.

But that isn't the point so much in this poem. The
first (name) poem is the thing. I have long wanted
some mind to write of the classics and to handle the
classic Greek and Latin material in our language as
against the English and English imitators—to whom

flock the Pounds and Eliots—like blind fish and bats from the caves.

More of this. Rexroth (King Red) has finally emerged into something very firm and perceptive—hard to say how good he is now (and how bad I found him formerly) It takes everything a man has to be a good artist and then he only succeeds by luck sometimes.

But I went to be cleansed last night, not a bitter tang in my whole system. This is on the beam

You see what I have realized all my life, something so very difficult to put over without help from the Universities and all its skimmed tribe who are no help at all, is that there is—as there must be—a genius of the American language. I mean not a human genius but an abstract of the language we speak which must be realized by everyone before we can have a literature. My anger at Pound first and then Eliot and all the less fry from [Robert] Penn Warren and that sort—is that they really know nothing of our language and its exigences, its unrealized forms and its possibilities. Whitman was a blind sort of frog that who saw something—he didn't know what and misinterpreted it as "democracy" never knowing that he was first an artist, a poet. He vaguely sensed that but just couldn't say it. Rexroth is a step in the right direction, not fully as yet realized, he is too bitter, not exalted enough by discoveries of method as the artist must be, the line, the turn of phrase etc etc ⟨the whistle has blown my lunch⟩

BILL

⟨But he is good.⟩

/ · /

The Phoenix and the Tortoise: A book of poems by Kenneth Rexroth (1905–1982) published by New Directions in 1944. The title poem also appeared in *New Directions 1944,* which is dedicated to Rexroth. WCW's poem "The Phoenix and the Tortoise," first published in November 1945, is a response to Rexroth's.

56. TLS-1   January 30, 1945

DEAR JIM:

I hope you received the Vazakas preface and that you will find it possible to bring out the man's book using what I have written to preface it in the near future. Drop him a note when you are ready to look at his script.

I'm glad you found the Rexroth piece satisfactory. I wish now, in a way, that I had asked you to send it on to him as it stands. Perhaps, though, it might be better for him to see it as a *fait accompli.*

The third item on my list is this. The first part of the *Paterson* thing is nearing completion. There will be four parts, each of fifty to seventy five pages. It is to be called, *Paterson: Introduction*—but that will be the end of it, just the introduction, life isn't long enough for anything else.

I'd like to have each part appear as a separate book, for each is, in fact, a unit in itself. I ought to be able to finish one a year at the rate at which I am going— quicker if possible. I've got to get the thing off my slate.

First I want to know how this hits you, do you still want it? And if so could you give me an idea when you think this first section should appear. Next fall (at the earliest), next Christmas or when? You once said you'd get it out within three months of receiving the script but times and men change and

I'm not one to hold anyone to old promises. My sole idea in mentioning the matter at the moment is that I believe a dead-line would be a good thing for me at this stage.

If you think I ought to wait until the four parts are completed, say so. But I'm afraid of that. I got to get going or it may prove too late. It's up to you.

Yours
BILL

/ · /

the Vazakas preface: WCW wrote an enthusiastic preface for *Transfigured Night: Poems by Byron Vazakas* (New York: Macmillan, 1946).

the Rexroth piece: WCW reviewed Kenneth Rexroth's *The Phoenix and the Tortoise* for the *Quarterly Review of Literature* 2, no. 2 ([1945]): 145–49.

57. TLS-2   Feb. 4, 1945

DEAR JIM:

When I finish the *Paterson* thing (sometime before St Patrick's Day) where do I send it? New York or Utah? It frightens me a bit and, as always, I don't think it's real; I wonder if it's really there—among those pages of words. It doesn't seem likely. And if so, WHAT is there—gravel for critics? I hope it cuts their hearts out. It won't; they're too grooved in their protected tracks ever to turn aside to see the dulled world close about them—always whistling into the distance.

It was as you say a good evening, I liked the feel of the little girl nestling (among her dachshunds) against me on the couch. She said she didn't feel very well and no doubt appreciated the physician in me—poor deluded soul.

Yes, the Joyce is of the essence. In Ireland they call such men "spoiled priests", a horrid epithet—it reveals the place. Yet Joyce could never go far from it—in his mind. He might have gone farther if he had been a continental instead of an islander. His island choked him in the end, made him clutch his throat out of which the garbled speech flowed whereas he might have spoken in magnificent measures—if there had been such measures in his day. We have the opportunity he perhaps made for us.

This early work shows him speaking with a personal voice, as a man—later he became seraphim or cherubim or cousin to God—but here he was a man. It is warming, brilliant stuff. I am glad you brought it out and I am very happy to have it to enjoy. I haven't even finished the book as yet, in the midst of my pleasure with it. Good, very good work—in spite of what he calls it.

Let me know where to send my contribution to the meal of the gods, perhaps a radish—they call this [New Jersey] the Garden State you know. I want to get this away from me so that I shall be able to start the second part. As I have told you all four parts are sketched and partly written. All I need now is time, time, time. If I could only permit myself to take six months off!

Yours
BILL

I hope you like the thing, that's always the danger—that you won't. I know you'll like parts of it.

/ · /

This early work: New Directions published James Joyce's *Stephen Hero*, an early version of *A Portrait of the Artist as a Young Man* (1916), in 1944 and republished Joyce's play *Exiles* (1918) in 1945.

58. TLS-1   March 9, 1945

DEAR JIM:

When you return on the 20th to N.Y. the script
(of *Paterson* I) will be awaiting you. Look it over and
for the love of Joyce's Jesus do let me know within
a reasonable time just what you plan for it. I am
hardly yet able to realize that, though only in a fourth
part, the thing has finally been completed. I know
now how a silkworm must feel the day after, though
my hopes are not so high.

The Latin is amazingly to the point, No ideas but
in things—it comes to about just that! I may even
use the tag in book two. Who—from whose lips did
that elixir drip? The exact translation should be,
Nothing in the mind that was not first in the feelings.

What in hell has happened to Weiss and his two
promised issues of *The Quarterly*. Why not even his
Fall issue has yet appeared. I hope he has not been
dragged into the Army. If he has and if he will be
forced to suspend wouldn't it be a grand gesture to
bring out his issue *as it stands* in *New Directions 1945?*—
the issue, that is, containing my small anthology of
new poems.

BILL

/ · /

The Latin: In a postcard to WCW dated March 8, 1945, JL quoted the
Latin maxim *Nihil in intellectu quod non prius in sensu* (Nothing is in the
mind that was not first in the senses). The saying is a commonplace of
medieval, neo-Aristotelian epistemology, often ascribed to *De Anima*
but not actually found in any surviving manuscript of that treatise. In
response to WCW's query about authorship, JL said in a letter of [March
1945?] that he had encountered the maxim in a "fairy story by Roditi."
Edouard Roditi uses the quotation as the epigraph of his prose poem

"Letters from a Lost Latin Empire," which is dedicated to JL and published in Roditi's *Emperor of Midnight* (Los Angeles: Black Sparrow Press, 1974), p. 81. In a letter to Hugh Witemeyer of May 29, 1988, Roditi describes this poem as "a revised version of an earlier one," which JL might have seen. However, Roditi cannot now recall where or when the earlier version was first published, nor is he certain where he first encountered the Latin maxim. WCW does not use it in Book 2 of *Paterson*.

59. TLS-1   March 28, 1945

DEAR JIM:

The signed contract enclosed, I realize the difficulties attendant upon book making today (in spite of the fact that we are flooded with mediocre books of verse, pamphlets etc) but do at least make every effort to get the book out by September at the latest. A book 9½ by 5½ would be most attractive, a little longer and a bit narrower than *Partisan Review*. An issue of 800 copies at $2. would be about right. Put me down for 50 copies, if you like, now. I'll buy all copies you wish to dispose of at the end of a year at the regular trade price.

Speaking of *Partisan Review,* the type face used in their Winter, 1944 issue, spacing (as in Warren's "Billie Potts") etc would suit me perfectly. Please use that face. Use it, that is, for the verse. Your suggestion that we use newsprint typeface for the prose strikes me as very much to the point. The two faces look good together. Space the prose also as the news is spaced in, say, the *N.Y. Times*. Give me an O.K. on this if you will.

In setting up the page please indent the verse variously as indicated in the typescript. The prose shd run all across the page.

Notice that the book is divided into 3 parts. Make those parts distinct beginning each part well down from the top of the page the first word in each case being initialed with a distinctive capital. There shd be bold Roman numerals indicating each part. And notice also that the individual verse segments, separated by at least 4 or 5 spaces in the script are distinct one from the other and had better begin in each case with a capital slightly larger than that used in the ordinary line.

Nothing can discourage me because I start from complete discouragement; just you give me a clean looking, legible page without cramping and showing a good open type face—that's all I ask. And if the critics say anything to the point (or even vaguely perceptive) something which is as much as to say, if they should break their backs—I'll incorporate their findings in the next book of the series. There are 3 more to come.

Please keep me posted on the progress of the book. A card from time to time costs little in patience or time and means mountains to someone who is waiting for an appearance.

Sincerely
BILL

/ · /

the book: *Paterson (Book One)* was published by New Directions on July 1, 1946.

Warren's "Billie Potts": Robert Penn Warren (1905–), "The Ballad of Billie Potts," *Partisan Review* 11, no. 1 (Winter 1944): 56–70.

60. TLS-1   May 15, 1945

DEAR JIM:

So the old goat beat you to the summit—oh well, it's his element. I'm glad the *Paterson* has gone to the printer, makes me feel good. That's a summit too, for me; hope I don't find a neat little pile of fresh crap there after the critics have departed though as you suggest, it's likely.

As to the Miller thing: it isn't that his piece resembles mine that shd be particularly noted, of course it resembles what I did, he wishes merely to emphasize the form, that's what counts. But, of course, if what he has done is stale then it must be thrown out. I didn't find it stale. I am willing to follow your suggestion, send it to a third party, someone not known to be antagonistic—let's say Weldon Kees—and abide by his decision. I'd like to see the thing printed in *N[ew] D[irections]*.

Has the double volume *White M[ule]* and *In the M[oney]* been published, the clipping seems to say so? I'm having fun reading the history of Greek lit.: *Studies of the Greek Poets* by John Addington Symonds. Looking up a few elements of the grammar as well. It relieves my mind. May do another play, simpler format than the last—I've been wanting to do it for many years. But, to reassure you, the *Paterson* Part II is well on its way. Or maybe you'd rather not be reassured as to that.

Did I tell you I recorded my interpretation of my own verse at Library of Congress? Three discs, both sides 5 sides of verse and one of prose *(Life Along the Passaic R[iver])* Robert Penn Warren was my host. Had a nice time, they had guests for lunch, 3 good guys and everything. It's quite a project but I wish the discs were to be available after, they're not—unless Harvard goes in with the gov't to finance it. At present they merely go on file after I get for myself the only copies released. They played part of one disc back to me, it sounded better than I expected, quite a thrill. Old Warren paid me the compliment of saying: I had no idea they read so well! He treated me

as tho' I were Homer redivivus (with certain reservations). I read for about 1½ hrs what with pauses
to readjust things, here and there.

Let me know about that *White Mule* volume, I want
one if it's out. Do keep me posted on everything—
as of course you do for the most part.

Yours as ever
BILL

/ · /

the Miller thing: A manuscript submitted to New Directions by WCW's
friend Fred Miller but rejected by JL.

Weldon Kees: The poet, short story writer, and editor Weldon Kees
(1914–1955) contributed frequently to little magazines. *New Directions
1944* contained six of his poems.

Symonds: John Addington Symonds (1840–1893), *Studies of the Greek
Poets,* 2 vols. (New York: Harper and Brothers, n.d.). The first version
of Symonds's often reprinted book was published in London by Smith,
Elder in 1873.

I recorded: In 1944–45, Robert Penn Warren was consultant in poetry at
the Library of Congress. The recording session took place on May 5,
1945.

61. TLS-1   June 14, 1945

DEAR JIM:

Something I'd like to add to the *Paterson* thing.
Yes, I know and all that but I'd still like to include it
somewhere in the script. I'd suggest that it be put at
the very end, a note at the bottom of the last page,
in small type, the single foot-note to the entire poem.
Here it is.

I'll be up in Connecticut the first two weeks in
July. The address is, 201 Ocean Ave., West Haven,
Conn. Shd be back in the saddle by the 16th. I men-
tion this on the chance that there may be some gal-

leys to correct while I am away, and that they might
be sent there instead of here during that time. Not
that I'm overly optimistic. Merely for your information.

The enclosed from Joe Gould—with a decent letter—I might as well enclose that too. No, I won't,
I'd like to keep it as it is.

> Once lost, now found
> Poor Ezra Pound
> Is not a hound.
> His mind's unsound

Joe insists the poet as well as other men has a right
to act the damned fool on occasion. He's right.

My grandson is raising hell with me. He wants to
play "bang" on this machine.

Paul want to do it.

I got to quit.

> love
> DAD

Final note at the bottom of the page, the last page,
Paterson, (Or if preferable, in the opinion of
J. Laughlin, the note may be placed on the back of
the last page as a sort of post scriptum.)

i.e. In order apparently to bring the meter still more
within the sphere of prose and common speech,
Hipponax ended his iambics with a spondee or a tro-
chee instead of an iambus, doing thus the utmost
violence to the rhythmical structure. These deformed
and mutilated verses were called χωλίαμβοι or
ίαμβοι σκάζοντες (lame or limping iambics). They
communicated a curious crustiness to the style. The
choliambi are in poetry what the dwarf or cripple is
in human nature. Here again, by their acceptance of
this halting meter, the Greeks displayed their acute

aesthetic sense of propriety, recognizing the har-
mony which subsists between crabbed verses and the
distorted subjects with which they dealt—the vices
and perversions of humanity—as well as their agreement with the snarling spirit of the satirist. Deformed
verse was suited to deformed morality.

—*Studies of the Greek Poets,* John Addington Symonds,
M. D. Vol I p. 234

/ · /

a note: WCW's quotation from Symonds appears at the end of *Paterson*
1, where the page number is correctly given as 284. WCW used another
passage from vol. 1 of *Studies of the Greek Poets* (p. 425) as the epigraph
of *A Dream of Love* (1948).

Joe Gould: Indigent Greenwich Village writer and colorful character,
who visited WCW from time to time, exchanging gossip for handouts.

now found: Pound was captured by Italian partisans and detained by the
United States Army in early May 1945. On May 24 he was incarcerated in the Army's Disciplinary Training Center at Pisa.

62. TLS-2   July something or other
                                                    1945

DEAR JIM:

   In a daze, in a dream we too are in Connecticut
but at our palatial hutch on the shore this a crystal-
line day of ancient Lesbos or Cos or anywhere you
may care to imagine along the Aeolian coasts and
seas—I barefooted, dirty pants, tasting (if any should
care to try) of the salt dried upon my hide from the
sea: but you have noticed that I brought my type-
writer with me. Your last note came today.
   I want to be in *N[ew] D[irections]* the next if I can
make it. What is your deadline? If I have a little time
for it I'll round out a piece of the biography of my

mother if it should come to that. I am doing the new play now but I do want to give it a fling first with the theatrical agents. However, if you're in no hurry and the chipsmen turn me down it's all yours: prose, 2 acts, no impracticality—might be a hit if it could be intelligently and thoughtfully presented. Who knows? I'm making the try.

It would be more than congenial to me if you'd use the "Comedy Entombed." I can't see why you can't use it since though it has appeared in a little mag published by the U[niversity] of Chicago called *Trend* I'm not sure one in a thousand has seen it. That's your business, not mine.

As to verse, I've a good group of that, some of the best stuff I've ever done (my private opinion) but it's gradually being taken up here and there—as by *The Pennsylvania Gazette,* Benjamin Franklin's own child, the routine publication of the u[niversity] of P[ennsylvania] Corporation of which an admirer of mine, Sculley Bradley, has recently become the editor. I've wanted to send some stuff to this and that review—but I despise all the bastards that edit them and so, I wait and dream of greatness.

Had Ted Weiss and his round little wife here at the shore last week (New Haven is just a step). They seem out of place in nature—that is, nature as we hermits of the spirit know it. They seem antagonistic to fish (except gefulte fisch) He had never until a few days ago eaten a lobster. I was amazed. Soft, of the city—Though he did say something I remember, that the sea would last longer than the Catholic Church. Which, however, I doubt. I like him and her, they're good eggs but it was odd in my present mood seeing them here at the shore with all the smells and sights, the carelessness that goes with the sort of life we are leading here.

We leave for home, alas! on Sunday. That reminds

me, why, oh why! Mr. Laughlin do you not use
Quevedo's *The Dog and the Fever* which I have translated (with Mother's help) at enormous pains and
which, I can assure you, is far more "modern" than
ever Hemingway or even Gertie [Stein] ever thought
of being. It's good and I mean good any way you
look at it. I could get it ready by late Fall. It is absolutely "new directions" in its manner of writing and
hot as hell besides. You ought to do it. The boys at
Cummington want it but I'm afraid it's too much
for them and they'd take two or three years I am
sure to set it up. You could use it with a clear modern conscience, take it from me.

Oh let me add that the "M.D." which I was so
proud to add to the signature at the end of the foot-
note I want you to use at the end of *Paterson*—is
unjustifiable there. It is Symonds' father who was
the M.D. so please delete that if you can remember
to do so or I'll do it when finally I see the galleys.
The old Doc must have been a wonderful old guy
to do the translations which his son quotes in the
book. And, by the way that book, *The Greek Poets*
has been my constant reading during the past two
weeks. What a thrill to me! I can now spell out the
verses, the actual words of the originals and come
somewhere near understanding them while getting
the actual feel of the language. Oh I could write on
that for a month—that in the entire literature of
ancient Greece with all its magnificence there is not
one rhyme! Not one! And when will we Yankees
ever stop imitating English and go on and do the
things that are open to us—in illimitable time.

Had a nice letter from Bob McAlmon who has
gone to the mountains of Mexico for a rest, one of
my best pals.

Have enjoyed the Scott Fitzgerald book though
why such a man thought the world, his world, came

to an end in Hemingway is beyond my thought. I
can understand though how he felt, the best of Hem
is very, very good but it isn't a Banzai charge at that.

Keep me posted. God how I wish I could go on
under circumstances such as this for a few years before
I croak; it would be the dream of my life come true.
I'd work my guts out with all the stuff that's stewing
around there seeking exit from that whore's nest of
a womb.

Floss sends a smile and a curl from her lovely grey
head of hair. I get a big kick out of seeing her looking ten, fifteen years younger under this sunlight.

Yours
BILL

/ · /

the new play: A Dream of Love, published by New Directions in September 1948 as number 6 in the *Direction* series. It was first performed
in late July 1949 at the Hudson Guild Playhouse in New York by We
Present, a small, off-Broadway company.

Pennsylvania Gazette: Three poems by WCW appeared in the *General
Magazine and Historical Chronicle* (Philadelphia), 47, no. 4 (Summer 1945):
220–21. Edward Sculley Bradley (1897–) was professor of English at
the University of Pennsylvania and an authority on nineteenth-century
American literature, best known for his editing of Walt Whitman's
poetry and prose.

Scott Fitzgerald: In 1945 New Directions published Edmund Wilson's
edition of *The Crack-Up,* a collection of autobiographical essays, notes,
and letters by F. Scott Fitzgerald (1896–1940), the American novelist
and friend of Ernest Hemingway.

63. TLS-2   Sept 7, 1945

DEAR JIM:

I'm sorry but the *Paterson* looks pretty bad to me.
I don't know what to do. What I have done (avoiding dramatics) is to slash it unmercifully. No use

trying to rewrite. I'll have to stand or fall on whatever merits may exist in the thing now. I feel like
hell over it.

As to whatever extra expenses may be incurred by
what I have done I'll bear them most willingly. The
cuts must be made as indicated on my set of the galleys. There are few other changes or errors.

Either that or, as Floss has suggested, withdraw
the thing completely. She wants me to hold it back
until the full four parts have been completed. I can't
do that. It's now or never or I'll chuck the whole
God damned mess—as I feel tonight.

I've written to Creekmore and sent him the corrected galleys in separate containers. I've told him
substantially what I'm telling you. The changes must
be made no matter what the cost and that you will
back me up in this.

Your own book, which I received this p.m. is
O.K., entertaining and well composed. I like it and
shall say more another time. At the moment I feel as
if the Navy had started shelling me on my desert
island—and I hope they hit me with the last shell.

Bill (Lt Commander now) and Paul had the luck
to run into each other at Pearl Harbor. Wish they
were home—but am glad they're not tonight.

I wish I had the guts to say to burn the whole
Paterson script.

Yours
BILL

/ · /

Creekmore: The poet, short story writer, translator, and editor Hubert
Creekmore (1907–1966) worked in the Norfolk and New York offices
of New Directions, which published his *The Long Reprieve and Other
Poems from New Caledonia* in 1946.

Your own book: James Laughlin, *Some Natural Things* (Norfolk, Conn.:
New Directions, 1945).

64. TLS-2   Nov. 18, 1945

DEAR JIM:

Thanks for the Rimbaud by Varèse. Now you're talking—Very different from the first. By the way, did you see the Anais Nin book recently out. I think it's bad, all but the first piece—maybe I don't get it but to me it seems as if a serious disintegration is taking place there. I'm sorry. And while speaking of books of course you've seen the Miller booklet, privately printed, from California (I'm terrible on names.) This thing of Miller's starts off in a puerile fashion but toward the latter half of it turns into a masterpiece. That's writing—really the best I've seen of Miller—ever.

It particularly interested me not only to notice that Miller twice mentioned me in this book but particularly mentioned my *Novelette* as one of the books he brought along to read on the ship. If ever you get around to my name again in your Modern Reprints I wish you'd bear in mind the *Novelette.*

PM is running an article by me on Ezra Pound in next Sunday's issue. I had no enthusiasm for the article when I wrote it but I believe it will do Ezra more good than harm for me to have said what I said—if anything a man in my position says has any weight in public affairs.

The play's finished except for being typed and copyrighted. As soon as that business is finished and I'm having a job getting the typing done—at night by an old pal—I'll send you a carbon of the thing for your enjoyment and advice. I intend to join the Author's League again (I resigned two years ago) then seek an agent and begin the grind seeking a producer. You spoke of Tennessee Williams having a hot shot agent who might take me on. Let me have any dope you think pertinent. I read the play last night to Floss, Jinny and Floss's sister Charlotte—an old Hollywooder. They didn't say too much but it seemed to knock them for a loop one way or another. All agreed it needed touching up here and there but advised me not to change a word—rather to seek the advice of a professional expert. That's rather high, if indirect, praise. Sounds on reading aloud to me as though it has possibilities for the stage which is my whole objective this time. The things I can't possibly know, of course, are questions of timing, of relative length in production to reading time etc etc. Everything else in the play is plain sailing. There is though, the question of obscenity—but even there I am pretty sure I'm within the bars. A word or two may have to be deleted but nothing more than that. It may be though that the whole thing is beyond the pale. I hope not and I don't think so. I meant to stay within the limits—but you never know.

Any news about *Paterson?* I'm not trying to force you in any way but it would be very important for me to see the page proofs before you go on with the book. Any information as to progress would be much appreciated.

Finally I wish you'd make a note of this: Fred Miller—you have heard me speak of Fred Miller—is pretty much on the loose these days. He's finished his war job but before he goes back to his tool designing or whatever it is that he does he would give his soul you might say to take a shot at supporting himself by some writing job. Has New Directions any place for him? He's a tough egg in many ways but a hard worker and I don't think he wants much money. If you could use Fred you'd find a loyal assistant and one, I think, with great potential abilities. He's never had a break in the literary game, he's overdue and right in his prime for something that would bring out his latent qualities.

Glad you liked Bunk Johnson and his band—Floss and I had a beautiful evening together listening to him week before last. An almost religious atmosphere you might say.

I have also an article on e.e. cummings coming out in *Harvard Wake*—and some poems. Do you know about that sheet?

I'm speaking at Briarcliff College Nov. 29 at noon, no less!

Saw Kenneth Burke at Andover, N.J. last week or so. That's something you should take in, a visit to Kenneth Burke at Andover, N.J. I'd like to see that—me in the wainscoting watching you and Ken sitting at his family table in a busted down chair. That would be something.

Yours
BILL

/ · /

the Rimbaud by Varèse: Arthur Rimbaud, *A Season in Hell,* trans. Louise Varèse (Norfolk, Conn.: New Directions, [1945]). In 1939, New Directions had published a poor translation by Delmore Schwartz.

the Anais Nin book: Possibly *This Hunger . . . with . . . Woodblocks by Ian Hugo* (New York: Gemor Press, 1945).

the Miller booklet: In *Aller Retour New York* (Paris: Obelisk Press, 1935), Henry Miller mentions WCW on pp. 11 and 87–91. The earlier passage describes their first meeting at Hilaire Hiler's Twelfth Street studio in New York. The later passage is an open letter to "Doc Williams" praising the prose style of WCW's *A Novelette and Other Prose* (1932), which Miller read on shipboard while returning to Paris. A privately printed American edition of *Aller Retour New York* appeared in 1945. WCW's signed copy, number 27 of 500, is in the Beinecke Library, Yale University.

an article: "The Case for and against Ezra Pound," *PM* (New York), November 25, 1945, 16.

a hot shot agent: Audrey Wood (1905–1981) and her husband William Liebling operated the Liebling-Wood agency in New York from 1937 to 1954. She was Tennessee Williams's agent from 1939 to 1971. She read WCW's *A Dream of Love* and conferred with him about it in May 1946.

Bunk Johnson: Leader of a black New Orleans classical jazz band that was playing at the Stuyvesant Casino in New York City. WCW heard them play twice in November, once with JL. His poem "Ol' Bunk's Band" recalls the occasion.

an article: "Lower Case Cummings," *Harvard Wake,* no. 5 (Spring 1946): 20–23.

Kenneth Burke: WCW and FW visited the philosopher and critic Kenneth Burke (1897–) at his Andover farm on November 9. WCW's poem "At Kenneth Burke's Place" recalls the occasion.

65. TLS-1   March 22, 1946

DEAR JIM:

A rather exciting bit of detail came up today, *The New Republic* purchased a 4 page poem of mine called, "Russia." That they should take the thing at all floored me completely. I played a hunch of Flossie's—must remember that. It's a hot poem topically, I can't yet understand how they came to consent to show it. I think it'll make a bit of a stir. And it's a wonderful thing for me just at this time. Better grow up to be old, Jim. Good free advertising, too, for *Paterson.*

Now I'm envisioning a new book of poems to be called, *Russia & Other Poems,* plunking the "Russia" thing in the middle and including everything since the *Collected Poems;* taking in, that is, *The Wedge* also— or the best things in that book. There's a lot of stuff.

For instance, I've got one poem coming out in *Arizona Quarterly,* a group in *Contemporary Poetry* (Baltimore), a group in *Yale Poetry Review,* a group in *Harvard Wake,* a single poem in *Briarcliff Quarterly* and there are the things that came out in *Quarterly Review* several of which will appear in a Knopf

Anthology due soon. I also have a back log of stuff in my portfolio that will serve after I doll them up a little. Oh well, there's the challenge. But as you will say, Where's the paper? Or as one of my schoolboy friends used to yell derisively when some ass made a stupid crack—PAPER!

In addition we have *Paterson* on the ways and a play at an agency.

But wait a minute, that ain't all. I had a letter from a Washington Square book store proprietor telling me she had just read *First Act* and that it was the greatest novel ever written in America. I got so excited that I sat right down and wrote the chapter of the next in that series to be called *The Buildup*—sixteen pages. For God's sake do something about this, I can't be allowed to go on and kill myself at this young age. For I got to finish my mother's biography one of these days.

Yours
Bill

I hope I haven't forgot anything. ⟨oh yes, the 3 additional parts of *Paterson!*⟩

/ · /

"Russia": WCW's poem appeared in the *New Republic* 114, no. 17 (April 29, 1946): 615. It was reprinted in *The Clouds, Aigeltinger, Russia, &.* (1948).

Arizona Quarterly: "The Horse," *Arizona Quarterly* 2, no. 1 (Spring 1946): 4.

Contemporary Poetry: "The Mind's Games," *Contemporary Poetry* 6, no. 1 (Spring 1946): 6–7; "Raindrops on a Briar" and "The Light Shall Not Enter," *Contemporary Poetry* 6, no. 4 (Winter 1947): 3–4.

Yale Poetry Review: "East Coocoo," "Ol' Bunk's Band," "The Savage Beast," and "At Kenneth Burke's Place," *Yale Poetry Review* 2, no. 1 (Summer 1946): 19–22.

Harvard Wake: Nine poems were published under the title "The Peacock's Eyes," *Harvard Wake,* no. 5 (Spring 1946): 80–82.

Briarcliff Quarterly: "The Visit," *Briarcliff Quarterly* 3, no. 9 (April 1946): 1–2.

proprietor: Bonnie Golightly operated the Washington Square Book-store; see letter 69 below.

66. ALS-4   6/10/46

DEAR JIM:

We're stationed, for a week, on this old estate. The main house has been semi-abandoned since the crash of '29 (probably), the old man of the place died thereafter, his wife moved to the city, Buffalo, and two of the children, Mrs. Abbott one of them have remained here to carry on.

It's a superb spot for a rest—if one could get it. I mean if I could be taken care of here (like the prize sheep) for a year or two I think I could catch up on myself & thereafter go to hell quietly.

I've read *N[ew] D[irections 19]46* since arriving— not all of it but most. Miller on Rimbaud is impressive, one of the best appreciations of a writer I have ever read and one of the best statements of our positions today as writers I ever hope to read—a few of his paragraphs are superlative. I have been deeply moved, thoroughly convinced of the soundness of Miller's address to his task as a man writing in our day. When he is good (not always) there's no one better.

I shan't try to describe this place or the lives led by the charming people who are our hosts. I wish there were more like them in the world. They are the complements to the wild men who do the work: they live. Very few live as far as I can see in America today, they merely fuck & have nerves.

By the way I enjoyed these poems of Tennessee

Williams more than I have enjoyed any other poems of his I have ever seen.

I liked your own poem as I think I have already said; one of your best.

What will happen to us now? to Floss & me. I wish I knew or could predict it. It will not be as it has been in the past.

Yours
BILL

/ · /

this old estate: This was the second of eleven visits to Gratwick Highlands in Linwood, New York, made by WCW and FW between 1940 and 1958. The Gratwick children were Theresa, who married Charles Abbott in 1936, and Bill, a horticulturist and sculptor, whose wife, Harriet Saltonstall Gratwick, was founder and director of the Linwood Music School.

Miller on Rimbaud: Henry Miller, "When Do Angels Cease to Resemble Themselves: A Study of Rimbaud," *New Directions 9* (1946), pp. 39–76, later incorporated into Miller's *The Time of the Assassins: A Study of Rimbaud* (New York: New Directions, 1956).

Tennessee Williams: "Three Poems," *New Directions 9*, pp. 77–83. The poems were "Camino Real," "Recuerdo," and "Lady, Anemone."

your own poem: James Laughlin, "Above the City," *New Directions 9*, p. 38.

67. TLS-1   June 20 [1946]

DEAR JIM:

I pulled a fast one this week that has given me no little satisfaction. It started by my receiving the enclosed letter from a French-Swiss asking me for a short story, as you'll see, he wanting it in his hands before leaving for Europe at once! Geezus, what the hell do they think I am?

As I have already told you, I think, I made up my

mind he'd have his God damned story if it killed me so I told him I'd write him one that night and put a special delivery stamp on my letter, adding that it would be in his hands Saturday morning.

So last Tuesday I punched out the story writing without stopping from 8 to 11 p.m., sixteen pages. Flossie looked it over and gave me the green flag. Wednesday night and Thursday before breakfast I revised and retyped the whole thing, become twenty three pages. Yesterday I revised and cut and today it is being typed clean for me.

But the damned French-Swiss has already left the country—after writing me another letter saying there was no hurry etc etc.

O.K.? Now I got the story which Floss says is one of my best and I've got also the satisfaction of feeling I can still do it. It was wonderful to feel the wheels clicking again after all those years—straight narrative with a beautiful theme to follow so that it took no effort whatever except to my ass from sitting in one place so long.

What about this guy Simon? Do you know him? He says he represents some new group. Shall I send him the story to translate into French? In his last letter he states that he wouldn't mind if it came out also in English in this country or elsewhere. But I'm not just throwing this work around carelessly. It's hot, but I mean hot—and in the pants—who do you think ought to get it?

Yours
BILL

/ · /

a short story: "The Farmers' Daughters" was not published by Jean Simon of Geneva, but he helped to arrange the first French translations of other stories by WCW; see letters 69 and 72 below.

68. TLS-2   July 17, 1946

DEAR JIM:

Many thanks for the check. And thanks also for the bid to the city, Floss and I will make it a point to be there "week after next" which will be the last week in July—if you make it either the 30th or the 31st. Those are the only possible dates for us. After that we'll be away on our vacation.

Have been hearing fairly frequently from Ezra of late, brief but more or less coherent letters based on the assumption that I need to go to school, study prose style and generally do more reading—all of which has a certain amount of truth in it. But if I suggest that he go back to the 6th grade and learn to write a simple declarative sentence and study the prose style of a barred window—he is silent. He's never got over the pedagogic frenzy when it is to be applied to others. A mind completely arrested in a past age— still speaks of the progress made by Hilda, of Ford Madox Ford (who was so much wiser in the world than Pound ever could be) etc etc But there the guy is and he still knows how to strut his fake poses of domination. He's dangerous too if allowed to indulge his deficiencies. All partially blocked-out minds endanger the community if permitted to impose their private abnormalities. It's an old story of genius. He can't learn therefore he is (obviously) all-knowing. We've seen it before this. I've hinted that he go to Monseigneur Sheen. What a comedy that would be! And logical too. Maybe Ezra could convert the bastard then the world would indeed be saved.

A frenchman asked me for a story, said you had steered him to me, a french-swiss, Simon by name. I'm trying to get one up for him, as usual they are always "sailing for Paris tomorrow" or something

of the sort. And no pay, of course. Geezus! I don't
see why the good Lord didn't make some men with
cocks grown into their mouths instead of tongues
and some Millays with them sewed into their vaginas
and done with it.

What else? "A Choral" which Zukofsky's wife has
set to music. *Partisan Review* would be glad to print
it—sometime, but not soon. I demanded it back. Sent
it to Ransom, He returned it saying he didn't care
for me in that mood. Now Vivienne has it—one of
the best things (of a sort) which I have ever written.
It is a bit long, runs four or five pages double spaced.
With Celia's music—or a few pages of the best of
her music it would make a fairly worthwhile exhibit
with plenty of punch to it. It is bawdy and perhaps
a bit blasphemous. I don't see how *Briarcliff* can use
it with all those young ladies looking on—to say
nothing of the faculty.

So what? I wish it could be brought out as a bro-
chure, music and all. I'd pay for part of it if it could
be done. It wouldn't take much paper and there'd be
no need of binding. Could it be done under New
Directions sponsorship and head? I'll ask Vivienne
to send you her copy of the poem. If it comes to a
show down I suppose *N[ew] D[irections] 1947* (if
there's to be one) might use it with some profit. But
at my age I'd rather let that be devoted to the young
uns. I can't see myself there.

Who was the son-of-a-bitch who reviewed *N[ew]
D[irections] 1946* in *Times Book Review?* I've forgot
the name, Welsh or Mapes or something like that.
What a bastard he was—left out Miller and Eluard
completely. I wrote the "editor" the hottest letter I
knew how to compose calling him and his weekly
the cowardly bastards they are for operating in the
first place without an editor—they appear to have
none—and then admitting to their columns such an

obviously vicious writer. They did not reply—there is no one to reply from such a source. I'm going to stop reading their dirty sheet. My only reason for reading it at any time has been that it gives the names of certain things published.

So until the week after next. Got anything of Carson McCullers' for me to read? Lend me something. I know of her work but don't remember anything at the moment.

Yrs
BILL

⟨Ez says "Studs Lonigan" called on him. No comment.⟩

/ · /

a barred window: Pound was imprisoned in St. Elizabeths Hospital, the federal hospital for the criminally insane in Washington, D.C., from December 1945 to May 1958.

Hilda: The American poet Hilda Doolittle, or "H.D." (1886–1961), met Pound and WCW at the University of Pennsylvania in 1905. She was later associated with Pound in the London Imagist movement of 1912–14.

Ford Madox Ford: The English man of letters Ford Madox Ford (1873–1939) introduced Pound to literary London in 1909 and influenced his thinking about literary style. WCW first met Ford in Paris in 1924 and saw him frequently when Ford lived in the United States from 1935 to 1939. Ford's memory is evoked in a number of WCW's later poems, including "To Ford Madox Ford in Heaven" (1940), "The Birth of Venus" (1948), and "Incognito" (1950).

Monseigneur Sheen: The Very Reverend Dr. Fulton J. Sheen (1895–1979) preached in St. Patrick's Cathedral, New York, and on NBC Radio from 1930 to 1952. Sheen's sermons mixed Catholic doctrine with a strongly anti-Communist political message.

Millays: Women poets, presumably, after Edna St. Vincent Millay (1892–1950).

"Choral": WCW's "Choral: The Pink Church," with a musical setting by Louis Zukofsky's wife, Celia Thaew, was first published in the Williams special number of *Briarcliff Quarterly* 3, no. 11 (October 1946): 165–68. The *Quarterly* was edited by Norman Macleod (1906–1985)

and published at Briarcliff Junior College for women, in Westchester County, New York.

Ransom: The poet and critic John Crowe Ransom (1888–1974) was editor of the *Kenyon Review*.

Vivienne: The critic Vivienne Koch was married to Norman Macleod from 1939 to 1948 and helped to edit the *Briarcliff Quarterly*. She also taught in the Division of General Education at New York University. On September 30, 1945, she interviewed WCW in Rutherford for her critical biography *William Carlos Williams,* published in 1950 as part of New Directions's Makers of Modern Literature series.

Times Book Review: Philip Wylie reviewed *New Directions 9* in the *New York Times Book Review,* June 16, 1946, p. 4.

Miller and Eluard: New Directions 9 contained Henry Miller's essay on Rimbaud (see letter 66 above) and "Paul Eluard—Poet of France: Some Preliminary Translations," which presented thirty poems by the French Surrealist poet and resistance worker (1895–1952). WCW and JL were each responsible for six of the translations.

Carson McCullers': New Directions had published *Reflections in a Golden Eye* (1941), by the American novelist and playwright Carson McCullers (1917–1967).

"Studs Lonigan": James T. Farrell (1904–1979), author of *Young Lonigan* (1932) and *The Young Manhood of Studs Lonigan* (1934).

69. TLS-2   Dec. 28, 1946

DEAR JIM:

Glad to hear from you, it's the first since your return. And sorry to hear you're laid out with whatever it is that has laid you cold. You've probably snapped out of it by this time.

That's great news from abroad and I'll comply with the conditions and send the additions to the short stories at once—in a week or two, that is. For I've been laid out myself, just back from the hospital in fact. It's this way, the bums who sewed up my hernia the first time didn't reckon on my prowess (so they say) with the result that the damned thing broke down and I was in a worse situation than before they operated on me. I got disgusted, decided I didn't want to go through the winter that way (with one hand in my right pants pocket holding my guts in) so I went to Bill's hospital in New York City and had myself sewed up right this time. I had a hell of a good time of it, on the 16th floor overlooking the East River, an auburn haired nurse and everything! I wanted to get home before Christmas so here I am, home and practicing Medicine again at the end of ten day—that is it was thirteen days after the op. when I saw my first patients again. I'm not being foolish—haven't been making outside calls yet. What a place that hospital is, magnificent. I couldn't have had a better vacation—it would have been perfect if Floss could have enjoyed it equally.

One day on her way in to see me Floss left the rewritten play (a new 1st act added) at Audrey Wood—at her request. You ought to see it now all professionally typed and refurbished—though I'm not kidding myself about it. It's just a good play but I know perfectly well what I'm up against. If I don't beat 'em one way I'll beat 'em another. It's a good play, I think you'll like it, a much better play than when you saw it last.

I've started to work on *Paterson,* Books II and III which I plan to have ready for you late next spring— I hope. It was a big thrill to me to have you say you're all set to go ahead with the next installment. I want to save Part IV for separate publication, I have to do it that way for private reasons linked with the story as well as because I want to study that book carefully before releasing it.

It saddens me and humiliates me to have to say that I have broken with old Ezra finally. I feel somewhat small about it since he is under confinement in a mental hospital at the moment but my own self respect (whatever the hell that is worth) demanded it. I just couldn't go on swallowing his guff—even for old time's sake, it depressed me to try to read his letter since, from his point of view, I don't doubt that he is at least arguably in the right. But I'll be damned if I have to take that kind of twaddle from him or anybody else. I know he's got to talk down to somebody, especially his close friends, in order that he may feel up. And I know that a person is morally bound at times to "play dead" for one's friends. However there is a limit to all that and, finally, I reached it with dear, asinine ol' Ezra. I couldn't take it any more—even to help him over his difficulty. Fuck him—the way to hell is open to us all.

A woman named Bonnie Golightly who owns and runs a bookshop at the corner of Washington Square and Waverly Place in the big city gave a coming out party for me over the appearance of the recent issue of *Briarcliff Quarterly* on the Sunday before I went to the hospital. I kept a firm grip on my hernia and had a swell time. She's a fine girl, one of the best—look in on her sometime if you don't already know her and be nice to her, you hear me? Poor kid we just heard from her assistant or secretary or something that she had to rush back to Kentucky yesterday, her mother is seriously ill. It was a good party, ask Vivienne Macleod about it. There's a swell girl too, Vivienne—and a hard worker. What's she up to concerning me, I can't get a word out of her though she keeps boring in as if I had oil in my pants somewhere.

Randall Jarrell sure gave me a boost, didn't he. He's turned out to be a firm friend. Auden also came to the party. What do you know? And Oscar Williams! Geezes, I must be getting somewhere.

Now, if this new seam in my belly really holds I'll

be in a position to get some really BIG work done. My Ma was 90 Christmas Even!

> Same to you
> BILL

⟨Happy New Year!⟩

/ · /

great news: In a letter of December 25, 1946, JL informed WCW that through Jean Simon he had sold the rights for a French translation of *Life Along the Passaic River* to Editions de l'Abbaye du Livre, in Lausanne, Switzerland. Translations by Susanne and Jean Vermandoy of ten stories were published in 1948 under the title *Passaic, Passaic!*

Bill's hospital: The New York Hospital, where WCW's elder son, William Eric Williams, was interning. The earlier operation had been performed on May 1, 1946, at the Passaic General Hospital, in New Jersey.

Randall Jarrell: Jarrell's glowing review of *Paterson* 1, entitled "The Poet and His Public," appeared in *Partisan Review* 13, no. 4 (September–October 1946): 488–500.

Oscar Williams: A prolific poet and anthologist (1900–1964), whose name was sometimes confused with that of WCW.

70. TLS-2   Feb. 9, 1947

DEAR JIM:

There have been a number of things on my mind lately concerning books, publication projects, new work and so forth as they concern both of us that need highlighting a little at the moment etc etc

The translation of *White Mule* done in Buenos Aires and published there makes an attractive book. I don't know what the sales there would be but it looks like good reading. I don't know anything of the man who did the work. Must be a good guy. Who gets paid and what—not that I care much but I suppose I'm protected?

I've been collecting short stories, everything that didn't appear in either *The Knife of the Times* or *Life Along the P[assaic] R[iver]*. There's enough for another book—almost. Since both the books mentioned above are out of print, what about it? I'm having the new stuff typed out so as to have a single script of it. What do I do next as far as Lausanne is concerned?

Someone in New York also wrote asking me for new prose material ⟨for French translation⟩? What the hell goes on? You ought to be around or we should at least be in closer contact for a while in order to get all these loose ends gathered together.

To clear up another point, the long story I told you about several months ago has been finished—more or less—but it's too hot for use at the moment, the man not yet having been brought to trial so that I'm afraid to do more with the writing. We'll drop that for the moment.

Two Italians, one a prof at Brown and Harvard, are after me for verse. I sent a copy of the original *Collected Poems* to Italy but the guy at Harvard is still on my neck. Do you know anything about him? I do what I can but my time is extremely limited and all this involves much work for me.

My principal chore is, naturally, *Paterson* Parts II & III. My theme for both parts is fairly well worked but the detail of typing and retyping the various passages as I advance is really taking it out of me—especially since they have elected me President of the Medical Board at the hospital. I tried my best to get out of it but nobody would listen to me. The more excited I get over Part II the more I am in despair knowing the work involved. I feel isolated and browbeaten—but I am thrilled with what I have mapped out. A good sign I suppose.

The play was turned down ("I'm *very* much interested in that play!") by Audrey Wood. The same day a card from Eric Bentley who said you had spoken to him of the thing. He wanted to see it, asked for production and publication rights—or rather asked if I had granted them to anyone. I sent him the play.

To continue with the matter of the play, what are your interests in it, if any? Would you bring it out in *New Directions 1947* if everything else fails? You said you would bring it out as a book if it gets stage production. Suppose it gets put on some experimental stage, would you still make a book of it? What the hell anyway? I need light on all these matters.

Norman Pearson asked for a copy of the play, I sent it to him, he says the Yale proff of dramatics is looking for something ⟨to⟩ experiment with. They might put it on there.

Finally another bid has come in (possibly through something Audrey Wood may have said to the *View* group) from *The American Company*, Sam H. Grisman, who has "organized a permanent acting company made up of distinguished actors, actresses, directors and stage technicians . . to produce new plays, reflecting the American scene, which may or may not appeal to the so called "Commercial" value . . in the text". I sent them a copy also—the revised text which you have not seen. Even Audrey said it was "much better but still too surrealistic (which it is not) for N.Y. production". Shit.

And what about some cash from recent sales old and new? Or is that out of tune?

Collected Poems out of print, *In the Am. Grain* out of print, *Life along the P. R.* virtually out of print, *The Wedge* out of print. ⟨Issue of *Briarcliff Q[uarterly]* concerning me, out of print. W.C.W. himself almost out of print.⟩

I haven't had time to collect the stuff for the *Selected Poems* not with all the rest of the stuff to do—but I suppose when I have a definite date to shoot at I

could do that in a week. No stimulation. I asked
Randall Jarrell if he'd do a preface. He said he'd like
to but it would be, he thought, like Little Lord
Fauntleroy introducing Henry Wadsworth Longfel-
low to heaven! Not a bad slant for a young man. He
and his wife are coming out for supper next Saturday evening. He says Robert Lowell (is that the right
name for the poet) has also gone off the deep end for
Paterson Part I and is doing an enthusiastic (?) review
for *Sewanee Review*. That's a good thing.

The thing is, Jim, I'm all balled up over this. I
don't know where the hell I stand from a practical
viewpoint. All I know enough to do is write, after
that I'm sunk. I have to count on you to straighten
out the business end—and I think you are interested—but where in hell am I. And why? It's no fun
sometimes.

Yrs.
Bill

⟨Give me some sort of detailed promise & plan to
follow so I won't get lost. What, practically, am I
writing for?⟩

⟨Macmillan thru Putnams wants a book. This one
wants the next in the *White Mule* series. Wish I knew
what to do.⟩

⟨& when, & what is the deadline for *N[ew] D[irections]*
for 1947? I have—various things.⟩

/ · /

The translation: *Así comienza la vida,* trans. Federico López Cruz (Buenos Aires: Santiago Rueda, 1946).
another book: WCW's *Make Light of It: Collected Stories* (New York:
Random House, 1950) contained three groups of stories: "The Knife

of the Times," "Life Along the Passaic River," and "Beer and Cold Cuts."

the long story: "The Farmers' Daughters" was published in the *Hudson Review* 10, no. 3 (Autumn 1957): 329–52.

a prof at Brown: The critic, editor, and translator Renato Poggioli (1907–1963) was moving from an assistant professorship at Brown University to an associate professorship of comparative literature at Harvard University in 1947. He was foreign editor of *Inventario*, a literary magazine published in Milan.

Eric Bentley: In 1947, the critic, translator, and playwright Eric Bentley (1916–) was professor of literature and drama at the University of Minnesota and author of *A Century of Hero Worship* (1944) and *The Playwright as Thinker* (1946). New Directions published Bentley's translation of Bertolt Brecht's *The Private Life of the Master Race* in 1944.

Norman Pearson: Professor Norman Holmes Pearson (1909–1975) joined the faculty of Yale University in 1941 and became a distinguished scholar and editor of nineteenth- and twentieth-century American literature.

the View group: The New York Surrealist magazine *View* was founded by Charles Henri Ford in 1940. Parker Tyler, Andé Breton, Nicolas Calas, Pavel Tchelitchew, and Philip Lamantia were all closely associated with *View*.

Grisman: Sam H. Grisman (1891?–1955) was a New York producer and theater owner whose greatest success was a production of *Tobacco Road* that ran for 3,182 performances in 1933–39. By 1947 his career was in decline, and the American Company mounted only one production that reached the stage, a circus musical by Halsted Welles called *A Temporary Island* (1948).

Selected Poems: WCW's *Selected Poems,* with an introduction by Randall Jarrell, was published by New Directions in March 1949.

Robert Lowell: "Thomas, Bishop, and Williams," by the poet Robert Lowell (1917–1977), appeared in *Sewanee Review* 55 (Summer 1947): 493–503.

71. ALS-4

Feb 17/47

DEAR JIM—

After reading the enclosed—I almost puked—Did you really at any time pronounce your name as they say—*you* or the family?—you never did to us.—I have a feeling that the *N.Y. Times* is just not up to what you are doing—and pick on a trivial matter—even if it did occur.—A moronic attitude for a major paper to take.—

Like the afternoon I spent with Joyce—when he asked me about the pronunciation of the Norwegian language in various districts of the country and he had been informed "tho I suspect he knew better" that they all spoke alike!—Like hell they do.—When I said a few words in "Oslo Norwegian" & the same in West Coast accent he pretended to be surprised!— Possibly your visit with him had the same implications. Any way it annoyed me. Mebbe you can laugh it off. Bill; busy—but mad as hell that his books are out of print. The demands for *The Wedge* are a daily annoyance.—and *you* wouldn't print it—but Jesus what you *did* print! *Life Along the Passaic*—people asking for it all the time.—It's all very well to say— as you did some time ago—"Your grandchildren will live on the Royalties of your books"—but we'd like to add to our slim dividends while we are alive—and enjoy a few years of easier living. So—get the work going!—Where can one buy *In the American Grain?*— *Why* is it out of print?—

Enjoy your skiing—but don't break your neck— yet!

Best wishes—
FLORENCE WILLIAMS

/ · /

the enclosed: "People Who Write and Read," an anonymous feature in the *New York Times Book Review* for February 16, 1947, recounts an anecdote of a meeting in Paris at which James Joyce corrected JL's pronunciation of his own name from "Lofflin" to "Locklin" (p. 8).

Joyce: WCW and FW dined with James and Nora Joyce at the Trianon in Paris on Saturday, January 19, 1924. Joyce was then working on the early sections of *Finnegans Wake,* which use Norwegian words to evoke the Viking occupation of medieval Dublin.

72. TLS-1   March 6, 1947

DEAR JIM:

Paterson II has me sleepless so I have to believe the Guy Up THERE is working on it; I always feel disturbed when He's doing a job. At the moment the 2nd or "full" version (assembling of all notes etc) is nearing completion, may be finished any day now.

The next step is to cut the thing down to workable limits. I don't know how long that will take, the way I go at it, but not more than a month I hope.

Then copies will have to be made and the final disgusts surmounted.

I'm not waiting for Bentley but sending you a copy of the play now. Bentley can send his copy back to me when he's through with it. The play needs some cutting. One suggestion, by Yale Dramatic Dep't, is that I eliminate two entire (as they say "unneeded") scenes. The very first scene of all and the one showing the two negresses. They say the first scene is misleading besides, makes the auditor believe that gal, that appears there is the hero. Shit with them— but then . So, cut those two scenes. I can use both separately as playlets elsewhere.

Sent the stuff to Jean Simon in Geneva—wish I was there today—and ol' stupid Ezra along with me if it would do him any good: which I doubt. I was reading some of his Chinese Cantos this A.M. Nice writing, nice squeezing up of history (as it might well be done) but, my God, what an occupation for an erstwhile brain. I'm afraid he never really grew up, not really. Still a bright boy. A musical "intellect". I mean a "musical" intellect.

This March sun . ! the sap is spilling

BILL

73. ALS-4   July 7, 1947

DEAR JIM:

Got your letter about *Pat[erson]* II this a.m.—after
my first "workshop" meeting at which I struggled
through Ezra's 83d Canto & discussed it briefly. This
is a tough life. A fair success with the pay members
but at least I brought the question before them.

Partisan Review accepted 3 excerpts from *Pat[erson]*
II, about 3 pages. *Poetry* accepted the short lyric about
Altgeld—first they've taken of mine in years.

[Eric] Bentley has offered to take us to Alta over
the next week-end. I'll see your banker some evening.

We're *not* going on to the coast—too far and too
hot—but plan to return via Taos as I told you.

It pleases me that your impression of *Pat[erson]* II
is favorable & that Van Vechten is willing to go ahead
at once, does that mean it will be out by Christmas?
I hope so.

It's hellishly hot here during the day as you know—
a city full of unusual associations.

                                             Best
                                             BILL

The drive across the country was a tremendous
experience for Floss & me. With Charlotte (Floss'
sister) sharing the wheel we averaged 400 miles a
day—which wasn't bad at our age & with our old
faithful 1940 Buick. Really, to see the States one after
the other that way from the hills of Jersey over the
Mississippi & Missouri & Platte Valley & the Rock-
ies & past them is something I wouldn't trade for
several good vacations at a quiet resort. And the trip
home still coming up—The desert country is something not to be imagined—glad to sock that away in

my coco—& the towns we stopped at!! & the people
there!!! New York is pretty dim compared to those
strange places & creatures.

WCW

/ · /

my first "workshop": WCW was paid $500 to participate in a writers'
conference and workshop at the University of Utah in Salt Lake City
from July 7 to 18, 1947.

Ezra's 83d Canto: Pound's "Canto LXXXIII" had recently appeared in
the *Yale Poetry Review* 6 (1947): 3–8. It was republished in the following year as one of the *Pisan Cantos*.

3 excerpts: These appeared in *Partisan Review* 15, no. 2 (February 1948):
213–16.

lyric about Altgeld: WCW's ironic fifteen-line lyric about Governor John
P. Altgeld of Illinois ("America the golden!") appeared in *Poetry* 71,
no. 1 (October 1947): 30.

Alta: Since 1939, JL had owned a ski lodge in Alta, Utah. His letters
had whetted WCW's appetite to see the place, which he did on Saturday, July 12. JL's banker was Mr. Stuart Cosgriff of the First Security
Bank in Salt Lake City.

Pat[erson] II: WCW finished *Paterson (Book Two)* in the last week of
May 1947 and sent it to JL on June 14. It was published by New Directions in April 1948. The printer was George W. Van Vechten, Jr., of
Metuchen, New Jersey. Van Vechten deserves much of the credit for
the striking visual layout of *Paterson*.

74. ALS-2   [On stationery imprinted:]
                                   Hotel La Fonda de Taos,
                                   Taos, New Mexico
                                   July 21/47

DEAR JIM:

We were taken out by a man named Berg of the
Blue Door, a gallery here in Taos, to see Brett &
Frieda Lawrence this afternoon. It was one of the
best moments of our two day stay in the place.

Earlier we had gone out to the Pueblo, shopped

for gifts for our grandchildren, visited the Kit Carson house and all that.

This evening we went to a Spanish movie in Ranchos de Taos—not too bad. Ranchos de Taos also produced for us the east transept of the little church with its decorated wood screen in red, black & white in 9 panels—primitive but very beautiful

All in all, what with the prevailing Spanish color and mood of the place, we have been very happy over our two day stand here.

Frieda has never seen my elegy on Lawrence. I've got to dig up a book that contains it for her perhaps you can help me.

Best
BILL

/ · /

Brett & Frieda Lawrence: The English writer D. H. Lawrence (1885–1930) and his wife, Frieda (1879–1956), first came to Taos in 1922. The English painter Dorothy Brett (1883–1977) joined them there in 1924. After Lawrence's death, both Brett and Frieda made Taos their permanent home.

the little church: The Spanish colonial adobe Church of San Francisco in Ranchos de Taos was often painted and photographed by modern artists who visited New Mexico between the two world wars. WCW was impressed by a *retablo,* or painted wooden altarpiece.

my elegy: WCW's "An Elegy for D. H. Lawrence" was first published in *Poetry* 45, no. 6 (March 1935): 311–15.

75. TLS-2   November 28, 1947

DEAR JIM:

It was a pleasure to get your letter. Yes, I'm really afraid the old boy *is* off his wack. But I don't see how they can keep him where he is indefinitely, it costs the state too much money and he isn't that

dangerous to it. And how can they try him as a traitor, he just won't be able to stack up against it? He'll
go off the track in court. Then they'll confine him
again for a while. Finally they'll just release him I
suppose. It'll take a long time though.

I'd be delighted if you'd print the play as an issue
of *Direction* rather than in the next *N[ew] D[irections]*.
But if you do that I'd want it in full again, it's abridged
now you'll remember. I'd want the first scene rein-
cluded for as I see the play now that would become
the second scene—with a very slight change in the
wording of the text. Also I'd want the short attic
scene in the 3rd act. AND I'd like to add a note at
the beginning saying how the complicated sets might
be avoided. You never did see Margo Joneses enthusiastic praise after a first reading, did you? Oh well—
but it's good to omit the play from *N[ew] D[irections]*
and give the space to some of the young boys. One
thing tho' Jim, I don't think you did right in turning
down Fred Miller this time. I wish you could review
your decision and give him space for that piece is
tops to me in many ways—you know the one I mean.
Come on, write him again.

As to the *Spearhead* party, I feel badly about not
having remembered about it. For some asinine reason I thought it was to be held a week after the actual
Tuesday (Election Day) on which it took place. I
had even suggested to several friends that I wanted
them to go with me. I'm glad it went off so well, I
was disgusted with myself for my lapse of memory.

Paterson II has been taken nicely in hand by Van
Vechten during your absence, it is being printed up
now and will, I understand, be bound and finished
without further consultation with you. He and I
together fixed up the galleys and the page-proofs. It
has come out tops. Robert Lowell who was here over
a weekend saw the page proofs, read them over twice

and pronounced them the best long poem ever written by an American not excluding Eliot—which he may have added knowing my feelings about the Eliot (who, by the way, I hear, is coming to the U.S. more or less permanently this year, God help us! we'll have to fight harder now than ever to maintain ourselves untainted) Be that as it may I think you can count on Book II as being more appealing to an audience than Book I ever was. Make your edition large enough! I'll get at Book III after the holidays.

All right, bring it out after Christmas and New Year—but if it's all printed up a month before that I'd sure like to have at least one finished copy in hand so that I may gloat over it, sleep on it and use it as a take-off for the next.

One drawback to using the play in *Direction* is that I had planned, more or less, to launch an assault on you with a view to getting you to use that long-short story of mine of which I spoke to you about a year ago as a *Direction* subject. But that can wait. I am convinced the play should have its chance first.

Remember, the play as you now have it in hand needs careful revision before it comes out under the new plan.

There's much news about all sorts of magazine invitations that come to me for short articles, poems etc etc. Sam Kootz has a book to be out Dec. 15 with reproductions of paintings accompanied by written materials in which I am represented—oh there are a dozen small things. I was asked to review Robert Frost's recently published *A Masque of Mercy* for *Poetry*. Sent it away day before yesterday. I spoke at N[ew] Y[ork] U[niversity] last night, or night before last, with Vivienne [Koch] and Allen Tate at a Round Table Conference, "The Poet and His Audience". Wow! I got loose and, I'm afraid, spoiled the show. Allen withheld in haughty silence. But I had some friends. The question period lasted an hour—it was a hot party—about 300 present.

And so forth. I guess that's all. Except, when I look at some of the stuff that gets printed I have to remember the work of Bob McAlmon who, though you hate him and with some reason, should be brought out again as he is at his best, say in *The Indefinite Huntress* and *Distinguished Air*. Many of the selections in your Modern Classics are nowhere near as good. Try and overcome the bitterness left by your first very decent attempts to work with Bob. He's a son-of-a-bitch in many ways but he is also a sick man psycho-somatically as well as sociologically and his great work of twenty years ago cannot in all fairness be overlooked today. You should give him honor in the only way you can do it, put aside your dislike and publish him.

Sincerely
BILL

/ · /

the old boy: WCW had visited Ezra Pound at St. Elizabeths Hospital on October 18, 1947.

Direction: Formerly published as *Pharos* (see letter 53 above), *Direction* was a series of paperbound books published quarterly by New Directions. WCW's *A Dream of Love* appeared in September 1948 as the sixth in the series.

Margo Joneses: Margo Jones (1913–1955) codirected the first production of Tennessee Williams's *The Glass Menagerie,* in 1945. In 1947, she founded a repertory theater in Dallas, Texas.

Spearhead: Spearhead: 10 Years' Experimental Writing in America: A New Directions Book was edited by JL and published on November 10, 1947. It contained selections from the first nine anthologies of *New Directions in Prose and Poetry* together with some previously unpublished writing. WCW was represented on pp. 525–46 by both old and new work.

Eliot: In October and November of 1948, T. S. Eliot was a visiting fellow at the Institute for Advanced Study, in Princeton, New Jersey. He returned to Europe to receive the Nobel Prize in literature on December 10.

that long-short story: "The Farmers' Daughters"; see letters 67, 68, and 70 above.

Sam Kootz: Women: A Collaboration of Artists and Writers (New York: Samuel M. Kootz Editions, [1948]) pairs WCW's essay "Woman as Operator" with Romare Bearden's painting *Woman with an Oracle* (1947).

A Masque of Mercy: WCW's review of Robert Frost's *A Masque of Mercy* (New York: H. Holt, 1947) appeared in *Poetry* 72, no. 1 (April 1948): 38–41.

Allen Tate: The poet, critic, and biographer Allen Tate (1899–1979) edited the *Sewanee Review* from 1944 to 1946. WCW had seen him recently at the Utah writers' conference.

Huntress: The Indefinite Huntress and Other Stories (Paris: Crosby Continental Editions, 1932) and *Distinguished Air: Grim Fairy Tales* (Paris: Three Mountains Press, 1925).

76. TLS-2   January 18, 1948

DEAR JIM

Sorry about your back, try one with a little more wadding on her next time to keep you out of the gullies. With this snow we're having this year I'm tempted to try the Finnish bath treatment on a few of my own patients with sacro-iliac strain. I'd damn well like to throw at least one of them out the window for the bellyaching she keeps handing me—but she didn't get it skiing, just parturating.

I've been sitting on a pillow myself for the past few days. Mine came from shovelling this fluff we've been bucking for nearly a month now. I got stuck in front of the hospital two weeks ago at 1 A.M. and couldn't even find a shovel in the damned place to fight myself out with. I did finally locate one near the ambulance entrance and nearly ruined myself digging. I feel now that nothing will kill me.

It snowed again last night!

I called up Van Vechten a few days ago. *Paterson* II hasn't yet been printed. He said he was waiting until he had the cloth for the binding before going ahead as he needed the presses for other work. The cloth has now arrived. He promises that the job will positively be finished by the middle of February, sooner if he can make it.

Yes, I'll make up a list of influential names for advance sending out of the book, I'll enclose a small list with this letter. I don't think there's any need of covering the country, ten names would be plenty but if you want more, let me know.

I've been over the ground and made up my 5000 lines for the *Selected Poems*. Let me review it before sending it to you. If you have other lists (I have one I think from Norman Pearson) let me lay them all on the table modifying my own list according to their promptings. I think that's the way to do it: not for me to "correct" the other lists but to use my list as the base and add to it whatever poems force themselves in from the outside. I have consulted Floss and shall continue to do so as I think it important to get her non-literary opinion on what will be read.

No word from Jarrell. In fact I have never heard from Jarrell since he was here a year ago.

Floss has suggested and I think it a good suggestion that you give the 3000 francs to Sylvia Beach with our love and best wishes. Do that, please. Tell her we never forget her nor Adrienne Monnier tho', God knows, we do little enough about it. We once had a superb chicken dinner at Adrienne's apartment the bird having been cooked (behind locked doors) by Adrienne herself in her own style, after her own recipe—whatever she did to it it was delicious. Maybe she pissed on it. At least it worked.

What else, what else, what else?

Bill [Williams] finishes at the New York Hospital July 1. That will be the signal for big doing here if ever we can get the carpenters and plumbers and painters to sell us their priceless services. I'm or we're going to enlarge my office, making a double job of it, after which (theoretically) Papa will be freer (poorer) to go his way to the demnition bowows—or bow wows. Naturally the transition period will be somewhat uncertain but at least Bill has indicated that he'd like to come here and practice with me. That's the big step. He's still unmarried (I don't, begging Flossies pardon, blame him) so that—oh well, there we are. Money, as usual, will be the first hurdle. The kid ought to weather that after a while then we'll see.

One of the English proffs at N[ew] Y[ork] U[niversity,] a man named C. G. Ross, has been showing interest in my plays. He says he thinks something can be done with them and has initiated several moves, separate for each play by which he thinks I can have one or both put on for at least an experimental hearing. And speaking of the play, the last play, do get Creekmore to send me the copy as you have suggested so that I can get it ready for *Direction*. That would be my next job. Let me know more of that: when you'd want the thing finished and all that. I think I can make quite a bit more of it than now shows.

I wrote a piece on the Eliot for a little 4 page sheet printed by a disgruntled and disgusted guy named [Dallam] Simpson from Galveston, Texas. It'll be out any minute now, as soon as I get hold of a copy of his sheet I'll send it to you. What I said about Eliot has nothing to do with his inheritance of the King's old underwear but dates from his advice to us in this country that we may now read Milton without fear of damage to our testicles. Geez what a shit he has turned out to be—to the enhancement of his charm, I must confess and drawing power among the American snots. Not that he isn't a sort of a good poet or a good poet of a sort but from the way they

bend down to kiss the hem of his metaphorical gar-
ments—cerements, I was going to say—you'd think
he possessed the universal genius of a Saint Anthony
or . instead of being a very frail sister indeed.

And Auden has been inducted into the American
holy of holies, The Academy of American Letters—
or Arts and Letters. Holy, Holy. Holy. Lord God
Almighty—even thy shit shall be preserved in silver
chalices for time to dote upon. More power to the
boys—but not for me. I'll bet Oscar [Williams] gets
it before long and he really should get it except that
he's a Jew, poor guy. I'm really beginning to like the
guy. He knows what makes 'em tick. I see even
Laughlin included him in his *Spearhead.*

I'll speak to McAlmon again. I confess I still don't
understand Bob. I've been apprehensive recently that
he may not be feeling so fit. I hope he isn't going
downhill physically.

Floss sends her salutations.

Yrs.
BILL

/ · /

Sylvia Beach: During their trip to Paris in January 1924, WCW and FW
met Sylvia Beach (1887–1962) and Adrienne Monnier (1892–1955),
publishers of Joyce's *Ulysses* and proprietors of the famous bookshop
Shakespeare & Co. Writing to WCW from Switzerland on January 11,
1948, JL conveyed their greetings and explained that the Paris publisher
Pierre Seghers had just paid 3,000 francs (about $10) for the use of
poems by WCW in the magazine *Poésie.*

a piece on the Eliot: WCW's "With Forced Fingers Rude," *Four Pages,*
no. 2 (February 1948): 1–4, responded to T. S. Eliot's lecture on the
English poet John Milton (1608–1674) at New York's Frick Museum
in 1947. "Milton the unrhymer" is evoked in WCW's "Choral: The
Pink Church" (1946). See also letter 84 below.

Auden: The English poet W. H. Auden (1907–1973), a citizen of the
United States since 1946, was not elected to the American Academy of
Arts and Letters until 1954, although he had received its Award of
Merit in 1945. WCW was elected to the academy in 1958.

77. ALS-4   3/14/48

DEAR JIM:

Your secretary called to enquire for the date of the
cremation but Floss had to put her off, too bad. I
hope you get to Germany. For myself if it weren't
for the erections I get in my sleep I'd be on my feet
long ago, but they set me back just when I'm about
to partake (in my dreams) and I find myself awoke
with new anginas. But on or at the hole I'm doing
better, they let me sit up in a chair for half an hour
twice daily. It's a slow process.

The one great thing about all this is that I've been
able to read—I read everything except mysteries—in
fact the tougher & more recondite it is the happier is
my mind. I've just finished a manuscript by my old
pal Zukofsky (you really ought to bring out his novel
Ferdinand) a thesis entitled: *Bottom: on Shakespeare*. I
acknowledge you've got to have good will to get
through it but, hell, all path making is difficult and
I enjoyed & profited by it in many ways. It's good,
scholarly but *not* academic, thank God. I'm now in
the middle of Eric Bentley on Shaw. That too is tough
going but extremely good.

As to the *Selected Poems*. Let me not boil over about
your removal to Suisse! I have my selection made.
The list of the already published poems is enclosed.
The difficulty will be with the as yet unpublished
work, the poems now in the hands of the Cummington boys, poems that either have already
appeared in periodicals or are about to appear there.
I don't know what to do about those.

I suppose the proper thing to do would be to make
my selection, get copies made & send the scripts to
you—but I'm in bed! And although my various girl
friends who can type are willing I can't look them

up indiscriminately. But I'll have to do something, I'll decide in a day or two.

Spring is here! What does the future offer? Well, for one thing I've been made Custodian of Poetry at the Library of Congress for 1949–50 *but don't use the information in any advertising blurb quite yet if you please.* Lowell has been very friendly.

I expect to be up & out pretty soon but, damn it, I still feel that damned "lump" in my chest, under my breast bone. Oh hell, no use cussing at that. They say I'll be all right so let's hope for the best.

Yrs
BILL

/ · /

the cremation: WCW had suffered a heart attack on February 10 or 11, 1948.

Zukofsky: Louis Zukofsky's *Bottom: on Shakespeare* was published in 1963 by the Humanities Research Center of the University of Texas at Austin. *Ferdinand* was published in 1968 by Jonathan Cape of London.

Bentley on Shaw: Eric Bentley, *Bernard Shaw: A Reconsideration* (New York: New Directions, 1947). WCW's poem "For G.B.S., Old" (1948) grew out of this reading.

Custodian of Poetry: Robert Lowell was consultant in poetry at the Library of Congress in 1947–48. He arranged for WCW to succeed him in the following year, but poor health prevented WCW from taking up the appointment.

78. TLS-2   March 25, 1948

DEAR JIM:

You better go bust your neck and have it over with. I called up Van Vechten just now. He told me *Paterson* 2 has been bound, packaged and stored in a warehouse a month ago. What the hell do you mean, Get after him?

He also told me he had 75 or 80 copies of *Paterson* I which he [word missing] been unable to bind in 1946 because of lack of cloth but that now he had got hold of the cloth for II he had been able to finish up the extra copies of I.

He asked me about III. I told him this fall.

As to what we're to do about republishing *Paterson* I & II. To hell with it. When the four parts are finished you can make a book of that or sell it to Harcourt, Brace for a trade edition. Maybe then I'll make some money.

I haven't a single copy of *In the American Grain* left, new or old, except personal copies belonging to me, to Floss or to the kids. Why can't Creekmore get one second hand from Gotham Book Mart or somewhere else and ship it to you? Besides if I remember rightly somebody in Paris is translating the book. Do you remember the woman who did the Champlain chapter. What the hell was her name, she's back in France now, I'm sure someone wrote saying she wanted to do the book. I don't know what happened.

Oh, when you think of it stick some pretty Swiss stamps on your air letters as you did last time. Bill's crazy about them. Give him a variety—and place them well back from the edge of the envelope so they won't be damaged.

I'll fix up those last 30 pages of the *Selected Poems* for you this week and ship them to Creekmore for relaying to you. They'll probably be the best in the book.

I'll follow up the proofs of the guy from Boonton as you suggest. I'm glad he's getting going. Many thanks. The name of the play will remain, *A Dream of Love*—corny as it sounds to me sometimes. But I agree with you it's the only correct name for the thing.

Have started on the 3d volume of *White Mule*. As
I think I told you it's to be called *The Build Up*—it
amuses me no end. Have done about three more
chapters. They aren't bad.

Do you know, Jim, I've had a crazy idea that may
some day pay off for someone. It's "my secret book".
No, I didn't write it. It's a wildly mushy romance
done by some unknown in about 1868 or somewhere around that time called *The Sylvan Year*. It's
a beauty—something I read when I'm low. A truly
secret book that would knock 'em cold if it could
suddenly be put into their insane hands today and
sweet! sweet as sugar. You wait and see for I tell you
I refuse to let it out of my hands. Influence of Poe;
But beautifully written, long swelling periods like
sobs—but completely unknown. A "beautiful"
style—all in a forest in southern France, lost in the
woods—adults lost in the woods!—like sweet children, but—Raoul is the hero. Yummy.

I got the checks. Thanks.

I'm to be Custodian of Poetry at the Library of
Congress in 1949–50. What do yuh know! Bill's
going to—Oh yeah you know that already

Wut else? Nuts to you. I'm feeling better and may
walk to the garage this afternoon—where I'll look at
the desert water bottle you gave me last summer.

Glad you're having fun. Did you get to Germany?
Why don't you jump off an Alp and land there?

Sincerely
BILL

So the Eliot is to be my neighbor next year. Why
don't you marry him to Oscar Williams and raise
pups with long ears and snotty noses? It ought to
make a hit—and be SUCCESSFUL! Such antipodal
juxtapositions—But I'm really glad poor ol' Eliot is

getting some sense. Or is it just cash? And don't think
for a minute I don't appreciate the *Quartets*. They are
about the only poems (as I have come to find out)
that are truly inventive (Pound not writing much)
today. As for Williams, I like him too—as a poet (1
or 2 poems) but that aside. Nix. I like the idea of
[Edouard] Roditi doing a blurb on him, it ought to
be good—good for Roditi.

/ · /

the woman: Dolly Chareau's translation of WCW's "The Founding of
Quebec" was published as "Dialogue sur la fondation de Québec,"
Fontaine (Paris), nos. 27–28 (June –July 1943): 89–95. Chareau did not,
however, translate the whole of *In the American Grain.*

Boonton: WCW's *A Dream of Love* was printed by Dudley Kimball's
Blue Ridge Mountain Press, in Parsippany, New Jersey. Kimball was
also mayor of Boonton, New Jersey.

The Sylvan Year: First published in 1873–74 by Philip Gilbert Hamerton (1834–1894), *The Sylvan Year: Leaves from the Note-Book of Raoul
Dubois* went through at least four editions by 1891. Having lost all of
his family but one son in the Franco-Prussian War, Dubois, the narra-
tor, retires for a year to *le Val Sainte Veronique* in "the heart of the
forests between the vine-lands of Burgundy and the course of the river
Loire" (2d ed., London: Seeley, Jackson, and Halliday, 1876, p. 1).
According to Hamerton's preface, the narrative "is intended . . . to
exhibit the value of external nature as a refreshment to a spirit which,
though it has suffered greatly, has still strength enough to take a hearty
and healthy interest in everything that comes within the circle of its
observation" (p. viii).

79. TLS-1

June 1 [1948]

DEAR JIM:

Thanks for your kindness. *Genet. Cheval d'Espagne.*
⟨Cross-breed Sterile.⟩ I enclose the Fitzgerald letter,
please return it at once. I enclose also the article which
I am sending to *P[artisan] R[eview].* What is your
impression of it?

I weary, Jim, but only in the flesh and not of this world. Never, I believe have I been so moved or more moved than I was yesterday on my way to and from your office by the world I beheld (so different from the one I knew in the same locale 50 years ago) on the train, the ferry, the subway and the street— the playground across the street from your office.

Then to have Genet's sweet novel, sugary with the odor of perversion, on top of that to give the final icing to my cake! And the nice gang you have assembled to do your work—with their gastric ulcers and strange eyes—looking out of the corners of their eyes at me as if I were a curio. It is childlike and wonderful.

But, Jim, I ain't no religioner. What I saw, however, shows me that there's a whole batter of new men and women—and children—making up what used to be called America (at least as far as New York represents it—and I'm sure it does) who have a yeast in them will show us something pretty soon that we don't expect. It's very simple and very much alive and, I must confess, I love it.

Best of luck to you, old man. I hope you can ride with it all when it comes. It makes me think of my grandchildren.

> Your ancient friend
> BILL

Did you like the *Imagi* bit?
A nice letter from Joseph Macleod, enclosed. Please send him *Paterson* II and charge it to my acc't. And *return,* please, his letter. Seems a good guy.
Remember, please, also, that the Fitzgerald letter is confidential. Not that it contains much that is new.

> W.

/ · /

Genet: When WCW wrote this letter, the French playwright, novelist, and poet Jean Genet (1910–1986) had published four novels: *Notre-Dame des Fleurs* (1942), *Miracle de la rose* (1946), *Pompes funèbres* (1947), and *Querelle de Brest* (1947). None of them was a New Directions book, and none contains the phrase *cheval d'Espagne;* it is therefore difficult to know which of the four WCW was reading. In French, *genet* means "jennet," a small Spanish horse. In English, *jennet* can also mean "mule," a sterile crossbreed between a stallion and a she-ass. WCW is probably alluding to Jean Genet's self-proclaimed homosexuality.

the Fitzgerald letter: Probably either F. Scott Fitzgerald (see letter 62 above) or the poet, classicist, and translator Robert Fitzgerald (1910–1985).

the article: No article by WCW appeared in *Partisan Review* for 1948 or 1949, although several poems did.

the Imagi bit: WCW published two poems, "April Is the Saddest Month" and "Song," in *Imagi* 4, no. 2 (Summer–Fall 1948): 1–2. For more information on *Imagi,* see letter 86 below.

Joseph Macleod: In 1948, the poet and former BBC newsreader Joseph Gordon Macleod (1903–1984?), author of *The Ecliptic* (1930), was a free-lance theater director in London and Scotland.

80. TLS-2   July 28 [1948]

DEAR JAIMES:

Just in from Seattle this A.M. and after mailing to Switzerland a letter I had written you en route I rec'd your card from N.Y. a moment ago.

My letter was about the little blue book for which and its dedication I thank you. It's a good book, I showed it around out there, they liked it too.

The conference was a smacking success. I'm glad you're doing *Pat[erson]* I over again as I'm sure there'll be a market for it. They're eating *Pat[erson]* II up out there and want to know how they can get the earlier volume—if that's any indication of the general interest. I read to an audience of about 150 attentive listeners the whole of Book II as one of my "Lectures". They fell fine. I'm getting to be a reader of poetry of note; wait till you hear me some time.

Don't overlook the North West when you're sending out books and notices, they are burned up for new things and right now is the time to strike for I can tell you this: it is a live territory that wants to know and the commercial boys are out there working the field for all its worth. Their advance agents are sneaking in NOW looking for cheap manuscripts and anything else they can snap up before they get wise. Send some advance notices to the Univ[ersity] Book Shop. They're absolutely ripe for it at this moment.

I went out by train since the medicos told me not to fly. I went alone because of the expense and what not, stayed a week and lectured every day. At first I was scared not to have Flossie near to hold my hand but I survived and to tell the truth feel better now than when I left.

Stopped off at Chicago to see the *Poetry* people both going and coming. They sure need snapping up—but I can't see much can be done about that. I talked and talked and talked.

I got an idea re your offer to do me a little book like yours, the gist is to use "The Pink Church"—to which I should have to add a considerable chunk—which I already have more or less in mind. For the Wells College people who are sponsoring the new book of mine which Cummington is just about ready to publish—deleted that, "The Pink Church," from it before okaying the script. Imagine! So we'll give it a whole book if you say so.

That's enough for a hot day. Hope to see you sometime soon. My legs are still cockeyed from riding the cars.

Glad you're home.

Yrs.
BILL

/ · /

little blue book: James Laughlin, *A Small Book of Poems* (Milan: Giovanni Scheiwiller, 1948).

The conference: WCW attended a writers' conference at the University of Washington in Seattle July 19–24, 1948.

Pat[erson] I: Books 1 and 2 of *Paterson* were published together in the New Classics series early in 1949.

a little book: The Pink Church was published as a chapbook by the Golden Goose Press, of Columbus, Ohio, on April 1, 1949. It was dedicated to JL.

the new book: The Clouds, Aigeltinger, Russia, &. was published jointly by the Wells College Press and the Cummington Press in August 1948. Wells is a small, private women's college in Aurora, New York.

81. TLS-2   [August 1, 1948]
                                              Sunday A.M.

DEAR JIM:

Yes, come out Wednesday or Tuesday or Friday if you can, come for supper; any time after 5 or 6 or whenever you please—we shan't make any fuss. I've never been quite clear what you want of me relative to the *Selected Poems,* we'll get that down in black and white.

Things are in a hell of a mess here because of the office being all ripped up but just this morning Bill helped me get my old desk set up on the second floor so that I can begin to get some typing done. Things will go forward from now on. There's plenty to do.

I'll bang *Paterson* III out in the next couple of months, it's already well started and about finished in general plan. Looks all right to me as it stands though, naturally, difficulties will develop as I progress. It'll hold the interest.

Glad to see ol' Ez get a favorable review for his *Cantos* in today's *Times Book Review*—not that he will care too much (or do I kid myself!)—knowing

Ez. At least it shows a fairly tolerant view of his case prevalent in the *Times* office. You deserve tremendous praise for what you have done in bringing out those books, the *Cantos* and the *Pisan Cantos* under present conditions and in Washington the admiration for your accomplishment was outspoken and widespread. Those people are right minded, a fine clear sighted crew. And we must not forget that they represent an area that goes from San Francisco well up into the western part of Canada. They're alert and eager to learn and to do; I think they'll buy books if they can get to them.

At the daily luncheons in Seattle where the regular publishing houses were heavily represented, houses like Doubleday Page, Random House and Little, John & Co. the stress was always upon *selling,* how to get people to buy and all that crap. But the *people,* those that had come to the conference to learn and to seek publishers for their work all said over and over again that there were not enough bookstores, that they'd buy books if they could get them etc etc and that the bookstores didn't have the kind of books they wanted.

I happened to be at one luncheon when someone from the local publishing group was holding forth on the necessity for the publisher being "tough", he wasn't interested in anybody's "soul", all he wanted to do was to publish a list of 4 to 6 entertaining books that *paid.* I happened to have your little blue book in my pocket. I stood up, showed the crowd the book and asked him if he could produce and sell it for 50c. He turned it over in his hand, handed it back and said, "Sure I could probably produce it for a nickel. But would anybody buy it?" Many looked at the book.

Bill

/ · /

favorable review: In 1948, New Directions published *The Pisan Cantos* and *The Cantos of Ezra Pound,* both of which were reviewed by Lloyd Frankenberg in the *New York Times Book Review,* August 1, 1948, p. 14.

82. TLS-2   Sept. 16, 1948

DEAR JIM:

What do *I* know? I'll be 65 tomorrow and what have I ever made out of writing? No more than a few hundred dollars a year (when I make it) with an occasional prize thrown in. That's the sum of it. When I was flat in bed I had a letter from *Poetry* asking me for some autobiographic notes. I took it as a joke and a time killer, I have no interest in an autobiography and never have had but when they asked for something I bought a 15 cent copy book, took up a pencil and diddled away. You know the size and resources of *Poetry,* what could they expect of me?

But when the issue containing the first installment came out I had a telephone call from Covici. He was all off base, thought the writing wonderful, asked me if he could have the book and virtually promised me a Pulitzer prize on it. I replied that I had no interest in books or prizes, that I was doing a very brief thing for *Poetry* that would run to perhaps 50 pages at the most and that that would be all. Besides, I told him, I have commitments, I have to finish *Paterson* Books III and IV together with several other things and that an autobiography didn't interest me anyway.

But he wouldn't quit. If I did finish the thing some time would I let him print it? Sure, why not? I told him. And that's the entire story.

And while we are speaking of this let me add that

not another single person has so much as mentioned that I wrote that piece in *Poetry,* not one. Not a single peep have I received concerning it from anybody. That's what I am up against, not from you not even from some enthusiastic young poet, male or female. I have been asked to give them the next installment when I get ready and there it stands. I've been busy and worried as hell about this and that, I have written a few pencil pages in the copy book and not even copied them out. Instead I've used what time I had on *Paterson* III which is well advanced. The rest of the time I've been plugging at my practice.

But let's get down to brass tacks. All I've promised Covici (by phone, not writing) is what I'm doing for *Poetry,* no more and no less. It might run to 50 or 60 pages taking in my whole life. But his enthusiasm set me going. I have planned a big book if anyone wants it, a full book really telling the whole story. Covici could still do a flash booklet and not have any hold on me for anything else—if I ever find time for either. I am in no way obligated—even tho' it might be to my financial interest to throw him the whole thing (which I am not inclined to do). There you have it.

Now as to your own heavy financial obligations. If you [word or words missing] $75,000 dollars into the publishing game at the moment it can't all be final loss. Some of it is bound to come back. I am pretty sure you're not losing (even if you're not making) anything on the *Paterson* publications. You're not asking my advice on what you publish and never have asked my advice on it—nor would I want you to. But I tell you frankly you've published a lot of unsaleable crap in my opinion. Maybe you have to do that to pick up a good one now and then but you haven't pushed the good ones or backed them hard enough, really driven a few promising items home. Instead you've gone on to some other project. That's where you've thrown your money away—if you have thrown it away. Which I do not believe—even if for the moment you are in the red.

If you drove your items home and followed them more closely, kept them in print and pushed the booksellers harder on the few good items you have you'd be better situated in my humble opinion. Damned if I'll accept blame for my doings.

I have thought I saw and I believe I do see a long range plan on your part but a difficult one to carry through and one involving a considerable investment which will not pay off on short notice. It is that you are digging in where possible on writers with a name to make who will within a span of years bring in the chips for you. It is smart and it is recognized here and there as good business. But you've got to prune the non promising and you've got to drive harder on what is good, You've got to polish your own taste and you've got to work like hell day and night at it. Otherwise the whole venture is just a rich man's foible. You've never worked at it, in my opinion, as hard as the job requires. You've had too many other interests.

I don't know that Harcourt-Brace will want the *Wedge-Clouds* book at this moment. You know that any publisher prints a book of poems only because he hopes to grab off something rich later. I went through it with the Boni Brothers and some others. Duell, Sloan & Pierce have been after me for years to do my mother's biography. I've wanted you to do several things that you refused to do—like the Quevedo thing. Your judgement was that it was no good. But my judgement is that you were wrong. That's a matter of taste but that's the sort of thing that has sent me to others.

If you want the full autobiography it's yours—if you think you want to handle it but the short thing, if he wants that sort of thing, goes to Covici. If you don't give a damn I doubt that I'll ever even write the long story. And don't think for a moment that I don't deeply appreciate what you're doing with the *Collected Poems,* the Koch book and the reprints. But I tell you frankly that if you think you're going to lose money on them I'd appreciate it if you'd chuck 'em in the fire.

Best
BILL

/ · /

the first installment: "Some Notes toward an Autobiography," *Poetry* 72, no. 3 (June 1948): 147–55.

Covici: In 1948, the former publisher Pascal Covici (1888–1964) was an editor for the Viking Press; however, Viking did not publish WCW's *Autobiography* in any form.

the Wedge-Clouds book: In a letter to JL of September 11, 1948, WCW reported, "[S]omeone at Harcourt-Brace approached me last spring with the proposal that they bring out a 'trade edition' of *The Wedge* and the new Cummington book *The Clouds* in one volume." No such book was ever published.

the Boni brothers: Albert and Charles Boni published WCW's *In the American Grain* (1925).

83. TLS-2   Sept. 21, 1948

DEAR JIM:

Probably the so-called autobiography will never even be written or if it is you will publish it. In any case I'm in no hurry: I wish it had never come up. But if I get the chance to write consecutively and hard again at any time we'll decide then what is to be done. Certainly I won't throw it away and I will definitely protect my copyright and your interests in the material.

Many thanks—I was going to say—for the poem. But thanks would not be the word. There's something else, Jim, that isn't to be spoken lightly of and never in any personal context. Our despair in this age is total and that's what we've got to build on. Name, fame even reputation mean just nothing. Even mastery, in a limited way as we may enjoy it, isn't the thing either. To be able to do is only a small and usually self centered part of the satisfaction. Did I say satisfaction? There isn't any that's lasting.

You know I've been thinking a lot recently about the old dreamers, the men who did nothing but loaf— if they could do it. Pure idleness and what the artist does are very closely akin. Perhaps it's my age and my desire to give up all labor—for I have worked hard at times in my life. But that isn't it either. I couldn't loaf if I wanted to. There's another aspect to the damned thing, it's the dream all right but it's to be lost in the dream, to be so taken up by what I term the reality of the dream that appears to me to offer the greatest satisfaction I can imagine.

But, somehow, in my case it doesn't seem to connote irresponsibility. It's more a love dream. You know, in a symposium in the *P[artisan] R[eview]*, an unlikely place to look for anything satisfying, I came across a statement by Lionel Trilling, a man I can usually scarcely bear. But it was a good statement. He said the more our lives are chemically determined by our environment to despair and destruction, the greater the need for the poem. Now that's a profound thought. It's been working in me lately to astonishing effect. It corrected my own determinism and pessimism and taught me that between pessimism and despair there is a tremendous chasm. Despair, yes, but not pessimism and the difference is the dream. *That* they cannot hold by a halter and that, by God, is the real.

I'm going to start a series of 4 lectures at the 92nd St Y[oung] M[en's] H[ebrew] A[ssociation] on October 14th. My first topic will be, "A Few Hints Toward the Enjoyment of the Modern Poem." I don't want you to come—unless you happen to drift in, I just tho't I'd tell you.

If we cannot relax before our fate we aren't men. Let the old balls roll.

Best
BILL

How's this from me old Ma, approaching 92? I was telling her how my little grandson Paul loves to fish (and eat the fish afterward, which I admire). She replied:

> They say when the fish comes!
> (gesture of getting a bite)
> It is a great joy!

/ · /

Lionel Trilling: A critic, novelist, and professor of English at Columbia University, Lionel Trilling (1905–1975) published his study *E. M. Forster* in New Directions's Makers of Modern Literature series in 1943. Nowhere in "The State of American Writing, 1948: A Symposium," *Partisan Review* 15, no. 8 (August 1948): 855–94, does Trilling (or any other contributor) actually make the statement that WCW attributes to him.

84. TLS-2   Sept 22, 1948

DEAR JIM:

Once more ye laurels and once more ye myrtles ever sere I come to pick your berries harsh and rude— Here's this. How about it?

I leave it in your hands with my best wishes to the guy. He sounds very pleasant.

I get a fever when I get stirred, not a real fever but a fever of the face and top of my head. My ovaries I'm sure.

I had a peculiar dream the other night: a twelve year old blond with a shovel nose and heavy as a horse appeared before me lying on my examination table. I know her well, her mother is pushing her up for some reason. So there she lay. I pushed up her dress for an ordinary examination, just routine stuff but thought—better take a look just for luck. So I shoved down her pants and looked. What the hell do you think I saw: a cock about seven inches long, erect but very slender—practically vibrant and beneath it a handsome pair of balls in a lovely scrotum. Geez! I was amazed. I looked quickly at her breasts (in my dream) and said to her: (I felt embarrassed) well, Marjy, I guess you'll have to tell your mother that we've made a mistake. You're a boy!—But the breasts had me stymied.

I dunno, I dunno I dunno. Maybe Seattle did it to me.

BILL

/ · /

Once more: WCW misquotes the opening lines of John Milton's pastoral elegy *Lycidas* (1638).

85. TLS-2   [November 3, 1948?]
                                              Wednesday

DEAR JIM:

Some German speaking friends of mine looked over the translations and found them pretty good.

They thought one word (in the poem "These") was a little off but didn't suggest an improvement.

I didn't answer the guy. Would you do that for me? Tell him to go ahead on an occasional basis, not a blanket permit. I don't see that I have anything much to lose either way—not in MY lifetime.

The proofs of the *Selected* looked very exciting. I had one slight regret, that I didn't include one of the very early pieces, from *The Tempers,* but that can wait until the omnibus edition comes out—even if I'm not here to see it. The book is especially interesting to me in the way the poems seem to gain mature interest, if not stature, as the book progresses.

I'm very much interested in seeing the Koch book in print but I'm no pig and can well wait until other things are out of your way. *Paterson* III is going ahead (I hope not backward) now. I'll finish it shortly. I get moments of despair over it, the usual thing, a feeling that I'm through for life, just a wash-out. Something lower than the lowest. Then again I spark along for a few lines and think I'm a genius. The usual crap. I'll do the best I can.

Poetry has just accepted 25 pages of the autobiography taking me through the first or infantile stage, up to my marriage. They'll publish it in two installments, one next April and one in May.

There will be 3 parts: "The Childish Background." "The Middle Years." "A Fresh Start." It will run about 150 pages. We'll have to talk it over. I don't give a good God damn about Covici, as you know, the only thing is that he got excited and phoned me—Kitty Hoagland got herself mixed up in it too. I said he could have it. On the other hand I have no contract, I'd never go back on my word but he might be induced to drop his interest if I told him I overlooked an earlier promise to you. But whatever comes of it the real biography would be ten times the book this is, this is only a topical hop skip and jump. There you have it. Maybe I won't live that long.

My good friend Wettereau has written you about the play. He's a grand booster and has sold copies of it to five or six Hollywood shits. He seems determined to do more. Wish him luck.

Rexroth is a strange sinner isn't he. Not at all what I thought him, much more erudite, well informed—but he sure has a loose connection somewhere—a fear. He isn't willing to follow his classical hardness but wants to be romantic in a bad sense, I think. His writing and himself are not the same person. But I realize he's a stranger to me still. I can't quite make him out, hard and soft, I can't tell quite where it begins and ends. Now Mr. Eliot, for instance, can you imagine an argument between Mr. Rexroth and Mr. Eliot—I'm afraid it would result in a love match.

BILL

/ · /

the translations: In a letter of October 29, 1948, JL forwarded to WCW "a letter from a bird in Germany, together with some translations which he has made of your poems." The translator remains unidentified.

The Tempers: WCW's second book of poems, published in London by Elkin Mathews in 1913.

Paterson III: Paterson (Book Three) was sent to New Directions in April 1949 and published on December 22 of that year.

two installments: There was only one installment: "Notes toward an Autobiography," *Poetry* 74, no. 2 (May 1949): 94–111.

Kitty Hoagland: WCW's good friend and neighbor Kitty Hoagland typed parts of *Paterson* and the *Autobiography* for him.

Wettereau: Bob Wettereau left the Department of English of the State College of Pennsylvania to become a bookdealer in Los Angeles.

Rexroth: WCW had just seen Kenneth Rexroth on November 2 at a conference held at Bard College, in Annandale-on-Hudson, New York.

86. TLS-2   June 14 [1949]

DEAR JIM:

I feel that I owe this woman something, both as myself and a fellow poet, and naturally I can't ask you to bear the responsibility; but I must continue to ask you to give her a book (a baby) with the added possibility that you will advance her whatever cash you think advisable under whatever pretext in order to help her in what seems her very real distress. I shall myself do what I can for her along the same lines acknowledging at the same time that I cannot do much. I think she comes legitimately under the aegis of New Directions—she's a good writer: even Parker Tyler (while hating her as a woman) had to acknowledge that her writing had literary merit—of a sort, said he green with a sort of envy.

No, I did not see the *Sat[urday] Review of Lit[erature]* but am making every effort to get hold of a copy especially since I rec'd a note from Dorothy Pound speaking bitterly of it. Apparently Ez was deeply hurt. And you know yourself that as between T.S.E. and the S.O.B. who attacked him I consider Eliot practically a St John—the one that Jesus loved. That other bastard is out to murder us all and I have known it a long time, emphasized as by his paper at Kenyon two years ago when he said that the english language had long since been fixed in immovable forms which cannot and should not be altered: a mile of such stuff. Like all fools he slipped in his terminology thinking "english" to be coterminous with the language we speak here. And so all his conclusions were false

But to return to Dorothy Pound—she was bitter over the article. She also voiced Ezra's pleasure with

the young man Cole, the publisher of *Imagi* and asked
me to ask Cole to go see Ez at St. Eliz[abeths Hos-
pital]. That's a lovely gesture both ways. I'm writing Cole to go.

Best luck in everything and please don't forget
Marcia.

Yours
BILL

⟨I called up Van Vechten, who told me he'd try to
get proofs [of *Paterson* 3] to me before July 15—when
I go to visit Chas Abbott at Buffalo for 2 wks.⟩

BILL

/ · /

this woman: Marcia Nardi wrote to WCW from Woodstock, New York,
on March 30, 1949, after finding her letters in *Paterson* 2. WCW and JL
had not secured her permission to use the letters, because they had not
been able to locate her. JL accepted four of her poems for publication
in *New Directions in Prose and Poetry XI* (1949).

Parker Tyler: The poet and critic Parker Tyler (1907–1974) was associate editor of *View* from 1940 to 1947 and film correspondent for the
Kenyon Review from 1947 to 1950.

the Sat[urday] Review: The Pulitzer Prize–winning poet, novelist, and
critic Robert S. Hillyer (1895–1961) published "Treason's Strange Fruit:
The Case of Ezra Pound and the Bollingen Award" and "Poetry's New
Priesthood" in the *Saturday Review of Literature,* June 11 and 18, 1949.
Hillyer was visiting professor of English at Kenyon College from 1948
to 1951. In 1949–50 he was associated with Virginia Kent Cummins's
attacks upon WCW's political loyalties in a magazine called *The Lyric.*

his paper at Kenyon: No paper on poetic form appears to have been
published by Hillyer in 1947 or 1948, but his views are made clear in
"Two Poets on the Teaching of Poetry," *Saturday Review of Literature,*
March 23, 1946, pp. 13–14: "In my own teaching I am careful to separate what for convenience I call dogmas, unbreakable and very few,
from principles, which can be broken but should not be broken merely
through ignorance. . . . My practice is to teach the principles strictly
and to require exercises in detailed conformity with traditional rules.
. . . We studied each form of English verse in chronological order and
wrote examples of each. . . ."

Imagi: A poetry magazine edited by Thomas Cole and published from 1946 to 1956 in Baltimore, Maryland, and Allentown, Pennsylvania. WCW contributed several items to it in 1948–53. Pound liked the issue of spring 1949 (vol. 4, no. 4), which contained WCW's review of the *Pisan Cantos* (pp. 10–11). Cole first visited Pound at St. Elizabeths on June 30, 1949; see Thomas Cole, "Ezra Pound and *Imagi,*" *Paideuma* 16, no. 3 (Winter 1987): 53–66.

87. TLS-2   June 20, 1949

DEAR BILL:

Please forgive my delay in answering you about Marcia Nardi, but I have been simply swamped with work, and haven't had the chance to study properly the little sheaf of poems which she sent in to me a few weeks ago. As you know, I am definitely sympathetic and favorable to her, and I feel sure that we can include some of her poems in the next *New Directions* anthology, and on that basis, I will include with this letter an advance check of $15.00 to her order. This isn't much but possibly it will help her out a little bit.

Now, as to doing a whole book of her poems, I would like to but I don't see how I can possibly finance it. At the present time, the book market is taking a terrible slump along with everything else and we are desperately pressed for cash for day to day needs. There is no question but what, in recent months, New Directions has got a little bit over-extended. We did more books than we ought to have done and now we are paying for it.

You must not reproach me by making the comparison between Roditi's poems and those of Marcia Nardi. The fact of the matter is that Roditi paid for the entire production of his book himself and it didn't

cost me a penny. Naturally, under those circumstances, I was very glad to help him out with the
distribution because he is an old friend whom I like
very much. Possibly things will pick up a little bit
in the fall and then we can consider doing a little
book for Marcia Nardi.

I've asked the *Saturday Review* people for some
extra copies of Hillyer's disgusting attack and will
send them along with this letter if they have come
in by the time I sign it. I'm glad to have this additional data about the swine Hillyer which you give
me in your letter. Personally, he is a pitiful figure as
everyone around Harvard has known. He started out
with all the breaks, getting the biggest professorship
that they have up there at an early age. But he drank
himself out of it and they had to fire him. But of
course, the people who read *The Saturday Review*
don't know his personal history and he can do a lot
of damage.

I was glad to hear that Van Vechten is working
along on *Paterson*. It would be fine if we could bring
it out this fall.

I'm going out to Aspen for the Goethe Festival for
a couple of weeks beginning next week, but when I
get back, I'll call you and possibly we can arrange an
evening together again. It certainly was fun and I
always enjoy seeing you.

With best wishes,
JAS.

/ · /

Roditi's poems: In 1949 New Directions published *Poems, 1928–1948* by
the writer, critic, and translator Edouard Roditi (1910–). Roditi's study
of *Oscar Wilde* had appeared in New Directions's Makers of Modern
Literature series in 1947.

88. TLS-1   [August 29, 1949?]
                                                        Monday

DEAR JIM:

I've managed to pick up a group of poems which
rather surprises me; I didn't, even, know they were
there. And of course they weren't—until I started to
work on them. One of them gave me a terrific battle
(day and night for a day and a half) but she came
through finally and well. All this shows that I will
not write, seriously, unless pushed to it. Your card
set me off. Without the card the poems would have
still lain lost in the matrix. I'll send them to you after
a few more days of polishing. Ten pages.

And I'd like them to appear in the order in which
I have them, including the one that *Poetry, Ireland*
has taken, for it is necessary to the group. Please. I
will not send the long poem, the 20 page one of which
I spoke in my last letter.

The poor Bollingen prize has been killed—by a
woman, a Congresswoman from New Jersey.
Princeton should now give her free access to its
ovarian extract supply and the Pope make her a Dame:
those things run together. But you may be sure my
native state will give ME no prize in the matter—
unless it should come from Rutgers whose School
of Agriculture raises the very best tomatoes, the most
germ resistant, the roundest and tastiest (for market
purposes) to be found this side of Eboli.

Oh weel, Oh weel, oh weel! the thing is to write
well, to write as we think well.

                                              Best
                                              BILL

⟨How about the enclosed letter, cute, huh? Use it on
your blurb for the new *Complete*(?)⟩

/ · /

a group of poems: "Fourteen New Poems" by WCW appeared in *New Directions in Prose and Poetry* XI (1949). The poem entitled "May 1st Tomorrow" was also published in *Poetry Ireland,* no. 7 (October 1949): 20.

the long poem: "Two Pendants (for the ears)"; see letter 90 below.

Bollingen prize: On February 20, 1949, the Bollingen Prize in poetry was awarded by the Library of Congress to Ezra Pound for his *Pisan Cantos* (1948). The fellows in American letters, who made the selection, included Léonie Adams, Conrad Aiken, W. H. Auden, Louise Bogan, Katherine Garrison Chapin, T. S. Eliot, Paul Green, Robert Lowell, Katherine Anne Porter, Karl Shapiro, Theodore Spencer, Allen Tate, Willard Thorp, and Robert Penn Warren. The resulting controversy led the library, acting in accordance with a resolution of a Joint Committee of the United States House of Representatives and Senate, to drop all prizes and awards. The Bollingen Prize was subsequently awarded by the Yale University Library.

a Congresswoman: In 1949, Representative Mary T. Norton (1875–1959), a Democrat of the thirteenth New Jersey Congressional District (Bayonne and part of Jersey City), chaired the House Administration Committee, which oversaw the Library of Congress. The protests of Representative Jacob K. Javits and others against the award of the Bollingen Prize to Pound were therefore addressed to her. A prominent Catholic, Mrs. Norton was unable to bear children after her first-born died in infancy.

Rutgers: Rutgers University in New Brunswick, New Jersey, did in fact award WCW an honorary doctor of letters degree on June 10, 1950.

the enclosed letter: A sweet fan letter dated August 20, 1949, from Dolores Pirec of New York City. WCW no doubt wanted JL to see the following passage: "It's too bad they let your complete poems go out of print. Couldn't you get them republished? The poems you write should be altogether. The little ones with the big ones." In his response to WCW of September 1, JL urged him to begin the work of assembling his "really definitive complete poems."

89. TLS-2   December 9, 1949

DEAR BILL

Please forgive me for having been such a lousy correspondent these past weeks. We have been simply up to our necks in work, as usually happens at this time of year. I'll try to get all the loose ends caught up before Christmas.

I want to enter both *Paterson* and the *Selected Poems* for the Pulitzer Prize, and they ask the date and place of your birth on the blank. I suppose we have this written down somewhere, but possibly you could just fill it in and save me the search for it.

New Directions Eleven has come from the bindery and copies are being mailed over to you soon. I hope you'll like the book. You look very nice on the cover.

Paterson III is also in stock now, and will you let me know whether you want some extra copies besides your six free ones. Then I can send them all over together in one package. ⟨Tell Miss Florio, as I'm in Boston next week.⟩

The little "New Classics" reprint of *Paterson* I and II together has also been bound, and we are printing up the jackets now, and should have books next week.

We have had an awful time with that Koch woman and her proofs. She has held everything up, and we'll be lucky to have her book [*William Carlos Williams*] ready early in January. So I don't know yet exactly when the official publication date for the three volumes will be. However, for purposes of copyright and eligibility for the Pulitzer Prize, I intend to fake up a fake publication date for *Paterson* III on the last day of December. I believe it will be sufficient simply to send a copy to the *New York Times* and tell them it is a publication date and they will announce it as such. Actually, we won't have the books in the stores until a little bit later.

It's a shame that we had to get the dates balled up like this but that woman kept fooling around with her proofs.

Well, that's all for now, and I hope we can get together again soon.

As ever,
JIM

90. TLS-1   February 3, 1950

DEAR JIM:

Now look what they've done to me. It looks as though I'll have to make a run for it pretty soon or end up in the stuffed shirt brigade.

In other words I'll have to produce three or four books in the next year or two, maybe five or six. Do you want to take them on?

It ought to begin right now with a volume of short stories. The demand is there, the works are there. All I need is a publisher. If you want it, say the word or if you're not ready give me the green flag to look elsewhere; it would take in *The Knife of the Times, Life Along the Passaic River* and about 12 other stories. I think that should be first.

Next, strange to say, comes the *Autobiography*. I'm being pressed for it and it's something I can turn out with a minimum of effort. It doesn't need to be a big book as I conceive it, just a hop-skip-and jump over my life from beginning to end—after which I intend to take my time to a follow up from 5 other angles looking at the same material. But that's not for now.

Next (simultaneously) comes *Paterson* IV, already on the way which is obviously yours.

Cummington is doing a small book now, called *Two Pendants, for the ears*. It should have appeared long since in *Botteghe Oscure* but the Princess seems to have been held up for some reason.

Fifth should come the half century *Complete Collected Poems*—of which you have spoken or I should not now mention it; a big job.

Then comes the big decision. I'll have to quit medicine pretty soon and really get to work. It may come next year. At that time I'll finish the *White Mule* sequence (at least the next book, *The Build Up*) and go on to . I'm not sure. I think it will be a Modern Prosody, badly needed today and of which I have much to say. The collected prose fits in and of course NEW WORK! the most important of all.

How about it? Are you really willing to go along, starting on the short stories right now or what? And what happened to McDowell, he seemed like a valuable piece of property? Sorry you let him go.

Best
BILL

/ · /

what they've done: In January 1950, WCW was elected a member of the National Institute of Arts and Letters and given the first National Book Award for poetry.

Two Pendants: WCW's "Two Pendants (for the ears)" was published not by the Cummington Press but by *Botteghe Oscure,* 4 (1949): 340–55. *Botteghe Oscure* was edited by the princess Marguerite Caetani and published in Rome.

The Build Up: The third novel in the *White Mule* or Stecher sequence was published by Random House in October 1952.

McDowell: At Kenyon College, David Ulrey McDowell (1918–1985) worked on the staff of a literary magazine called *Hika,* to which WCW contributed several items in 1939–41. McDowell was secretary of the *Kenyon Review* in 1940–41 and an editor of *transition* in Paris just after the war. From 1948 to 1950, he worked as sales and promotion manager for New Directions before moving to Random House. WCW was impressed by his efforts to publicize *Paterson* 3 and Paul Bowles's *The Sheltering Sky* (see letter 91 below).

91. TLS-2   February 7, 1950

DEAR BILL,

Thanks for yours of February 3rd. It does my old heart good to see you young fellows kicking up your spry heels with such an eruption of energy. I only wish I had half your vitamins. More power to you, I hope you get all those books written before Christmas so that you can start on a new batch before the 4th of July. But seriously, it is fine that you are planning to give up the medical work altogether and concentrate on the literature.

I'm sure you know that I would like to go along with you on the publishing of the books. My feelings would be very much hurt if you went anywhere else. My thoughts have been running toward a uniform edition of your works. How does that strike you? The *Complete Poems* would be in two volumes, of which we could get out the first one fairly soon, and there could be a volume of short stories to match it, and then later on other volumes of assorted prose in the same format. I think the books could be designed in such a way that material that you write in the next years could be added to subsequent bindings.

Why don't we start fairly soon on the volume of short stories and first volume of the really complete poems? If we began getting busy about them now they would be ready to come out by next fall or winter. But I hope you will really make the effort now to make these volumes definitive. Have you got all your stuff collected so that you can run through it and see what you want to preserve in these definitive volumes?

I haven't seen any reviews of Vivienne [Koch]'s book yet, but there ought to be some soon. Also some pieces on the *Paterson,* though poetry is always slow in being reviewed.

Yes, we are all very sorry here to lose Dave McDowell, but he received a very flattering offer from Random House, and I didn't think it was fair to try to hold him back from a bigger opportunity. After all, the kind of books that we publish here are never going to make much money for a young man who has a family and needs it. Now and then we have a bit of luck, like this Bowles book, or some of the Merton, but by and large the kind of things that I like to do are pretty thin pickings from the profit angle. Let's hope that your autobiographical book will prove to be one of the exceptions. I'm very keen to see that.

I'm off to the West for a bit of skiing, but don't let that dampen your ardor. We can carry on by mail. My address out there will be c/o The Hotel Jerome in Aspen, Colorado.

As ever,
JIM

/ · /

Complete Poems: New Directions published *The Collected Later Poems of William Carlos Williams* on November 30, 1950, and *The Collected Earlier Poems of William Carlos Williams* on December 17, 1951.

this Bowles book: In 1949 New Directions published both *The Sheltering Sky,* by the novelist, translator, and composer Paul Bowles (1910–), and *Seeds of Contemplation,* by the poet and religious writer Thomas Merton (1915–1969). The former sold 25,000 copies; the latter, 70,000. Earlier, New Directions had published three books of Merton's poetry: *Thirty Poems* (1944), *A Man in the Divided Sea* (1946), and *Figures for an Apocalypse* (1947).

92. TLS-1   February 9, 1950

DEAR JIM;

I'm glad to have you speak well of David McDowell, I liked him a lot and was particularly moved by his enthusiasm for pushing my work. That's what I need. I think I'll have a talk with him now that he's with Random House for I tell you frankly I'm not satisfied to let things run on the way they've been going.

It isn't that I've not been satisfied with our arrangements in the past. I won't go into details as well known to you as to myself. It's the future I have to think of. Let's draw a line across the page and begin again.

You once said your primary interest has been the poem and of my work what poems I should write—though you remember you didn't find yourself in a position to do *The Wedge* when I needed it brought out. So, if you'll agree, I'd like to limit ourselves to this: That you bring out, now, the *Collected Poems* as you have planned them and *Paterson* IV just as soon as I can complete it, everything else to be crossed off the list.

By this I shall gain a free hand to try myself out, to see just how far I can go with sales. For I tell you and you yourself confess it in the first paragraph of your letter, I'll never make any real cash through you. Nor have I wanted it until now when either I must go on with Medicine or somehow or other get me more income by writing, one or the other.

So there we stand, I don't see why we can't go along from here out much as we did in the past; you in some ways will be relieved and I shall at least give myself the satisfaction of trying out my own ideas.

What do you say? But I'm going to do it anyhow so what the hell?

By the way, I'm showing this to Floss and she agrees with me that it's now or never. So wish me luck and let's get to work on the new *Collected*.

> Have a good time.
> BILL

---

93. TL-2   February 12 [1950]

DEAR BILL—

Yours to the 9th to hand, and what a magnificent kick in the teeth that is—administered, I may say, with a touch that is definitely deft, and almost that, one might think, of a practiced hand at this sort of thing; which, of course, you aren't—the furthest thing from it—but how easily we drift into it when the devil has planted the seed.

Yes, a lovely reward for a decade of work and faith and sacrifice. More power to you. I love the human race. The more they try to kick me around the better I love them. Sure thing.

Frankly, Bill, I would never have dreamt that you, of all people, would fall this low. I suppose I have always carried you around on my special idealistic pedestal. You have always seemed to me the whitest of the white the real human being—complete with sense and feeling.

Well, I am hurt. I am terribly hurt, I won't conceal it, and from the quarter I most trusted. A hundred times when other publishers have told me what faithless bastards writers are I have held you up as an example of loyalty. I feel exactly like Gretchen's brother in *Faust*. Look up the passage and read it for me.

But go your way—with my blessing. You are a loveable cuss, and I'll be sore for a few weeks, but it will pass. What you are doing is only human, and I've done plenty of things myself on a par with it. I can't complain.

Still in all, it's incredible, unbelievable. Have you no insight? Are you totally blind about your work and its nature? Do you really think that you can sell yourself to the masses, no matter how hard you try to write what they want?

All right . . . go to the big boys. They were swell to you about publishing *White Mule,* weren't they? They did a beautiful job on the *Collected Poems* didn't they? They fell over themselves didn't they to get a critic to write a book about you? They overwhelmed you, didn't they, with offers to keep the *Am[erican] Grain* in print? Go to them. Rush. Run. Don't lose a second. Let them slobber their dirt all over your decency and your purity. And offer up to them as a little bribe *my* pride, and my life's devotion to an ideal. See how dirty they can make that too.

Ten years of patient work and expenditure. Just exactly two of your books have paid their way. But I don't begrudge the money. I had always felt that in the end I would get it back, that the time lag would turn and there would be a public, but I don't care about the money lost. I'm lucky that way. But you might think about this. I've never taken a cent out of the business and never intend to. But I have only so much a year to put into it, and when we do make a success of something it means there is money to take on a promising youngster. Thanks to Merton and Tennessee and Bowles I'm able to lend a hand to kids like Hawkes—to get out the *New Directions* annuals, which lose about three thousand a crack, and to translate French poets.

OK, go your way, make a nice chunk of money, if you can, for Bennett Cerf so that he can have lunch every day in 21 and get a few more good jokes for his column!

Oh Bill, when you do a thing like this to me I feel like quitting. If you of all people don't understand what New Directions is about and don't want to back me up, then what is the use of my going on with it? I might just as well quit and enjoy life. Do you think I like working every damn night, weekends included, till midnight?

But, get along with you, and as the old boy said to his pal with the beard, do what thou hast to do and do it quickly.

But let me throw in one stipulation, if I may. Make it a part of your contract that they *have* to consult with me on format and establish one which will do for that big definitive edition. We can make the *Complete Poems* to match them, or they can match us, but there must be the same page size, type layout and binding. Then when they have had their fun with you—and have you ever known them to keep a good man in print (Is there a collected edition of William Faulkner at Random House . . . is there a collected edition of Scott Fitzgerald at Scribners?)—I can buy the plates from them and put through my plan for a uniform edition of the works. You can treat me like the shit under your feet if you want to, but you won't get me to turn against you as a writer. I have given my word to the world that you are a good writer, while *their* good writers are bad writers, and I am sticking by that and fighting it through. You can make it easier for me by insisting on this question of format, so that I won't have to reset the books when they are through with them.

Well Bill, I'm sorry to have talked to you this way. It's not respectful, it's not friendly. But you have hurt me deeply and terribly, and the only way to get it out of my system is to talk right out, cauterize it, and then forget it.

You say you need money. Let me remind you that I offered to put you on a monthly check basis, as I do with [Henry] Miller, and you turned it down. I suppose you had your reasons.

/ · /

Gretchen's brother: In lines 3,620–45 of Goethe's *Faust,* Part One, Gretchen's brother, Valentin, recalls that she was always exempted when his fellow soldiers toasted their favorite girls. Now that she has been seduced, however, she is no longer the ornament of all her sex ("die Zier vom ganzen Geschlecht"). Valentin could tear his hair and climb the walls at the thought that every knave may now taunt him ("Soll jeder Schurke mich beschimpfen").

Hawkes: In 1949, New Directions published *The Cannibal,* the first novel by the American writer John Hawkes (1925–). Most of his subsequent novels have also appeared under the New Directions imprint.

Bennett Cerf: With his partner Donald Klopfer, the flamboyant publisher Bennett Cerf (1898–1971) founded Random House in 1925. He also published a regular literary column in the *Saturday Review of Literature.*

the old boy: In the King James version of the New Testament Gospel of John, 13:26–27, Jesus identifies Judas Iscariot as his future betrayer and says to him, "That thou doest, do quickly."

William Faulkner: Random House began to publish the fiction of William Faulkner (1897–1962) in 1929, and gradually became Faulkner's principal American publisher. Charles Scribner's Sons began to publish the fiction of F. Scott Fitzgerald (1896–1940) in 1920. During the 1940s, both of these large houses leased to New Directions the right to republish classic novels that were out of print: Fitzgerald's *The Great Gatsby* (1925) and Faulkner's *Light in August* (1932). New Directions brought out the former in 1945 and the latter in 1947. For the publication by New Directions of Fitzgerald's *The Crack-Up* (1945), see letter 62 above.

94. **TLS-1**   February 17, 1950

DEAR JIM:

That clears the situation quite a bit; I just don't think you're much interested in sales.

I'll go on working as usual during what spare time I can find for it. When I have scripts ready I'll submit them to you beginning with the final *Collected Poems,* followed by the short stories. I'm particularly anxious to get the short stories in print again, all of them. At that time we'll have it out.

Don't worry, if I go anywhere it won't be to Bennett Cerf whom I detest as much as you do. I had no idea when I last wrote that he was at the head of Random House.

I envy you the sight of those slalom races, it must be really something.

Best
BILL

On my way back from Goucher College where I talked yesterday I had a hell of a good idea for the *Collected,* something I've been searching for for quite a while. It's new and shd work out to good advantage. You'll see.

95. **TLS-1**   March 9, 1950

DEAR JIM:

I've made up my mind and having done so I write to you at once that you may know how we stand. I want you to do my poems as you have done in the past but my prose will go to someone else, probably

Random House, under McDowell's editorship. This may prove somewhat of a wrench to both of us but there's no escaping it.

This chance has got to be taken if I'm to go on as a writer. For I can't make any money with you and I've got to try to earn at least a partial living by writing.

With this settled in my own mind I'm getting the new, two volume *Collected* in order for Kaplan; it'll take me a few weeks to do it. The short stories, before I give them to McDowell, I shall hold for two weeks or until I can hear from you.

I hope this will satisfy you and that you will give the deal your blessing but it is final.

Yours as ever
BILL

/ · /

Kaplan: Maurice Serle Kaplan (d. 1951) designed both *Collected Earlier Poems* and *Collected Later Poems* for New Directions.

96. TLS-1   April 30, 1950

DEAR JIM:

I'm holding your very generous check for the time being or until we can nail down a few of the conditions which I think should be mutually agreed upon before we set up the new understanding.

In the first place I want whatever books you publish of mine henceforth to be copyrighted in my name. This is common practice and in fact a practice which you yourself have followed in most cases.

Next and really before anything else I think what you have said in your letter should be formally incorporated into a contract which we should both sign.

Finally I wish you'd give me some assurance that my books will have better distribution than has been the case heretofore. As you yourself grow older and more experienced I presume things of this nature will change for the better. At least I hope so. Too often I have felt unsupported in my efforts to get my books into the hands of those who manifestly want to buy them. Or you're in Europe or somewhere else just at the moment when I need assistance.

I shall not cash the check until I know where I stand on these matters. I can hand you the short stories any day. The *Collected* should follow them in a matter of two weeks.

This looks like the business.

> Yours as ever
> BILL

97. TLS-1   May 4, 1950

DEAR JIM:

While waiting for you to reply on the matter of the contract the question has become paramount in my mind whether it wouldn't be more to my advantage to follow the other proposal in spite of certain advantages on your side. That way, with a flat down-payment for certain books delivered, I'd feel myself to be a more independent agent, which is very important to me. Everything would be besides in my own name, which I absolutely require, I'd get a far greater distribution of my books, with larger editions and, in the end, the chance for a greater ultimate return. That of course is a gamble but it's an attractive one.

But with your scheme I'd be tied hand and foot on a practical salary beyond which I could probably expect nothing. I don't like it. All incentive to put on a drive would be gone. And when you take into consideration the improved business relationships I should expect to enjoy with a more established firm I find myself forced to consider that also.

It's all very well for you to treat me as a long term investment but that has no interest for me. For myself I'm a short term investment and during that term I've got to be satisfied. That's why I'm making my fight now. I've got to have it my way. So you'll find your check enclosed. Think it over.

The two items not so far affected by this letter are the *Collected Poems* and *Paterson* IV.

Sincerely
BILL

98. TLS-1   May 6, 1950

DEAR JIM:

I might as well tell you that I have signed a contract with Random House for three prose books. Dave McDowell will now take up with you the question of whether or not we shall be able to start off at once with the short stories. This will require your cooperation on whatever reasonable terms you suggest.

The next thing will be to get the matter of the *Collected Poems* on a solid basis—and by the way you haven't sent me the two copies of the *Selected* you promised me last week. The contract should come first in this case also. As with everything else it must be in my name. Then I want to know how many copies will be in the first edition and what the terms will be about keeping it in print. In fact it should be a regular contract with all details specified.

Paterson IV is well on the way as I have told you and waits to be finished only on what arrangements we can make generally with reference to all the books. As I've said before there's no reason that I can see why we shouldn't go into rapid production all along the line as soon as you and I can come to an understanding. There are rubs here and there of course, on both sides, but that won't prevent an amicable settlement and good feeling once we get certain details settled. I wait to hear from you.

Sincerely
BILL

/ · /

three prose books: WCW was offered $5,000 by Random House for *Make Light of It: Collected Stories* (1950), *The Autobiography of William Carlos Williams* (1951), and *The Build-Up* (1952).

99. TLS-2   May 8, 1950

DEAR BILL,

Many thanks for your good letter of April 30th which reached me in Washington, where I have been paying daily visits to Ezra out at the hospital. The old boy is certainly alive and kicking. He started giving me Chinese lessons this morning, but it didn't mean a thing.

I am very glad to hear that we are getting closer to a program which will be satisfactory for all concerned. I shall try to give you in this letter a few of the ideas which are in my mind for a long term, overall agreement, and possibly you can mull them over and then let me have your comments and additional suggestions.

First of all, there is no objection to having the copyright in your name. I would like, however, from now on to get my half share of the anthology fees, which you will find to be a general practice in all publishing houses.

As I visualize it, we would send you a check the first of each month for $250 for the next three years. These would be advances against royalties on all your books, and against our half share of all the permission fees. As new books come along we would make contracts for them at prevailing royalty rates. That is, 10% of the retail price up to 5,000, 12% to 10,000, and then 15%. We would also like our usual half cut on the foreign translation rights.

You, for your part, would give us first crack at all the books which you write from now on. If it should come along that you would wish to do one of these little specialty volumes with one of the small presses, you would offer it to us first, and then, if we didn't want to do it, you would let them have it, though with the understanding that the basic rights would rest with you so that the material would available for your collected edition.

I feel quite certain, however, from what you have told me of your plans that we will want to do all of those new books which you project, as soon as you have them ready. We would also want to do the collected poems and the collected stories, probably beginning with the poems, because that is the natural follow up to the book award, which was for poetry.

I don't believe that you need to worry about our distribution. It is getting better all the time, and I suggest that you come into the office some day and look over the records of our outlets. This is the way you ought to judge the matter, and not on the basis of yaps which come in from people who live in towns where there are no bookstores, or who are looking for a book that is out of print, or a first edition. When you see the number of outlets which we have all over the country, and for that matter all over the world, and the volume of business which we are doing with them, I believe you will be convinced that we can sell your books if anybody can. And I think that we can.

Let me know how these ideas for the long term contract strike you, and feel free to make any suggestions that you want. I want you to have the peace of mind and feeling of security necessary for you to do your best work.

See you soon,
JAMES LAUGHLIN

100. TLS-2   [August 20, 1950?]
                                            Sunday

DEAR JIM:

I've looked but I can't find anything outside the *Collected Later Poems* worth picking up for you for N[ew] D[irections] this year. All my energy has gone into trying to straighten out my literary affairs with you know what results.

I had a good workout at Yaddo where I about finished *Paterson* IV, which I believe is up to the level of the other 3 books, and put in a few good licks later at Chas. Abbotts' on something else but haven't been in the mood for many shorter poems.

There's much I could say perhaps upon our rela-

tionships during the past six months but since I have
put my affairs in Murray's hands they must remain
there without interference from me until he is
through.

One thing I will add. I have just written Murray
giving him my final views relative to the *Collected
Later Poems* which ought to be brought out separate
from the *Complete Collected* and at once. Will you
not please do your best to bring yourself to an agreement with this viewpoint and to close our deal on
that basis this week?

As ever
BILL

P.S. There's 40 to 60 pages of a novel Fred Miller
and I started to write together ten years ago that you
could have if you want to take on anything as big as
that. I reread it yesterday while browsing around and
found it still exciting and experimental in a good way
in technique. It belongs, in its unfinished state, to
N[ew] D[irections]. But you asked for poems not
prose. Ready to mail if you want it. I'd have to speak
to Fred first of course but I could do that by phone.

I was happy to see Pep West's book which I am
rereading and hope to write a note about for Barbara
Asch if it will not be too late.

W

/ · /

Yaddo: From July 15 to August 2, 1950, WCW visited Yaddo, the writers' colony near Saratoga Springs, New York, endowed by Mrs. Kate
Nichols Trask (1853–1922), a poet and widow of the banking and rail-
road magnate Spencer Trask. There, in the summer months, selected
writers were offered room, board, and quiet time in which to work.

Murray: From 1950 to 1960, WCW entrusted his literary business affairs
to James F. Murray, a New York lawyer who specialized in contracts
between artists and publishers.

a novel: In 1945–46, WCW and Fred Miller tried to write a collaborative novel influenced by the techniques of black American improvisational jazz. Tentatively entitled *Man Orchid,* it was never completed and never published. WCW's sole contribution to *New Directions in Prose and Poetry 12* (1950) was "The Self," a poem.

Pep West's book: In 1950, New Directions republished *The Day of the Locust* (1939), by the American novelist Nathanael West (1903–1940). WCW reviewed it for *Tomorrow* 10, no. 3 (November 1950): 58–59. WCW had known West in New York in 1931–32, when they edited the new series of *Contact* magazine together. Barbara Asch worked on promotion and publicity for New Directions.

101. TLS-1   October 4, 1950

DEAR JIM:

The date of my leaving for Seattle is rushing on me like an express train. They want me to speak on the campus at Los Angles U[niversity] when I am there etc etc Plan to visit Bob McAlmon in El Paso. Sorry you two can't get along. There's still a book to be had from Bob and a good one. Such is life.

Yes, I have written permission to use the letter in *P[aterson]* IV. I'll transmit it to Murray. I'll get permission in writing to use the material from the National Credit guy, he'll probably be tickled to death to have me take it over. The piece about the nurse doesn't name her. I cut the paragraph out of the *Journal of the Am[erican] Med[ical] Ass[ociatio]n.* But there's no harm in changing the initials. Do it. I guess that covers the 3 items mentioned.

Yes, change the Villon to the old spelling. It would enhance the text. I meant to do it myself but forgot.

Mostly though I'm glad you're pleased with Part 2. I was a little worried thinking it might be too specialized for general comprehension, not that people generally aren't sensitized to anything that touches money but they might just shy off. Curie should catch them however and make them read, she's a popular figure. It's brief, too and fits into the flow of the whole book. I count a lot on having the 4 books between covers so that the reader progresses from the beginning to the end. In that way many things not now acceptable will gather meaning from being in the sequence of the book itself. It'll go, I'm sure when read all together.

The last part, Part 3 of the last book is all blocked out but I'd like to keep it over Christmas if I can to smooth it out.

Best
BILL

/ · /

The date: WCW and FW left for Seattle on October 19, 1950.

the letter: Paterson 4, Part 2, was finished in late September 1950. It contains a letter sent to WCW by the Paterson poet Allen Ginsberg (1926–) on March 30, 1950.

the National Credit guy: August Walters of Newark, New Jersey, published a Social Credit editorial in the journal *Money* 15, no. 4 (June 1950): [1]. WCW includes an edited version of the document in *Paterson* 4, Part 2.

the paragraph: The paragraph headed "Report of Cases" in *Paterson* 4, Part 2, comes from Joseph Felsen, Alfred J. Weil, and William Wolarsky, "Inapparent Salmonella Infections in Hospitals," *Journal of the American Medical Association* 143, no. 13 (July 29, 1950): 1135–38.

the Villon: Describing Madame Curie in *Paterson* 4, Part 2, as a "pauvre étudiant," WCW applies to her the opening line of François Villon's *Le Testament* (1456): "en l'an trentieme de mon age." Though he accepted it here, WCW later (October 13, 1950) vetoed the change from modern to medieval French spelling proposed by JL.

Curie: The discovery of radium in 1898 by Madame Marie Curie (1867–1934) and her husband, Pierre, was the subject of a popular motion picture starring Greer Garson and Walter Pidgeon, which WCW saw in 1944.

102. ALS-6.

[On stationery imprinted:]
Hotel Edmond Meany,
University District, Seattle 4
Oct. 28/50

DEAR JIM:

By all means let Harvey Breit go ahead with the 500 word brief of the longer article on Dahlberg. We can then look around for a berth for the full spread somewhere else. Hope it does some good, its a unique & valuable book even tho' overpacked with wild metaphor.

I knew about the *Harper's Bazaar* bid to print something from the *Paterson* IV Part 3 script—but the business came up at the last minute before our leaving. All I could do was to dump it into Murray's hands with a carte blanche leave to go ahead as he saw fit. I haven't the least idea what the outcome will be. I told him, though, at the same time to turn the piece over to you as soon as you wanted it.

We've had a better time here than I expected. I was nervous, naturally, and tired at the beginning and not at all confident of my ability to carry on a week's program of lectures and conferences. To make it worse they sprang one on me that nearly knocked me off my feet: a public lecture Wednesday evening on the novel—of all things.

What was I to do? I decided to bluff it, open my big mouth and listen for what might come out of it. Floss said it went great, God knows what I said! There was a public lecture Monday on "The Creative Process"—talks every day on the short story, my main theme and a two hour session with Ted Roethke on my poems. I read parts of *Paterson,* the "Beautiful Thing" original from the *Selected* and then talked for an hour.

I've been reading scripts of novels (4!) poems and short stories, picked up a couple of good stories and one guy, 21 yrs on his way, who is a good poet—I told him when he was ready send about 10 pages to you for a look see—Can't remember his name.

The older gals have been looking after Floss, taking her out & being attentive generally. On a fine day (we had *one!*) this is a beautiful place & Floss has been impressed, the big Scandinavian population has much impressed her.

So next week the same thing at Reed College & after that U[niversity] of Oregon at Eugene. Then San Franciso for 2 days, Los Angeles (where I read once at U[niversity] of California) for 6 days, El Paso—to visit Bob McAlmon for 2 days—New Orleans & home.

Weel, there is, if I survive there's still a heavy winter ahead—or have I told you all this before.

> Best
> Bɪʟʟ

⟨c/o Eng[lish] Dept. Reed College, Portland, Ore-[gon]⟩

/ · /

Harvey Breit: Before departing for Seattle, WCW sent JL several pages of typed notes on *The Flea of Sodom,* a prose work by Edward Dahlberg (1900–1977) published by New Directions in 1950. The notes were never separately published, but they were distilled by the writer and journalist Harvey Breit (1909–1968). He had known WCW since at least 1940 and had interviewed him in January 1950 for the *New York Times Book Review,* of which Breit was assistant editor.

Harper's Bazaar: None of *Paterson* 4 appeared in this magazine.

the short story: WCW delivered the prepared text of his remarks on the short story to the Alicat Bookshop Press, of Yonkers, New York, in August 1950. The talk was published in December under the title *A Beginning on the Short Story.*

Ted Roethke: WCW first met the poet Theodore Roethke (1908–1963) at Pennsylvania State University on May 12, 1940. In 1947, Roethke moved to the University of Washington at Seattle, where he helped to arrange WCW's visits of 1947 and 1950.

103. ALS-4   Nov 9, 1950

DEAR JIM:

This is my last day at U[niversity] of Oregon; one more classroom hour to go and the trip, the work-trip, will be over. I shan't be sorry tho', as I have said, I wouldn't trade the experience for a carload of apples—and the apples up here are the finest in the world. But three weeks of speechmaking have had me, literally, in a fever practically continuously.

All my principal talks have been recorded but by whom or what authority I can't say. I know that those at U[niversity] of Washington were done by an amateur for I asked him about it. At Reed College I think it was someone connected with the school and here again it was some official agent: only the one big event, in the auditorium was recorded here (by a man who got his training at Fairleigh Dickinson College in *Rutherford* !!)

What to do?

I'd like you to have the records or transcriptions of these talks for whatever use you care to put them to—they may, of course, be lousy but thats as it may turn out. However I think I'd better work through Murray. I'm writing to him today, as my agent, giving him the names of the heads of the English Depts in each case & telling him to go ahead.

This is a world entirely separate from the rest of the U.S. We, in the East face Europe, the old world, but they face the new world to the west, the Orient & all that that implies. I think if you took the young of these parts, the young girls especially & they're beauties! to our east they'd die of suffocation just as the trees native here would die in our comparatively rainless forests. In some ways the young seem apathetic to me. They don't come alive emotionally & intellectually as our kids do but maybe it's just the inevitable time lag due to the slowness of the cultural drift.

One thing sure though, there's a freshness about the young writers that has not yet been corrupted by the dry rot of our pseudo sophistication. Oh well, there's a cream of younger writers that is doing some good novels & short stories. When the next *N[ew] D[irections]* anthology is beginning to be made let me know, I've got some good leads. Shd be home before Thanksgiving

Best
BILL

104. TLS-1   Tuesday, Nove 28 [1950]

DEAR JIM:

Herewith the proofs of *Pat[erson]* IV. Aside from minor errors and corrections they are astonishingly successful in presenting the text. What speed! The man's a wonder.

I returned home to find a large tree across the roof of the office with Bill and Paul both mounted upon it armed with axe and saw. They at least eased the weight off the house without injuring themselves. No great damage, no apparent leaks. Floss and I were on a plane coming up from New Orleans to Newark when the storm broke. The flight was terminated at Washington where we spent the night etc etc.

The trip was a success from a business-professional viewpoint and we enjoyed ourselves besides.

McAlmon at El Paso was very kind, took us nightly to Juarez. Charlotte, Flossie's sister and her son at Hollywood and John Husband and his wife at New Orleans were also superb hosts. We slept and ate to the queen's taste. Escaped storms and floods for the most part.

But there are mountains of letters to dismay me and this week and the next promise to lay me flat on my back if I do not watch my step. But Paul's house had its electric and phone connections restored and Bill, his wife and baby shd get into their apartment by the week end. They've all been here, more or less. Children! The baby is getting to be a really beautiful little thing.

But witnessing what one small storm can do to a community in these parts I am awonder over the thought of what a single small atom bomb might not accomplish. Disruption of every service, now become more and more centralized, would starve us out in 3 days—and no peasant resources of temper or goods could save us.

Take care of yourself and buy some pigs. We'll have to talk about publication dates when you're ready. It's up to you. If you want to (and can) get *P[a]t[erson]* IV out this year it might make a hit. But, as I say, it's entirely up to you: possibly on December 31? The revised and corrected and enlarged *Earlier Collected Poems* is ready for you for next year—you'll be surprised how much it is an improvement on the 1938 edition—in content, that is and arrangement. It couldn't improve on that in format. I notice the way you have matched the jackets on that and the present volume.

More later,

Best
BILL

/ · /

Pat[erson] IV: WCW's *Paterson (Book Four)* was designed and set by
George W. Van Vechten, Jr., and published by New Directions on
June 11, 1951.

McAlmon at El Paso: Since 1940, Robert McAlmon had been living in
El Paso, Texas, where his brothers owned a surgical-supply business.
He met WCW in Taos, New Mexico, in the summer of 1947, and their
reunion in El Paso on November 19–22, 1950, later prompted WCW's
poem "The Desert Music" (1951).

John Husband: John Dillon Husband (1909–) was a poet, anthologist,
and professor of English at Tulane University, in New Orleans, from
1947 to 1975. WCW had met him at Yaddo in July.

105. TLS-1   March 26/51

DEAR JIM:

Sent your letter to Murray for a decision on the
Emerson matter: to print or not to print. I urged
him to give you the green light if that could possibly
be arranged. You should hear from him at once.

I've written in detail to Barbara Asch about this
whole matter so you won't need to go over it again
with her. But let me repeat that the script for the
Earlier Collected Poems is all set to be delivered to you
(or to her) when you want it. I've been over it carefully this time rearranging and adding new stuff until
you would hardly know the old gal in her dress as
of 1938. It'll be a different and a far better book than
that one, good as that one was.

The *Autobiography* has had me nailed to the mast
since last fall. It's been a heavy job for me, my only
hope being that the heaviness shall not be reflected
in the style of the thing. At times I feel a little fright-
ened at the speed that I have had to show in getting
the script together; we are at the moment in the stage
of the final (semi-final, I'm afraid) typing of the three
parts: "The Childish Background," "Middle Life,"

"The Later Years." Let's hope it comes out readable.
Thanks for the check which I appreciate. And have
good skiing. The world's a place (as the Good Book
has it) of many mansions. Let's keep the windows
clean.

Best luck
BILL

/ · /

the Emerson matter: Richard Wirtz Emerson, co-owner of the Golden
Goose Press, in Columbus, Ohio, was upset because no permission or
copyright fee had been arranged or acknowledgment given for the
reprinting in *Collected Later Poems* of poems from WCW's Golden Goose
chapbook, *The Pink Church* (1949). It took several months for an
accommodation to be reached.

rearranging: WCW had decided to abandon the chronological ordering
used in *Complete Collected Poems* (1938). For an account of the differ-
ences between that volume and *Collected Earlier Poems* (1951), see A.
Walton Litz and Christopher MacGowan, eds., *The Collected Poems of
William Carlos Williams: Volume. I, 1909–1939* (New York: New
Directions, 1986), pp. xvii–xviii.

106. Telegram [March 31, 1951]

JAMES LAUGHLIN, TEMPLE LODGE. LAKE LOUISE.

THOUGHT YOU WOULD WANT TO KNOW BILL WIL-
LIAMS TAKEN TO PASSAIC GENERAL HOSPITAL ROOM 219
PASSAIC NEW JERSEY CEREBRAL HEMORRHAGE CONDI-
TION CRITICAL NEXT WEEK OR TEN DAYS SHOULD DECIDE
STILL HOPE

STANLEY MOSS

/ · /

Stanley Moss: WCW's stroke occurred on Wednesday, March 28, 1951.
The poet and art dealer Stanley Moss (1925–) was an assistant editor at

New Directions. *New Directions in Prose and Poetry* published six of his
poems in vol. 11 (1949) and two in vol. 13 (1951).

107. ALS-2 April 7/51

DEAR JIM—

Thanks for your note. Bill is doing well.—His
recovery is remarkable—but he will need a long rest.
He is to remain in the Hospital for three weeks—
then go away for a month June.—Then—we'll see!

The energy that burns in that guy is too much for
one human to burn up! He's rarin' to go *now*—and
is anything but a *good* patient. Thank God he's in the
Hospital!—I'd go mad if he were at home. He resents
the situation and tries to minimize it out of all pro-
portion!—

Alta must be beautiful now. Wish I could see it.
Don't break any bones—Bill said to thank you for
your note.—

Sincerely—
FLOSS

108. TLS-1 May 21, 1951

DEAR JIM:

I agree, let's omit the signed, limited edition.

The 25 copies of the pages to be added to the *Later
Collected* were here when I arrived, yesterday afternoon, from two weeks at Saratoga Springs. It was a
curious thing how they came to be omitted when
the book was originally printed but a fortunate one
that Babette Deutsch should have picked up the error

so quickly. There has been no such omission in the case of the *Earlier Collected*. I sent them to your office for Maury Kaplan three weeks ago.

You asked about the *Autobiography*. I just about made it before the lightning struck. At present I am waiting to see the galleys after the lawyers have inspected the script for libel but there will be very little for them to do as my interest was not in material that might prove libellous. I was anxious to give credit where credit was due but the main theme was a history of my books and what brought them on.

I get about more or less as usual but have not attempted to do any practice. Whether or not I return to practice this fall depends on the extent of my recovery. If as time passes I find that I am as able as I ever was I'll go back to medicine—especially if the *Autobiography* is a flop. But if I feel that physically and mentally I am unable to do a full day's work I'll reduce my living expenses in one way or another and do what I can without medicine. Time alone will tell.

Sorry you've been laid up. Harriet Gratwick, Chas. Abbott's sister-in-law, and one of her daughters are likely to turn up at Aspen this summer. If you are there and you get to meet them be nice to them for me. The mama is a good egg, works hard all the year round at a music project called The Neighborhood School of Music which she directs on her farm near Buffalo—which you know. She is a Saltonstall and has all the drive of that well known family. I'm very fond of her.

Oh, and before they're all sold out, please send me an additional five copies of *Paterson* IV. Don't forget. Why you don't print 2000 copies of that book as it comes out is more than I can say. The small edition is not half so attractive or efficient.

(You notice that the typing is not yet what it should be.)

> Sincerely
> BILL

/ · /

limited edition: One hundred copies of a signed edition of WCW's *Collected Later Poems* were issued in 1950, but no such edition of *Collected Earlier Poems* was prepared in 1951.

Saratoga Springs: WCW had been convalescing from his stroke at the home of Dr. W. Sullivan in Schuylerville, New York.

Babette Deutsch: The accidental omission of ten poems from the first binding of *Collected Later Poems* was first noticed in December 1950 by Babette Deutsch (1895–1962), poet, novelist, critic, and lecturer at Columbia University. A section of eight leaves entitled "The Rose" (pp. 233–45) was printed separately for insertion into the bound copies.

a Saltonstall: For Harriet Gratwick, see letter 66 above. Sir Richard Saltonstall of Yorkshire came to Massachusetts in 1630. For many generations, his descendants have played prominent roles in New England as lawyers, magistrates, clergymen, military and naval officers, state governors, and elected lawmakers. Most recently, Leverett Saltonstall (1892–1979) was governor of Massachusetts and United States senator.

small edition: Each of the first four books of *Paterson* was initially published in an edition of one thousand copies.

109. ALS-2   Oct 29 / 52

DEAR JIM—

The copy of *Perspectives* came this morning. It's a splendid collection and Bill asked me to write and tell you how much he likes it and how deeply he appreciates your giving him so much space.

You may not know that Bill had another stroke just before we were ready to go to Washington in September. He was pretty bad for a while—Couldn't talk—or use his right arm at all. Now his speech has returned pretty well & he can move his arm & fingers but can't write. His eyes too were affected so that he has difficulty reading. In spite of it—he has plenty of courage and determination—and we expect to go to Washington at the latest by the first of the year.

We have heard that you are in India—so possibly this letter will be long in reaching you if at all.—

Bill sends his best and says to thank you for him and hopes you have a fine journey, to which I add—ditto—

Sincerely—
FLOSS

/ · /

Perspectives: In 1952, JL became president of Intercultural Publications, Inc., which under the sponsorship of the Ford Foundation published a quarterly journal called *Perspectives USA* in American, British, French, German, and Italian language editions. The first number of the journal, edited by JL and published in fall 1952, contained fifteen poems, a short story, and a chapter of *In the American Grain* by WCW and a review of his two-volume *Collected Poems* by Randall Jarrell. Intercultural Publications also sponsored a series of supplements to the *Atlantic Monthly,* which profiled the contemporary arts and letters of foreign countries for American readers. The first of these was *Perspective of India,* ed. Harvey Breit (1953), in connection with which JL visited India in 1952.

another stroke: WCW's second stroke occurred in mid-August 1952, while he was staying at Gratwick Highlands. The consultantship in poetry at the Library of Congress had been offered to him again, and he was planning to take up the post in September. He did not do so, however; see letter 114 below.

110. ALS-2   Feb 7 / 53

DEAR JIM—

As Bill is not up to letter writing as yet—I am doing what I can.

Bill did get a copy of *New Directions XIV*. Also

Rexroth's book—which he liked and spoke up for at the Book Award Committee meeting.

Come out when you can—Bill *needs* to see people—who he likes and is at ease with. His vision is seriously affected—and his right arm is not carrying it's share of the load—so—he is for the most part in a deep depression—which possibly only some shock treatment will jar him out of. We are in the process of working that out—right now,—I am pinning *all* my hopes on it.

You looked well—and must be full of interesting talk—so when you can—stop out and cheer Bill up—

Sincerely—
FLOSS

/ · /

New Directions XIV: WCW's contribution to *New Directions in Prose and Poetry XIV* (1953) was a prose improvisation entitled "Exultation" (p. 345).

Rexroth's book: Probably Kenneth Rexroth's *The Dragon and the Unicorn* (Norfolk, Conn.: New Directions, 1952).

shock treatment: WCW was hospitalized for depression from February 21 to April 18, 1953, but he did not receive electroshock treatments.

111. TLS-1   9/4/53

DEAR JIM:

The proper handling of letters from friends certainly does present an unsolved problem when it comes to activities of a literary executor. Much has to be left to the discretion of the man on the job. John Thirlwall who has taken an interest in writing a new biography of me and as a matter of fact has already been working on it for half a year seems a person that can be trusted with any available materials. That's all I can say. Look him over and give him a chance. You have my permission to show him my letters to you but if there is any one of them you wish to withhold for personal reasons I think it should be understood that you will do so.

You realize, or do you, how close I have grown to Dave McDowell in the past two or three years. To be brief, I have let him have my new book of poems which he promises to bring out next year. It was only fair to let him have it in view of all that has taken place between us in the recent past. I hope you will understand.

At the same time I have no intention of severing my connection with you, too much is involved emotionally and in a business way for me ever as far as I can prevent it to permit that to happen. Specifically I still have plans for bringing out an additional volume in the *Paterson* Series, called *Paterson* V. This belongs to you, unless you do not want it. It has to do with the world after I am dead. It is already partly written.

I'll never forget your kindnesses to me, how you entertained both Floss and me at your aunt's house and how magnificent you were with the bringing out of the first edition of my *Collected Poems* [1938]. Those were great times for me. I am much interested in your activities in India and wish you luck with them, the young painters, from what I am told, are much interested in what is coming recently out of India.

Your family must be growing up.

Best of luck
BILL

/ · /

John Thirlwall: Professor of English at the City College of New York, John Connop Thirlwall (1904–1971) edited WCW's *Selected Letters* (1957) and "Lost Poems" (see letter 116 below). Thirlwall published a number of articles and notes on WCW, but the projected biography was never completed.

new book of poems: The Desert Music and Other Poems (New York: Random House, 1954).

112. ALS-2   September 8 [1953]

DEAR BILL—

I am terribly upset over your giving the new poems away. Really how can you be so brutal? I thought we had an understanding that N[ew] D[irections] would go on with the poems.

Quite apart from questions of sentiment and honor, it messes things up so to have poems which we will want to add to the *Collected* eventually under another imprint.

Can't you give David something else, Bill—your letters perhaps—and lets, in a world that gets lousier by the day, try to hold together what was, I think, a pretty fine relationship.

You didn't return Thirlwall's letter, which I need to answer. I'll go along with him.

Best,
JIM

113. TLS-1   9/9/53

DEAR JIM:

I'm sorry you feel the way you do about my decision to let Random House do my latest book of poems. You did not feel that way when I was trying to sell *The Wedge*. The publication of that book by a press other than your own did not and does not now prevent the assembling of the collected edition, if it ever comes about from appearing under one imprint.

The need of money, which you have never felt, is a determining factor in many of my dealings now-a-days. I get much more than I have ever got from you under the new arrangement.

But I can't for the life of me see why you have been upset in the long run. Sentiment is a factor to be dealt with but at times like the present it has to be laid aside especially if the rewards outweigh it. There is no real loss to you, save sentiment, that has been incurred but to me it is very nearly a life and death matter to which I trust you will accommodate yourself when you think it over.

Do not let your judgement concerning any of our relations be disturbed by our new relations but take it in your stride as you can so easily do and trust me as in the past to keep in mind the relations that have always pertained between us to our mutual benefit.

Yours sincerely
BILL

114. TLS-1.   September 30, 1954

DEAR BILL,

Do you have anything down on paper which outlines the chain of events in this disgraceful situation of the withholding of your Library of Congress position?

A friend of mine, W. H. Ferry, who is vice-president of The Fund for the Republic, has heard about the case and is eager to know more facts about it. As you may know, The Fund for the Republic is an independent organization set up by the Ford Foundation to work in the field of civil liberties.

If you have anything which you would care to send me to give to Ferry, I would be very grateful. Needless to say, Ferry would not take any action in the case without consulting you.

How have you been? I have missed seeing you and hope we can get together again soon. I have seen some wonderful new poems in various places. The one in the American number of *The Times Literary Supplement* was a real beauty.

How goes the continuation of *Paterson*? As you know, Bob and I are looking forward to that very eagerly.

With best wishes,
JIM

/ · /

Library of Congress: WCW's appointment to the consultantship in poetry at the Library of Congress was delayed late in 1952 when his loyalty to the United States was investigated by the Civil Service Commission, the Federal Bureau of Investigation, and the Library of Congress Loyalty Board. The investigation was inconclusive, but lasted so long that WCW was prevented from taking up the one-year term of office, which ended in September 1953. The case was mentioned twelve months later in the *Times Literary Supplement,* September 17, 1954, p. liv, under the heading "Prophets without Honour? The Public Status of American Writers." The same issue, a "Special Number . . . Devoted to American Writing To-Day," carried WCW's poem "The Ivy Crown" on p. 588. Because the *TLS* wrongly reported that WCW "was refused a security clearance," he told the *New York Times* (October 12, 1954, p. 20) that "he intended to take legal action to get the poet's post in Washington or at least the chance to defend himself." In the end, however, he did not sue or avail himself of the public-relations assistance mentioned by JL.

115. TLS-1   Oct. 1, 1954

DEAR JIM:

Using this paper reminds me of the old days—I can't tell you how pleasantly. Your letter was very welcome. A flood of memories comes over me that almost makes me want to weep, in other words I am not weeping. Forget it.

As far as the continuation of *Paterson* is concerned, *Paterson* V, it got side-tracked. It turned into something else. That doesn't mean the end of it. As a matter of fact it is stirring again in my imagination and when it begins concretely to take shape I promise you that you'll hear of it.

That notice of my situation in the London *Times* has certainly stirred up a whirlwind. As far as the particular raised by your letter is concerned Jim Murray is the man to see about that. I called him on the phone immediately on receipt of your letter. He said he would call you at once and has no doubt already done so. He has all the papers in his office and will no doubt give you access to them whenever you want to consult them. Awfully glad people in key positions are beginning to hear of what has been going on. Thank you for your part in the matter.

How many times have I thought of that idyllic two weeks we spent at Norfolk that summer so many years ago. We took some walks in the woods, down the ravine back of the house, that come to my mind thrillingly sometimes in the middle of the night. I can see every detail of it. And hear it too. It was the hermit thrush that was the chief musician. Sounds almost silly to think of as important to a man's life but it is not pleasant to think it will in all probability not come again. Well.

Oct. 2 / 54

Talked to Jim Murray on the phone yesterday then had to leave in a hurry. Hope he gave you the information you wanted. If not come again.

Best
BILL

/ · /

something else: The poem which WCW had thought would be *Paterson* 5 became "Asphodel, That Greeny Flower" (1952–55).

two weeks: In August 1938, WCW and FW spent their summer vacation in a cottage on the estate of JL's aunt, Mrs. Leila Carlisle, near Norfolk, Connecticut.

116. TLS-1   Jan. 26 / 56

DEAR JIM:

Glad to hear from you—about things. The new *New Directions Anthology* interests me, the new format is all to the good, I quite approve. When Jim Murray gives the word I hope the way will be cleared for the appearance of the *In the American Grain* in the new form.

I'm glad to hear you—or see you speak again of Marcia Nardi. Her address is as it has been of recent years simply Woodstock, NY. I had a letter from her recently enclosing a number of poems among which were some of the best I have ever seen of hers. Indeed write to her, I hope you will see your way clear to publishing a generous collection of her work.

As for myself I am in the doldrums of late after finishing a fifty page typescript of a long short story I have been working on for years. I don't imagine it's your meat as I want to sell it for as much as I can

get for it—if after I get the chance to look it over—
it is worth anything.

Jack Thirlwall who has been assiduously collecting my letters, as you know, has assembled a collection of unpublished poems written during the past
thirty years that have somehow escaped publication.
Some of them are interesting. If you like, you can
have those I think, with an accompanying note by
him. They have at least an antiquarian interest.

As for new work in verse, I ain't got none. The
well seems to have dried up. Prose c'est la vie, used
to be Marcel Duchamp's pseudonym. It has become
my confrontation of late. If I can dig up something
that I want to write about during the next two or
three weeks I'll send it on.

I haven't heard either from Ben Shahn or Dahlberg recently. Hope you can come to an agreement
with the former about his price without too much
delay. As I say, glad to have heard from you for
without your backing, and I know it, I would never
have succeeded in getting most of my books published.

Sincerely yours
BILL

/ · /

*New Directions: New Directions 15: An Anthology of New Directions in
Prose and Poetry* (1955) was the first paperback edition of the anthology.
It was considerably smaller and cheaper than its predecessors.

In the American Grain: The first New Directions Paperbook edition of
In the American Grain appeared on August 22, 1956.

Marcia Nardi: In a letter to WCW of January 26, 1956, JL had expressed
an interest in using some of Marcia Nardi's work in *New Directions 16*.
None appeared there, but the Denver publisher Alan Swallow brought
out a volume of Nardi's *Poems* in 1956.

a long short story: "The Farmers' Daughters"; see letters 70 above and
120 below.

unpublished poems: New Directions in Prose and Poetry 16 (1957) contained
sixty-three poems by WCW edited and introduced by John C. Thirl-

wall and entitled "The Lost Poems of William Carlos Williams or the Past Recaptured." Most of the poems had previously appeared in periodicals but had not been collected in any of the volumes of WCW's poetry. Only twelve had never been published before.

Prose c'est la vie: While living in New York during the winter of 1920–21, Marcel Duchamp (see letter 35 above) created a feminine alter ego named Rrose Sélavy (after "Rosse est la vie" and "Arrose, c'est la vie"). Man Ray's famous photograph of Rrose (Duchamp in drag) was incorporated into a Dadaist perfume advertisement, and she signed two of Duchamp's ready-mades, *Fresh Widow* (1920) and *Why Not Sneeze* (1921). For years thereafter, Duchamp used the pseudonym for a variety of purposes.

Ben Shahn: In 1957, New Directions published *The Sorrows of Priapus,* by Edward Dahlberg, with drawings by the Russian-American artist Ben Shahn (1898–1969). WCW met Shahn in Hightstown, New Jersey, on June 10, 1950, and was instrumental in persuading him to undertake the *Priapus* commission in 1955. Both Shahn and Dahlberg appear in Book 5 of *Paterson.*

117. TLS-1   Sept. 16 / 56

DEAR JIM:

Copies of *In the American Grain* reached me promptly after I had written you, many thanks. The cover is a knock-out and will, I am sure, sell many copies. Really wonderful.

We don't go to the city very often in the evening and on the 27th we are going up to Buffalo for a few days, but after Oct. 2 Flossie and I would be delighted to have you run out in the afternoon with your wife if you will let us know the date. Stay for supper, Floss says, we'll be delighted to have you.

Did you see my article on Rene Char in the last *New Republic?*

Best from us both
BILL

—and in Ferlinghetti's City Lights Series Ginsbergs *Howl* with an introduction by me. W.

/ · /

my article: WCW's "A Poet Who Cannot Pause" appeared in the *New Republic,* September 17, 1956, p. 18. It was a review of René Char (1907–1988), *Hypnos Waking: Poems and Prose,* selected and translated by Jackson Matthews, with the collaboration of William Carlos Williams and others (New York: Random House, 1956), a volume to which WCW contributed two translations. Char's poetry is evoked in WCW's poem "To a Dog Injured in the Street" (1953).

Howl: Allen Ginsberg, *Howl and Other Poems,* Pocket Poets Series, no. 4 (San Francisco: City Lights Pocket Bookshop, [1956]). WCW's introduction (pp. 7–8) is entitled "Howl for Carl Solomon." The poet Lawrence Ferlinghetti (1920–) was the proprietor of City Lights Bookshop and publisher of the inexpensive paperback series. A letter from Ginsberg appears in *Paterson* 5.

118. TLS-2   Oct. 28, 1956

DEAR JIM:

You have sent me, I thoroughly believe, the truest and most beautiful book in the world as well as one of the most feelingly translated ones in Osamu Dazai's *The Setting Sun.* Both Floss and I have been near tears, going around in a daze from the opening words of it until the bitter but triumphant close. I have just begun to speak of it to friends, Louis and Celia Zukofsky night before last were the first but everyone I know will hear of it in the end. I must congratulate you on the insight and initiative that has made the discovery and the publication of such a magnificent book possible.

The book itself is well written, even superlatively well written—I'm going whole hog in saying that I know but I don't think I will have to hedge on that in the time to come. The character of the mother who practically never opens her mouth (except to flutter the soup between her lips at the beginning) weaves a spell over us from the beginning. I have never been able to see the Japanese from Gengis Kahn (spelling?) to Pound's talk of the Noh (again spelling?) plays with much sympathy but this Dazai has won me over completely. I haven't yet read his story, "Villon," in the *New Directions* of a year or two ago, I'm ashamed to say, but I will at once. The character of that marvellous young woman his heroine, has been handled in such a way that I shall never forget her. The courage, the insight into our world, occidental and oriental, which she represents—the handling of the Christian myth which she represents is breathtaking in its fundamental human value. Aristocrats are born.

The young woman's final simplification of her female plight in the world leaves nothing to be said. Until woman makes free with her sex for the one purpose for which she is made we are both of us, man and woman, powerless in the world. Mary had to have her baby, who was a bastard; until that has sickered down in the consciousness with an acknowledgement of the dignity even the glory of that occurrence we don't know nuthin.

A fundamental experience for which I am deeply grateful to you.

Best
BILL

I want Louis (Zukofsky) to have the book at my expense if necessary as soon as you can send it to him.

He also wants the latest *New Directions* annual for his own use. Charge me again if necessary—but don't tell him for he has made me promise not to pay for it. Ha ha!

W.W.

/ · /

The Setting Sun: In 1956, New Directions published Donald Keene's translation of *The Setting Sun* (1947), by the Japanese writer "Osamu Dazai" (actually Tsushima Shuji, 1909–1948). In *Paterson* 5, WCW mentions "Osamu / Dazai and his saintly sister."

the Noh: Certain Noble Plays of Japan (1916) and *Noh, or Accomplishment* (1917) contained translations of classical Japanese Noh plays made by Ezra Pound from the notes of the American Orientalist Ernest Fenollosa.

"Villon": Dazai Osamu, "Villon's Wife," trans. Donald Keene, *New Directions 15* (1955), pp. 177–95.

119. TLS-1   Dec. 4, 1956

DEAR JIM:

The first rough, very rough, draft that I have been working on as my inspiration has permitted, was finished today. There is much still to be done but within the year it will be finished and put aside to ripen. The arrangements with Random House have still to be made but I have no doubt that they will be completed without any bad feeling—even if I have to write one additional book to satisfy them. *Paciencia.*

As for Thirlwall's book of poems that have been inadvertently omitted from my past volumes, for *New Directions 16* I am thrilled. Your suggestions as to copyright are perfectly satisfactory to me. As far as an advance payment of $100. I would like to split it with Jack who has had all the work of making up the volume, I'll tell him what we are going to do. A one time arrangement with permission to reprint is all I want. Maybe I've missed a point or two but I don't think so. I'm amazed at what Thirlwall has succeeded in collecting, glad you're handling the deal.

That was a good party the other night. I guess I have thought in the past 5 years that I was all washed up. When I see people like Martha Graham and Dorothy Norman I feel that I have returned from the dead. I am really shocked to see that the world still goes on. The intervening years since I disappeared from the scene seem to have disappeared in the void, I cant tell you how strange it feels. People have merely grown older (though many like Gertrude Stein have died long since), I feel that I remain an anachronism. But I'm just beginning! How long can it go on?

Glad to see your wife again and looking like a kid. Keep it up.

Sincerely yours
BILL

/ · /

party: On November 29, 1956, JL gave a party in New York at which Ravi Shankar and Chattur Lal played Indian classical music. There WCW met his old friends Martha Graham and Dorothy Norman.

Gertrude Stein: Stein, who died in Paris on July 27, 1946, is evoked in Book 5 of *Paterson* and in "Tribute to the Painters" (1955). See also letter 4 above.

your wife: JL's first marriage ended in 1952. In 1957 he married Ann Clark Resor. She helped to arrange the concert tour which brought Shankar and Lal to the United States.

120. TL-1 [March 2, 1957?]

DEAR JIM:

Awfully glad to have your letter and such a good letter, full of interesting detail to boot. I was specially glad to learn that you had met Stevens and had a chance to talk with him, he's a very attractive individual and a good "American", a really swell guy I thought. Flossie liked him too and that always means a lot to me. He's lucky to have a man like you to help him, you can count on me to keep all mention of your new relationship out of my letters or conversation. I hope you continue to get along. I hope he realizes how lucky he is. Thank you for returning his letter with the address.

Dave's new adventure with Obolensky, whom you probably know about, is very exciting. I hope they do well. The break with Random House came about, as far as I know, without untoward incident. Aside from the poem *Paterson* 5, which I have warned the new firm that you will do when it is ready, they will be my publishers from here out. Random House having turned me down on my letters McD[owell] & O[bolensky] will begin operations by bringing them out forthwith. I have already signed the contract. There will undoubtedly be other volumes later.

It was a real satisfaction to me to have you do the poems that Thirlwall had dug out of the past, as yet unpublished items which I had even in many cases forgotten existed. I hope they do well for *N[ew] D[irections]* when they appear, I know I shall be thrilled.

I'm waiting now impatiently for the next issue of *Hudson Review* in which they have promised to include my long short story "The Farmers' Daughters" on which I have been working for the last 15 years. That I am excited by the prospects is putting it mildly, I thought I was washed up on this score I had accepted long since. It is a 35 page item makes me lucky to have it accepted by any contemporary magazine.

The *Paterson* 5 (and I must ask you on your part to keep this also under your hat) has been finished in more or less the final draught but I will not be able to release it until Dave has published the letters. I'll continue refining until the last minute. Meanwhile, since life at my age is essentially uncertain, I want this to be my assurance that it is yours if, when you see it, you will still want it.

Take care of yourself and have a profitable time and an enjoyable one in Burma. Especially keep well. Floss sends her love. O, I almost forgot to tell you we just today got our reservations for the Mississippi River trip next May, it'll be hot but I think we can take it; New Orleans and points along the river and back for about 15 or 16 weeks. I think we'll enjoy it.

Sincerely yours

/ · /

Stevens: The poet and critic Arthur Wilber Stevens (1921–) met WCW at the University of Washington in 1949. Stevens was instructor in English and founder of *Interim,* a literary magazine published in Seattle from 1944 to 1955. WCW contributed several poems to *Interim* in the late 1940s. In 1956–57, Stevens was a Fulbright professor at the University of Mandalay. In a letter written from Rangoon, Burma, on February 23, 1957, JL told WCW that he had recently met Stevens. Since 1973, Stevens has been professor of English and humanities at the University of Nevada, Las Vegas. He revived *Interim* in 1986.

Obolensky: In 1957, WCW's editor David McDowell left Random House to form a company of his own with Ivan Obolensky. The firm of McDowell, Obolensky published *The Selected Letters of William Carlos Williams,* ed. John C. Thirlwall, in August 1957 and *Yes, Mrs. Williams: A Personal Record of My Mother* in June 1959. McDowell left the partnership in 1960 and later worked for Crown Publishers and Kraus Reprints. He received an honorary degree from Kenyon College on May 1, 1973, and died on April 8, 1985, as a result of a motor vehicle accident in Monteagle, Tennessee.

Hudson Review: WCW's "The Farmers' Daughters" appeared in the *Hudson Review* 10, no. 3 (Autumn 1957): 329–52.

15 or 16 weeks: WCW probably meant to say "15 or 16 days."

121. TLS-1   Oct. 14, 1957

DEAR JIM:

First, don't be incensed that the boys on the anthology program for England left me entirely out. I may not be old enough for them but will come along later. 'Tain't important. What the hell have I been yapping about all these years if we have to think of them?

About the Christmas card: I think the script should be bolder, in other words more prominent, larger more prominent (said that before). The decorative openwork letters make it seem somehow sentimental. Nuts with that.

What is written on the back suits me well. Let us have 50 copies with envelopes.

Starting to work on the final version of *Paterson* 5 today. Wish me luck.

Oh, we're flying to Berkeley ⟨Calif⟩ Nov. 7 to have my head examined by the professors there! a project they have dreamed up for themselves to find out if possible why writers tick. ⟨Five!⟩ specimens including me are to be examined. Hot cha!

                                    Sincerely yours
                                    BILL

⟨Edited by FHW.⟩

/ · /

anthology program: In a letter of October 11, 1957, JL told WCW that the Carnegie Foundation had not included "any book by you in the list of 300 titles that they are sending to Commonwealth Libraries."

Christmas card: WCW's poem "The Gift," *Hudson Review* 9, no. 4 (Winter 1956–57): 485, was reprinted by New Directions in broadsheet form as a Christmas card for the 1957 holiday season.

Berkeley: WCW was examined for three days at the Institute of Personality Assessment and Behavior. He did not find it a pleasant experi-

ence, but his expenses were paid and he subsequently visited a number
of California friends and relatives.

122. TLS-1   Nov. 3, 1957

DEAR JIM:

I am leaving the manuscript of *Paterson* 5 in charge
of my son Bill while we shall be away, with full
instructions.

This is a good time for me to tell you what I want:
1. $1,000 in advance. 2. Guarantee of 3,000 copies in
the same format and quality of printing. 3. Guarantee of an advertising budget of at least $1,000.

I don't mind telling you that I have been in touch
with Murray who has advised me on the statement.
If for any reason you will not agree to this, the deal
is off.

Sincerely yours
WILLIAM CARLOS WILLIAMS

/ · /

Paterson 5: On October 14, 1957, WCW told JL that he was "starting
to work on the final version of *Paterson* 5 today" (see letter 121 above).
The poem was signed, dated, and sent to the typist on December 4,
though further revisions were made in January. *Paterson (Book Five)*
was published by New Directions on September 17, 1958.

123. TLS-2   January 3, 1958

DEAR BILL—

I hope that you all had a good Christmas down
there, with the grandchildren rallied round. Up here
we have had the older children home from school—

Leila is now a very grown up young lady of 13—and the little new one, Robert, burbling and crawling about—he is eight months now, and quite a hulk.

As I wired you, I am most enthusiastic about *Paterson* V, and so is Ann. We both think it is beautiful, surpassing even the earlier parts in intensity and in the richness of the interweaving themes. It will take many readings, of course, to get to the bottom of it, there is so much there to think about, but even the first one is quite overwhelming.

No doubt at all about it, Bill, this is a thrilling poem and I want very much to publish it, first in the de luxe format, matching the earlier volumes in the set, and then later, when the time is right, adding it to the rest of *Paterson* in the New Classics Series.

The terms which you have offered are entirely acceptable to me: an advance of $1000 against royalties; a first printing of 3000 copies; and a guarantee of $1000 to be spent on advertising. All this is fine with me, and I'll ask Bob to write these terms into the standard contract form and get it over to you speedily, so that you can go over it with Murray.

I suppose that we ought to get permission from the authors of the letters that are included, or have you already done so? Who wrote the first one? I spot Ginsberg and Old Ez and Corman, but the first one eludes me. I dare say the requests should come from you, but we can help you prepare the letters, if you like.

I see nothing in the poem which gives cause for worry about a censorship problem. You have probably been following the recent court decisions, and I think they clearly give all the cover that is needed. I see nothing offensive in the references to the Virgin; it is all handled with dignity.

I have taken the liberty of marking on the script a few places where I think the typist may have misread spellings in your original, and also indicated, with little check marks, a few spots where the spelling may or may not be as you wish it.

Were any parts of the poem published already separately, so that we would need to clear permissions? I have a feeling I have seen the beautiful bit of Sappho before somewhere.

I hope that we can get the thing finalized soon so that we can start right to work on it. We will want to do a big publicity build-up and really launch the poem with a proper bang.

I'm returning the script by way of the New York office so that Bob will have a chance to look it over. He can make a rough cast-off of the length and start talking with the printer and the paper dealer right away, so that there won't be any delay.

And here is the check to your order for $1000, so that you won't be worrying about that.

With best wishes to you all for 1958!

As ever,
Jɪᴍ

/ · /

the letters: The first letter incorporated into *Paterson* 5, signed "Josie," is from the American novelist Josephine Herbst (1897–1969). Letters from Allen Ginsberg and Ezra Pound follow. At one stage, a letter from the poet Cid Corman (1924–), editor of *Origin,* was also included; but in the final revision WCW replaced this letter with one from Edward Dahlberg.

Sappho: Paterson 5, Part 2, begins with WCW's translation of "Peer of the Gods," by the Greek lyric poet Sappho (7th cen. B.C.?). JL could have seen the translation in *Spectrum* 1, no. 3 (Fall 1957): 57; in *Evergreen Review* 1, no. 3 ([Fall] 1957): 56–58; or in *Sappho: A Translation by William Carlos Williams,* a broadsheet edited by Stanley Kunitz and others and published in San Francisco in December 1957 as part of the Poems in Folio series.

Bob: Robert M. MacGregor was at this time JL's second-in-command at the New York office of New Directions.

124. TLS-1   June 18, 1958

DEAR BILL:

Thanks so much for your note of June 13th, and I
am glad to know that you might be able to make the
recording for the American Broadcasting Foundation in the fall. I'll suggest it to you again along some
time in September.

Yes, I met Harold Norse once, and know some of
his work. I agree with you that he is definitely tal-
ented. If he wants to submit something here, we'll
certainly give him very careful consideration.

Richard Avedon, the photographer, wants to take
a picture of Ezra before he gets away to Italy. About
the only place he could catch him would be out at
your house, on the 30th, since Ezra doesn't want to
come into town. I hope this is all right with you and
Floss. Avedon has been briefed that he is to work
very quickly, and I hope he won't make a nuisance
of himself and get in your way. Possibly Bob
MacGregor will drive out with him, as Bob wants
to say goodbye to Ezra, and he may also have things
to talk to you about on promotion plans for *Paterson
Five*.

My address during July will be Snake River Ranch,
Wilson, Wyoming. Drop me a card there if anything comes up. And I'll look forward to seeing you
again when I return.

                                           As ever,
                                           JIM

/ · /

the recording: In a letter to WCW of June 10, 1958, JL explained, "The
Ford Foundation has given a grant to an organization called the American Broadcasting Foundation . . . to exchange tapes of cultural broad-

casting materials between American and foreign radio stations." WCW
was willing to record some of his poems, but the recording was never
made.

Harold Norse: The American poet and translator Harold Norse (1916–)
was represented in *New Directions in Prose and Poetry 13* (1951). WCW
contributed a preface to Norse's translation of *The Roman Sonnets of G.
G. Belli* (Highlands, N.C.: Jonathan Williams, 1960).

Richard Avedon: Pound was discharged from St. Elizabeths Hospital on
May 7, 1958. He stayed at 9 Ridge Road on June 28–30. Richard Avedon (1923–), then a staff photographer for *Harper's Bazaar,* made several portraits of the two poets on June 29.

125. TLS-1   Sept. 23, 1958

DEAR JIM—AND HIS WIFE:

It was a beautiful party you gave Floss and me for
my seventy fifth birthday and the publication of
Pat[erson] 5. We sincerely thank you for it all. And
also for the return of the telegrams and other mes-
sages. It'll take me a week to catch up with them all.
I'm not as sprightly as I was.

It's a beautiful book you, Jim, have made for me.
Who knows anything of the future but if there is to
be a *Paterson* 6 in the next couple of years there is no
disloyalty in saying that I shall ask you to do it.

Glad that my final remarks at the supper table were
not taken amiss by Mrs. Laughlin.

Sincerely yours
BILL

/ · /

party: On September 17, 1958, JL and his wife, Ann, gave a birthday
party for WCW in the New York City apartment of JL's mother-in-
law, Mrs. Stanley B. Resor, who lived at 66 East Seventy-ninth Street.

126. TL-1   Oct. 15, 1958

DEAR JIM:

I have to report, regrettably, that less than a week ago, in fact last Saturday night I had another stroke—and if it were not for this machine I'd be sunk.

It came at a bad time. The show at Johns Hopkins had to be cancelled much to my disappointment and I take it—theirs and with other engagements. It is not too bad a shot but enough to lay me low. We'll see how much I am discommoded. Lucky it didn't come a week ago.

That's all I wanted to tell you. Best regards to your wife, she made many friends at "the Party". I'm getting on all right under the care of Floss. Nuff said.

Sincerely yours

P.S. Please notify MacGregor of what has occurred. I can still sign my name with my left hand—after a fashion. W.

/ · /

Johns Hopkins: WCW had been scheduled to read at a poetry festival at Johns Hopkins University, in Baltimore, Maryland, during the first week of November.

127. ALS-1   10/21/58

DEAR BILL—

Just a line to say how much I appreciated your writing, and to tell you that Ann and I are thinking of you and rooting for you to jump this new hurdle as you have done the others. It's wonderful to all of us to see how you meet these things, Bill—as if they were nothing at all—and I just wish I had ¹⁄₁₀th of your guts and savoir vivre.

Best to Floss!
JIM

128. TLS-1   Feb. 1, 1959

DEAR JIM:

I'm sending the enclosed original poem to keep as your own, may very well be my last, it says all I have ever wanted to say. Use it as you think fit. I did think to ask you to have a few copies printed up for keepsakes thinking Floss might be interested but that must be up to her.

I am at the moment involved in making not more than 10 poems using Brueghel's paintings as models. That will keep me busy I hope for some time to come.

I wanted you to see this poem and record it—after all I have been a writer, writing has been important to me.

Sincerely
WILLIAM CARLOS WILLIAMS

/ · /

poem: "To Be Recited to Flossie on Her Birthday" was printed as a broadsheet by Igal Roodenko in April 1959.
10 poems: WCW's ten-poem suite "Pictures from Brueghel" was first published in the *Hudson Review* 13, no. 1 (Spring 1960): 11–20.

129. TLS-1 October 23, 1959

DEAR BILL—

Just back from the other side, and glad to hear from you, though distressed that there has been some snafu on your gift orders. Will look right into it.

Bob is fine, though I often wonder how he stands the pressure. Many a night he comes back to the office after dinner and works away til midnight. It has been especially bad lately because two young ladies in the order department left at once. The head of the department moved to California to live, and one of the assistants produced an offspring. It was very difficult to find replacements, despite all we were hearing not long ago about unemployment. We have them now, but there were some bad moments, when the editorial crew were getting out the orders . . . and I think it must have been then that your requests got sidetracked.

I don't want to contact Bob on it this weekend— I hope he is getting some rest—but I'll have word to him on Monday and feel sure he will call you if the original orders can't immediately be found, or have one of the girls do so if he is tied up.

I am very much worried about Uncle Ezry, who is really sitting on the bottom of the black hole. A terrible depression and collapse of physical energy. He talks a lot about dying, and just lies around and broods. He is back up at the castle now with Mary. She writes that he looks well, but that there is no improvement in his spirits. I've been trying to persuade him to take some treatment—some of these new drugs—but he won't go anywhere where the specialists are. He lets the local man jab him with something—vitamins maybe?—but it doesn't seem to help.

Marcella, as you may have heard, couldn't take it any more—she hated Italy—and has gone back to Texas. Dorothy takes it, but is not at all strong any more. It's really a very tough situation, and I came away with a rather hopeless feeling about it, because Ez, miserable as he is, is still so damn stubborn, he just won't listen to sense.

Best to you both,
JIM

/ · /

the castle: Schloss Brunnenburg in Tirolo di Merano, Italy, purchased by Pound's daughter and son-in-law, Mary and Boris de Rachewiltz, in 1948.

Marcella: Marcella Spann, coeditor with Pound of the New Directions anthology *Confucius to Cummings* (1964), accompanied the poet and his wife, Dorothy, to Italy in 1958 but returned to the United States at the end of the summer of 1959. Now Marcella Booth, she is a professor of English at the University of Connecticut.

130. TLS-1   Jan. 4, 1960

DEAR ANN & JIM:

The pears were—and are still—delicious. Much thanks. They are really poems which Virgil according to his own witness had a preference for. At least he mentioned them in a poem. Nice of you to have thought of us.

In about another year I'll be submitting to you another book of my recently collected poems without any compunction, just for you to look at. It's a strange thing still to be writing poems. If I did not feel that I have something to contribute to the art I'd shut up tighter than a clam—but the young by their inability force me to keep eternally at it.

You have both been very kind. Flossie joins me in wishing you the seasons greetings.

Affectionately yours
BILL

/ · /

Virgil: Pears and pear trees are mentioned at several points in the *Eclogues* and the *Georgics* of the Mantuan poet Virgil (70–19 B.C.). JL had translated *The Fourth Eclogue of Virgil* for private publication in 1939.

131. TLS-2   January 7, 1960

DEAR BILL,

That's good to know that Virgil also liked pears! I'll have to track down the reference some day. I imagine it must be in the *Georgics.*

That is great news that you are thinking of another volume in the *Collected Poems* series. We certainly would like to add a third, in the same format, and I know that there is some wonderful stuff waiting to go into it.

And I think too that at some point we ought to be thinking about adding some pages to the little *Selected* paperback, drawn from the later individual volumes, if the necessary arrangements can be worked out with the two other publishers involved. The time to do it would be when we reprint that little volume, and I'll have a look one of these days and let you know what the timing might be.

I've just had a wonderful letter from Eva Hesse in Munich, describing Uncle Ezra's triumph at Darmstadt. He went up there for the opening of the *Women of Trachis.* It's so good that I'll copy off a bit of it for you: "Ezra was invited by the Mayor of Darmstadt to be a guest of honor of the city. Thus Ezra and

Mary turned up in Munich two days ahead of the premiere. Ez was very much a "reclining figure" at first, but very soon livened up. On the day of the premiere we took him to Darmstadt by car and he donned what he called his "fancy suit"—a sort of vintage velvet jacket in which he used to attend concerts in Rapallo before the war, and in which he incidentally makes an imposing figure. In the excitement of the journey he, alas, forgot to pack any shirt studs, and also the crazy invention his tailor had provided for keeping his pants up refused to function. However, the hotel management finally succeeded in making him seaworthy and so we all proceeded to the theater. The theater in Darmstadt is located in the wing of a baroque castle and, to Ezra's concern, does not have any private boxes. That meant that we had to sit among the audience. Ez was near to decamping on learning this, but when we pointed out that this was hardly what Mr. Eliot would do under such circumstances, he quieted down. Though not on the same high level as the one in Berlin, the Darmstadt production went over very well and Ez visibly enjoyed himself. Just before the end he suddenly rose from his seat and made a dash for the exit. However, instead of racing out of the theater as we had feared, he suddenly appeared on the stage, where the cast were receiving their applause. A great new wave of applause set in as Ezra showed up in the spotlight, and there were long ovations—he was called back to the curtain some five or six times. He cut a very fine figure standing out there—one critic described the incident as the "final appearance of the real Herakles", another referred to his "fuerstliche Erscheinung", yet another, in more ironic vein, referred to it as the "Satyrspiel". Afterwards, we went on to the Mayor's reception, where Ezra conducted lively conversations with the Mayor, the Minister of

Culture, and members of the cast. The Mayor was, it is true, caught unprepared when Ezra demanded a portion of ice cream with his Mosel wine, but he responded nobly and sent out for some."

I wish I could have seen it, and it's certainly nice that the old boy is having some fun after all he's been through. The last few months he seems to have been in much better shape mentally. What he really needs is an audience, and everyone over there says that he brightens up immediately when someone comes along for him to talk to.

By the way, in the same letter, Eva Hesse talks about your *Many Loves*. She wonders if it would be possible for her to see a copy of the acting version as it was put on at the Living Theater. She has quite a standing now as a translator and adaptor of American plays—she did one of Jeffers', and the MacLeish one on Job, as well as Ezra's—so I think it would be fine if she could do yours, if you wanted her to, and it would work out. Please let me know how to proceed on this, won't you?

I believe that we've already sent you the Levertov book, and the one by Corso will follow soon. Are you interested in Kerouac? We are getting out a little limited edition of one of his things, and I'd like you to have it if you are interested.

We've all been well, and we're expecting a new addition some time in February. Hope it will be a girl. They really are great. I get more fun out of Leila, who is now fifteen, and a real dandy. Took her skiing for a few days this past vacation in Vermont and we really had a ball together. But I suppose some young squirt will grab her off before long. Hope I can take it.

With best to you both, as ever,
JIM

/ · /

reprint: WCW's *Selected Poems* was reprinted as a New Directions Paperbook in January 1963. This edition was superseded in 1985 by a different, more inclusive *Selected Poems,* edited and introduced by the British poet Charles Tomlinson.

Eva Hesse: The critic and translator of modern American literature Eva Hesse (1925–) made German versions of works by Pound, Eliot, Marianne Moore, E. E. Cummings, Robinson Jeffers (*Die Quelle* [1958], *Medea* [1958], *Die Frau aus Kreta* [1960]), and Archibald MacLeish (*J.B.* [1958], translated as *Spiel um Job* [1960]). She did not, however, translate *Many Loves.*

Women of Trachis: Pound's translation of Sophocles' tragedy *The Women of Trachis* was first published in the *Hudson Review* 6, no. 4 (Winter 1954): [487]–523, and first performed on BBC radio on April 25, 1954. Eva Hesse's German version of Pound's translation (1958) had its premiere at the Schiller Theater in Berlin on May 9, 1959, and was also produced at the Landestheater in Darmstadt on December 12, 1959.

the Living Theater: Founded by Julian Beck and Judith Malina, this avant-garde repertory company performed in New York from 1947 to 1963. The Living Theater first sought WCW's permission to produce *Many Loves* in May 1948 and did stage it from January 13 to November 17, 1959 (216 performances). WCW attended on January 18; his poem "15 Years Later" recalls the occasion.

Levertov: In 1959, New Directions published *With Eyes at the Back of Our Heads,* a book of poems by Denise Levertov (1923–). Thirteen other books written by Levertov have since appeared under the New Directions imprint.

Corso: In 1960, New Directions published *The Happy Birthday of Death,* a book of poems by the Beat writer Gregory Corso (1930–).

Kerouac: In 1960, New Directions published *Excerpts from Visions of Cody,* part of a memoir of Neal Cassady by the Beat writer Jack Kerouac (1922–1969).

132. TLS-1   Jan. 8, 1960

DEAR JIM:

We laughed fit to kill at your account of Ez at Darmstadt. It is wonderful that he had so good a time as the guest of the city—and that his play or his translation of the play went so well: it puts me in mind of a play by Schiller I attended at Leipzig at the opera house there in 1906. It was *Die Räuber* one of the poets early plays in which he permitted his actors to rant and rave to their heart's content. I was shocked being more used to [word missing] restrained art of Ibsen at the time—but I was there and took it all in while the Zeppelins floated above us in the mist of the city.

I'll send you a copy of the acting script of *Many Loves* myself that you may forward it to Eva Hesse in Munich—if she does not already have, I'll get it off this very afternoon—I'll send it through the regular N[ew] D[irections] office.

So you have a 15 year old daughter, like to introduce her to my own 15 year old granddaughter, I bet they'd make an attractive team. It's amazing how they grow up Bill has nothing else but daughters, three of them the youngest 2! Very attractive.

We'll get to the other business, as I say, in another year. best to your wife.

Sincerely
BILL

/ · /

Schiller: During his term of study at the University of Leipzig in 1909–10 (not 1906), WCW attended a performance at the Altes Theater of *Die Räuber* (1781), by the German Romantic poet and dramatist Friedrich Schiller (1759–1805).

133. TLS-1   June 16, 1960

DEAR JIM:

It's good to be back again—for the last time. I've written Atkinson telling him our talk about the plays is all off except possibly their stage production, their printing or reprinting will be henceforth in your hands.

I'm through with Dave [McDowell]. We'll talk more about that at another time, the reissuing of a paper-back short stories with a 50 page introduction by me, already written will be also in your hands (if you want it?).

I'm relieved.

Sincerely yours
BILL

/ · /

Atkinson: On May 14, 1960, Clinton J. Atkinson directed a production of WCW's *Under the Stars* and *A Dream of Love* at Wesleyan University, in Middletown, Connecticut. In June, Atkinson offered to try to persuade the Wesleyan University Press to publish all of WCW's plays. *Under the Stars,* a one-act dialogue between George Washington and Lafayette, was published in the *University of Kansas City Review* 11, no. 1 (Autumn 1944): 26–28. It was not included in *Many Loves and Other Plays* (see letter 134 below).

short stories: The Farmers' Daughters: The Collected Stories of William Carlos Williams was published by New Directions on September 22, 1961. It did not contain WCW's introduction, which survives in a forty-eight-page typescript entitled "The Short Stories of William Carlos Williams" at the Beinecke Library (catalogue designation Za/Williams/223).

134. TLS-1   September 30, 1960

DEAR BILL,

I happened to be having lunch with Tennessee [Williams] today and I want you to know with what deep feeling he spoke of you, both as a friend and as a writer. He asked whether you came to town at all these days, saying that he would like to have a little very select party for you at his apartment, perhaps just Marianne Moore, or one or two other friends

whom you might like to have. Failing that, he wondered if he could come out to see you with me some
day.

He regretted very much that he had not seen *Many
Loves* when it was done at the Living Theater, and
said that he had heard such wonderful reports on it.
He is eager to read *Dream of Love* and I have sent
him a copy. It would be a big help toward a production, of course, if he could throw his weight behind
it, and also for the book of plays if he will give us a
statement on it. Of course, he may not like it—but I
don't see how he can fail to respond to its great
beauties and human truth.

As ever,

JL

/ · /

Marianne Moore: WCW had known the poet Marianne Moore (1887–
1972) since 1916.

*book of plays: Many Loves and Other Plays: The Collected Plays of William
Carlos Williams* was published by New Directions on September 22,
1961.

135. TLS-2   October 11, 1960

DEAR BILL,

I have been reading your friend Chigounis—very
carefully, and with a good deal of pleasure, for he
obviously has talent—but also with a good deal of
worry, for him, as the picture developed for me of
his situation.

What has happened, I fear, is that he has immersed
himself in your poetry—a good master to go to school
to, but dangerous where the person may not have
enough strength in himself to step on your head, as

it were. In too many of the poems, I feel that he has stayed right with you—not gone on to be himself yet. It isn't parody, because he has feelings of his own and a flair for words, but it is often too much, first, your intonation (not your metric, exactly) and your cadence, the way you have of leaving the sound hanging at the end of a line—truncating for emphasis—and, secondly, even sometimes your kind of observation, of statement.

I am very sympathetic to this lad's problem, because it is one I face myself as a poet—and may, or may not, have solved. You were always the one I felt the most drawn to as an innovator in verse (far more than Ezra, whose style is really very old-fashioned when you analyze it in terms of what you have done with "American"), and it would have been natural and easy for me to do what this boy has done—just take up your manner and method and work in them, with slight visual changes. Chigounis makes his page look different from yours but the "flow" in the lines forces the stuff to sound like you, no matter how he arranges it.

But I knew I had somehow to "fight" you—as well as draw from you. I didn't, of course, sit down soberly and think this out—it gradually, instinctively happened. I think there were two forms that this resistance took. First, there was the entirely artificial visual pattern, that the lines, when typed, had to be the same length with a latitude of two, or at most three, spaces. Of course, this pattern in itself would not do much, but submitting to it would; a poem might pop into my head in your cadence—because I was full of your sounds in my head from reading you—but by the time I had tinkered around to wedge the words into the tight visual form, these enforced word changes would slightly alter the cadence so that it sounded somewhat different—

the stresses and weights would be changed a little.

The second thing is that I try sometimes in my cadences for certain echoes of song or church hymn rhythms and beats—the kinds of tunes I had picked up and hummed as a child. Lilting the lines to myself as I work over the visual pattern helped, I think, to overcome the tendency I naturally have to sound like you.

I believe that Chigounis has got to face up to his derivations from you and take steps—somehow—to sever the cord. You have made yourself an idiom that is, I think, as perfect, for its purpose, as any poetic form. But it's yours—and it's you. Nobody else will ever be able to use it intact and in toto and be an original writer. Isn't this one of the tragedies— and also the glory—of art, that a man's genius creates something perfect, but, in one sense, it has to stop with him? Wasn't the sonnet really finished after Shakespeare had done what he did with it?

Your idiom, Bill, is so unique that no one following you can approach it without danger—it's high tension wire. Creeley and Levertov have run risks coming as close to it as they have. But both of them, I feel, are now finding their own way. They have taken your direct simplicity of statement and they use your ellipses and they write "American" (for the most part—Denise sometimes goes back to her London background)—but they are imposing their own sound patterns on the framework. Creeley helps himself to this by using a fairly formal little stanza, Denise by lengthening out her lines to longer cadences, to a more "chunky", less vertebral kind of structure. Chigounis has got to do something similar for himself. And I don't think anybody can tell him just how to do it. He must work it out inside himself.

But, of course, I would like to encourage him in

some way—not just tell him to start over. It isn't perhaps exactly cricket to find space in *N[ew] D[irections]* for someone who just turned up at dead-line date, when others whose stuff has been around on hand for months, or even years, are deferred to a later number—but—I see how much this fellow means to you personally, and that is a powerful plea for him. Not "inside influence" but respect for you.

So what I suggest is that we work in one or two of the short poems as fillers where prose pieces end high on a page. I think "End of the Cat as a Man" and "Backyard" are my favorites.

How about that? If you approve, I'll write him to that effect. But I think the advice about his future course as a poet would come stronger from you—if you agree that my analysis is right, and feel like tackling it.

> As ever,
> JIM

/ · /

Chigounis: The New Jersey poet and journalist Evans C. Chigounis (1931–) is the author of *Secret Lives* (1972). His poems "Backyard" and "End of the Cat as a Man" appeared in *New Directions in Prose and Poetry 17* (1961).

Creeley and Levertov: New Directions in Prose and Poetry 17 (1961) contained two poems ("Kore" and "The Rain") by Robert Creeley (1926–)and "A Sequence" of five poems and "A Note on the Work of the Imagination," by Denise Levertov, who was born in Ilford, Essex, and lived in London after World War II.

136. ALS-1   5-1-61 [January 5, 1961]

DEAR BILL—

Some good news!
Van Wyck Brooks writes that he *will* do the intro-

duction to the stories—and hopes to have it inside a month.

Isn't that *great?*

I see Zuk's boy Paul has his fiddle concert on February 3rd. Will you be going? Maybe we could go together? Have dinner in town first? Or would you prefer something more jazzy?

Ever,
JIM

/ · /

Van Wyck Brooks: The biographer, critic, and cultural historian Van Wyck Brooks (1886–1963) wrote an introduction for WCW's *The Farmers' Daughters* (1961).

Paul: WCW attended the Carnegie Hall violin recital of Louis Zukofsky's precocious son Paul, whose development WCW had followed since the boy's birth on October 22, 1943. Paul's first Carnegie Hall recital, also attended by WCW, took place on November 30, 1956.

137. TLS-1   Jan. 11/61

DEAR JIM:

Tell your Mother for me that the medicament which I have just begun to use is not designed particularly to induce sleep but as a mood tranquillizer when used in tablespoonful doses 3 times a day. It promises well as far as I have so far gone.

It is called—Alertonic (Merrell) made in Cincinnati a good house. You can get it by the pint without a prescription so far as I know. I'm sure your doctor will approve. It contains no narcotics.

As far as taking you up on your generous offer to house us on our vacation, we can't take you up much as we might like to. We should be too isolated without the free use of a car which with the best will in the world you would be powerless to supply. We're too old to let ourselves in for that sort of thing any more. We both thank Ann especially for her part in the project.

So things are going forward with the printing of the plays satisfactorily. That's good. You realize what a mess we have been going through this summer because of Paul's pending divorce from his wife. It's not over yet but we have high hopes that the end of that impasse may be approaching. We can't just break in and bring matters to an end on our own, Paul has to be his own agent. All we can do is wait a difficult thing for me to do under the circumstances—being constituted as I am.

Small things send me into the clouds or despair alternately. For instance I sold a poem to a magazine named *Epoch* (no pay!). It's really a fine poem, really good for reasons that I privately must respect. It gave me a thrill even to see it again.

If it were not so slow . . .

Affectionately yours
BILL

/ · /

Epoch: WCW's "Iris" was published in *Epoch* (Ithaca, N.Y.), 11, no. 1 (Winter 1961): 22.

138. TLS-1   [Enclosed with 139 and 140.]
March 1, 1961

DEAR JIM:

This is a short short story I got up for you, now. Floss hates it. It's all I have and all I am likely to have. I don't see anything pornographic about it, quite the opposite in fact—but you should hear my wife! Make up your own mind, I give you permission to destroy it if you want to. Make up your own. This is a unique copy. Do not alter except to correct dramatic construction.

Bull
Bɪʟʟ

/ · /

a short short story: On February 27, 1961, JL told WCW that *Esquire* magazine would like to publish a short story of his. WCW sent one entitled "Long Island Sound," but JL did not forward it. The story was first published by Theodora R. Graham in "A New Williams Short Story: 'Long Island Sound' (1961)," *William Carlos Williams Review,* 7, no. 2 (Fall 1981): 1–2.

139. ALS-1 Mar 3/61

DEAR JIM

This should be in your files. —Bill is still in a slump—a *very* bad one—as I *hope* you realized when you read what he sent you. I didn't touch it—so it came *pure!*

Fʟᴏss

140. Signed typescript-2

Long Island Sound

We had to take a boat named the Richard Peck to get there, a days journey paid for by my father on the day when he could get off from the office to make the trip, my younger brother 2 years younger than myself, always behind me—unless I could escape him in some clandestine adventure.

The sea was always beside me at the small boats rail. It excited me extraordinately, just to feel that it was there just out of reach at the ship's rail was enough to do it, even in New York harbor with it's buildings and smells was enough to do it but as the distances, not great at any time increased, my excitement increased. I was bound away from N.Y. on a vacation, on a vacation by the sea, not further than to New Haven where adventures awaited me of which I knew nothing.

But of one thing I was pretty sure, there would invariably be an encounter with girls as intimate as I could make it. I knew nothing about girls, timid as my approach to them would be, it was at that age when I would have given anything for a mere view of a girl in her skin toward whom I hankered with an eagerness which was not to be attained for many years later. Not that summer at any rate.

Just that summer what I discovered my interest in girls, to me at the time the most recondite of a man's interest in the world. And alongside that I had discovered their interest in me, that they were moved to seek me out and make much of me at all parties and dances wherever I should discover them. But at the same time, was it perhaps my own pretty face, I was still just a boy, attracted me to them—it was a dilemma which was resolved for me during my entire life.

I loved women and should continue to love them as I should to continue to love them to the edge of the grave. The males were there and I had to deal with them casually as it should happen as I went along but girls occupied my first interest.

This first summer at the shore was proof enough of my real interest and success with women. There was a small girl at the same boarding house with whom I was determined to get to bed with—just here I made my first observation: I didn't want to more than gain her consent to my fumbling man- oeuvers which accomplished nothing but from which I came away completely rested.

Something had happened completely disasso- ciated with any sexual I might presumably have pos- sessed which I was too young and inexperienced to link with love but vaguely identified with the divine passion and I knew it and made the correct associa- tions. Love! and close behind it the terrifying—but thrilling image which I didn't for a moment recog- nise as Poetry which should possess me for my entire life.

My childish companion got up from the hayloft where we had been lying and both relieved I take it, went out to play on a swinging ramp which I and the rest of the boys had erected. And we collected a variety of flowers which when we had had enough of that we chucked away and returned to our board- ing house dinner which we had completed for our morning adventure.

WILLIAM CARLOS WILLIAMS

141. TLS-1   Mar. 13/61

DEAR JIM:

Before it is too late I want to propose one of my final books together, a book of my as yet unpub- lished poems—in book form. I am now assembling them together with a foreword as you will see. Put this book aside to be published when the time is ripe— within a year from now as far as I can tell. I'll have the MSS collated and mailed to [word missing] as rapidly as I can. I think copies should be made of this without delay and mailed back for Floss to record, I'll be careful not to put the thing into typescript until I am ready to do so but count on you to make the final copy.

I don't know what is happening to me the last few days but it seems serious I dont want to over hurry myself but before I lose the opportunity to speak something warns me not to delay. Maybe I had best bundle everything together and get it off. If I decide in the end to do that the condition of the script will reveal it; I feel that I shouldn't delay.

Devotedly yours
BILL

/ · /

a book: WCW's *Pictures from Brueghel and Other Poems* was published by New Directions on June 26, 1962. It won the Pulitzer Prize for poetry in 1963, after the poet's death.

142. TLS-1   Mar. 17/61

DEAR JIM:

However great the difficulties there is nothing for me to do—in the spirit of St Patrick—but to continue to make a record of my poetry as long as I can looking toward better days which may or may not come. With this in mind I must tell you how pleased I was to get your last postscript to your letter saying you would print the recent and final edition of the poems. To keep my hand in, there is nothing for me to do but to continue typing as well as I can lest I lose the ability to put the record down at all, it's surprising, as has been brought in on me, how easily the ability can be lost. A last slip in the verbal ability and I would be reduced to an inability to communicate at all. This can be frightening it may happen, I'll do my best to keep you forewarned of the approaching event.

Meanwhile I must continue to type each day, because I realize that it is no more than a nervous phenomenon but nonetheless formidable. A transitory (I think!) pain in my kidney region may be warning of a catastrophe.

It is very understanding of you to have replied as you did.

Affectionately yours
BILL

143. TLS-1 April 15, 1961

DEAR JIM:

The check from *Harper's* was very welcome, suppose I should welcome it with open arms. I'll see what I can do.

I'm sending you another poem on the recent trip of the Russians to outer-space, just written, one of the best I have ever done, when Suzy has had a chance to copy it for me you shall have it disposed of as you think best. Send it along shortly.

Pretty uncertain on my pins lately, took a header recently, fortunately did not hurt myself over much.

Look for this new poem of mine.

Sincerely yours,
BILL

/ · /

Harper's: Two poems by WCW, "Song" and "The Children," were published in *Harper's Magazine,* June 1961, p. 85.

poem: WCW's "Heel & Toe to the End," *Saturday Review of Literature,* July 8, 1961, p. 31, celebrates the first manned space flight, which was carried out by the Russian cosmonaut Yuri Gagarin on April 12, 1961.

Suzy: WCW's granddaughter Suzanne was born to Paul and Virginia Williams on August 5, 1944. In 1960 WCW published a poem about her entitled "Suzy."

144. ALS-1.   [Return address:] c/o City Lights,
261 Columbus Ave, San Francisco
7/8/61

DEAR BILL—

I was so happy to have your card that you liked the book of plays. I do, too, and I think it is going to make a big impression. I am writing to Bob [MacGregor] to propose a special letter or circular that will go to drama people, theater directors, the profs who teach drama in the "beaneries."

When shall we start on the book of poems? I know it's tough for you to type—so ask Floss to let me have your thoughts on this in due course. Are there enough new poems that have not been in any book for a small paperback? Or should we group old ones (that Jack T[hirlwall] has found) with new ones?

San Francisco is great. I've rented a pretty little flat right on the water in Tiburon, across the bay, and am getting a lot of work done. I've "rationed" Rexroth. He's recently divorced and would like to go out every night with a different dame, but I've laid down the law—only twice a week for me. He really is very funny, though, and a big wheel out here now because of his newspaper columns in the *Examiner*. The restauranteurs all grovel before him.

Seeing quite a bit of [Lawrence] Ferlinghetti, too, who is a very all right guy—so modest despite his great success.

Best to you all!
JIM

/ · /

Rexroth: In 1961, Kenneth Rexroth was divorced from his third wife, Marthe Larsen. From January 31, 1961, to 1968 he wrote an informal column on a variety of subjects for the *San Francisco Examiner*.

145. TLS-1   Aug. 7, 1961

DEAR JIM:

Not that it would have made any important difference to the worlds peace but at just time of my sending you the final draught of the poems I thought my mind had finally given up the ghost. I made one last copy of the poems and called it a day destroying the record once and for all.

So that you the copies in the collection now still in your hands which Flossie rescued from the garbage man cleaned me out.

With the partial return of my wits I have realized close I was to losing the final touch with the world. I was sure that unless something drastic happened to the U S mails I was still safe but the margin was by far too narrow. One slip and I would have been lost. Stupid but the facts of the case.

And there are 5 or 6 poems written since the collapse of wits which warrant inclusion.

Therefore excluding the poems rescued from the garbage by Floss nothing remains. What a fool I have made of myself.

The one perfect copy of the poems is in your pos-

session. As soon as you are ready I shall be over-
joyed to see that you have started the composition.
    I am beginning to get reports of the other books!

Gratefully yours
BILL

/ · /

garbage: Having made a clean copy of the poems in *Pictures from Brueghel,*
WCW tore it into pieces and threw it into the garbage can. FW retrieved
the typescript, patched it back together, and sent it to JL.

146. TLS-1   Aug. 16/61

DEAR JIM:

    It's a great satisfaction to me to get news of the
new book of poems. By all means make it a paperback, always wanted it to be paper-back from the
first. Hooray! And I will be tremendously pleased if
Random House will grant you permission to include
Journey to Love under the same title—for that matter
I was about to say I wish *Desert Music* would come
under the same category but Flossie tells me Random House is still paying me royalties on that.
    I am making slow but definite progress in the state
of my health as my typing shows. I think. I should
be steadier in my psychiatric stability but that takes
time—maybe it is gone forever. These delicate
adjustments of psychologic balances take time but
with the removal of certain family imbalances there
is still a chance that I will right myself.
    When we come to finishing the book up, there
may be some minimal additions to make—a poem
out of the *Middlebury Quarterly* etc etc
    I don't want to strain my ability to the breaking

point so I'd better quit now. Best to Ann and your charming daughter whom I met earlier this year.

> Take care of yourself Jim
> BILL

/ · /

Journey to Love: Both *Journey to Love* (1955) and *The Desert Music* (1954) were republished in *Pictures from Brueghel and Other Poems* (1962).
family imbalances: The divorce of WCW's son Paul became final in 1961.
Middlebury Quarterly: There has apparently never been a magazine called the *Middlebury Quarterly.* It is not clear what poem or magazine WCW has in mind.

147. ACS

Jan 8/62

DEAR JIM—

The Braziller collection of the Brueghel pictures, spells Brueghel with the *u* before the *e,* and since that is the collection we have and that Bill used—let it stand.

Lower case the names of flowers & birds says Bill & make any necessary corrections in spelling. Wish I could do a better job in this matter—but everything irritates Bill—so I just spot the obvious things & let the rest go—and dump it in your lap!— Thanks.—

> As ever—
> FLOSS

/ · /

Braziller collection: WCW consulted several art books when he wrote "Pictures from Brueghel." One of them was Gustav Glück's *Peter Brueghel the Elder,* 6th ed. (New York: George Braziller, 1952).

148. TLS-1.

[Uncorrected]
April 3/62-31

DEAR JIM: (31)

I fnally got your letter enclosing your letter enclo-
cussing your letter which was so ompportant foe me,
thannkuok yuon very much. In time this fainful bsi-
ness will will soonfeul will soon be onert. Tnany
anany goodness. If S lossiee eii wyyonor wy sinfsigna-
ture.

I hope I hope I make it

BILL

⟨Dear Jim—Bill wants so much to communicate with
you—He has great difficulty as you can see—but he
insists that it be sent.

Best as always
FLOSS⟩

149. TLS-1

Nov. 11, 1962

DEAR JIM:

I received this morning the notice from england
about my books, it shows, according to what the
critics say, a lively interest in my books. If it only
showed a corresponding penetration on the part of
the critics I'd be made. Their leaders, or they that
should lead them have gone far astray—much to my
loss.

Maybe it is still not too late but I doubt it.

You have been very faithful, it is deeply appreciated. I wish I could write as I could formerly.

Affectionately
BILL

/ · /

notice: The English poet Tom Raworth (1938–) had expressed an interest in publishing a British edition of *Paterson*.

APPENDIX

[This autobiographical story was written by JL after a visit to WCW's home in Rutherford on April 8, 1960. It was first published in the *William Carlos Williams Newsletter* 4, no. 1 (Spring 1978): 1–9.]

A VISIT

MacDonald found a spot for his car not far from the house. The town was growing. Since his last visit, two years before, they had installed parking meters. He put in his nickel and crossed to the little frame dwelling that stood on a raised bank, with concrete steps going up to the door from the sidewalk. It was April but the bushes around the house weren't in bud yet, and the strip of lawn on the bank was more brown than green. The house had been recently painted—a light gray with dark green shutters—and looked neat if not handsome. MacDonald knew that it had been built for the Evanses just before the first world war and that they had lived there ever since. Although Evans had tapered off his practice some ten years ago, his faded shingle was still mounted

beside the door: HOMER C. EVANS, Attorney-at-
Law.

MacDonald rang the doorbell and in a moment a
small, old colored woman in a cook's apron let him
in. He threw his coat on a chair as she called up the
stairs: "Mister Evans . . . man here to see you," and
went back to the kitchen. MacDonald went into the
living room—it wasn't large but light came in through
tall windows—and studied the paintings on the wall
while he waited. They were all good ones—gifts to
Evans from painters he had known. There was a
lovely, delicate Demuth of red flowers and green
leaves—very abstract in its design and the colors
subtle. And a strange Graves bird—no kind of a bird
you could name but very much bird—a dark form,
only the feet and the beak drawn sharply, on a soft
gray wash; it had an oriental feeling. And a Hartley,
a forest scene, the logs and rocks like crude chunks,
thickly painted with heavy black outlines. And over
the fireplace a Marin, a view looking out over some
beach that must be in Maine—those wonderful free
slaps and slashes of the water-color brush, an inspired
jumble of bits and patches of pure color with the
white of the paper left showing between them. Evans
had been friends with all these painters. He had written poems to most of them.

The furniture in the room was in no way "interesting," no particular style and heavily worn. Evans'
daughters had grown up in this room and now
brought their children there for Sunday visits. At
one end of the room was a tier of shelves built across
the corner that always attracted MacDonald. There,
filling nearly four shelves, were all of Evans' books,
from the first little green pamphlet that had been
printed at his mother's expense by the local newspaper printer to the collected volumes of his poems
and essays. And the three books about him, and runs

of the magazines he had helped to edit, and the translations into foreign languages. MacDonald had read most of them and had copies of many of them at home. Five of them had been published by his firm.

As he moved about the room, taking it in, he heard a noise from upstairs that he couldn't at first identify. It was a series of regular, repeated sounds—first a kind of soft scrape and then a little thump . . . then another scrape and thump. Suddenly it struck him; Evans must be dragging himself downstairs, holding onto the bannister and dragging one leg that had lost its mobility. It had gotten to that, the poor man could hardly walk anymore!

MacDonald rushed into the hall to see if he could help him, but Evans was already down and moving carefully toward the living room. MacDonald had an impulse to embrace him, to throw his arms around him, but he checked it. He did take Evans' hand in both of his and held it as he greeted him.

"Gosh, Hank, it's great to see you, it's really great." And without waiting for Evans to speak, "You're looking wonderful!" MacDonald said this because it seemed the cheerful thing to say to a man who had been through the mill with his health—two years of one thing after another. But as they moved into the living room and he could study him in the light, MacDonald saw that his remark was true. Evans looked older and his hair, what there was of it, was white, but his figure was erect and his face ruddy and little lined for a man in his late seventies. He was wearing spectacles with much thicker lenses—the last bout in the hospital had been an operation for cataracts—but the magnifying effect of the glasses made his eyes appear even more lively than usual.

Evans had wonderful eyes. People remembered his eyes. He had always been rather handsome in a crisp, lean-faced, eager-looking way, but his eyes—gray-green with a dancing light in them, a merriment in them—were the dominant feature. He could never have been much of a poker player with such expressive eyes. Every movement from a mind that was constantly in motion came through them. And now the magnification of the lenses brought this play of feeling even closer to the person near him.

They sat down together on the old sofa and Evans told him, speaking very deliberately (MacDonald had been warned by Mrs. Evans when he telephoned to announce his visit that the worst effect of the illness was in her husband's speech), that he had missed seeing him and that he was glad he had driven out.

Evans was sprucely dressed—perhaps even for the occasion—in a rather sporty tweed jacket, a dark blue shirt and a pert little bow-tie of the same shade of blue. This must be the garb of retirement, the final break with the profession of law, for MacDonald couldn't remember ever having seen him before in anything but a conservative business suit.

In his poetry and in the essays—those "Letters from Nowhere" with which he had peppered the magazines for years, having his say in free-wheeling style about anything that caught his eye or crossed his mind, from the new book by a young unknown to the probable effect of syphilis on Beethoven's music, Evans had always been as unrestrained in language, as unconcerned with taboos, as the newest would-be Rimbaud in the Village or North Beach. He had kept young with the youngest, and this had been a part of his appeal to successive generations. He didn't date. In his writing there was neither pontification nor withdrawal to a protected height. At seventy he could still be playful, at times a little ingenuous. But in his personal life he was very much the respectable, small-town lawyer, and he had always dressed the part.

To his neighbors in Hampton Evans was still more the man to whom they had gone to write their wills, or whom they could still call for free advice if some woman driver dented their fender and her husband wouldn't pay up than the poet who had won a Pulitzer Prize. Of course there had been quite a stir in Hampton when Evans had been homogenized with a picture story in *Life* (an accolade of banality which had had the curious effect of prompting some of his townsfolk clients to pay their bills for his services which had gone forgotten, and undunned, for years), but he had never in the least resented this lack of local recognition of his literary stature, this public separation of the halves of his life.

In fact, the busy mixture of two full careers had been the taut spring that kept the mechanism turning. A vintage portable Corona had always sat at one side on the desk in his law office and phrases for a poem or ideas for a "Letter from Nowhere" would be pecked out on it between calls when they drifted into his head. And some of his best poems had had their birth in the county courthouse in pencil scrawlings on the margins of a brief.

With Evans creation was a matter of spontaneous (and sometimes almost continuous) combustion. Even on weekends he seldom had time to sit down to write with an open space of a whole morning before him. He had to catch the sparks as they flew. And how they flew! It was as if he were under a rain of cosmic rays, invisible pellets that showered him from God knew where, leaving marks on the sensitive plate in his mind which were immediately translated into images made of words. And the greater the pressure of law work, the more intense the bombardment. On vacations, when he did have free time, he wrote less than during the crowded rest of the year.

This way of writing had certainly influenced his style. With its ellipses and leaps from image to image it was almost a poetic shorthand. There was something skeletal about his poems, even the long ones. Evans had no time to hammer out ornamentation, or to fashion much flesh between the bones. Part of the power of his poetry was in its very rawness, the fresh bite of the perception coming through to the reader as directly as it had to the poet in the simple, uncluttered phrasing. Of course, there was an elegance too; a man with an ear doesn't work with words fifty years for nothing. And it was not automatic writing; Evans did revise and rework. In the evenings, or on weekends, he would tinker with the sheets of drafts, trying different sequences and combinations. But he had never won the good opinion of the professor-critics for whom a poet must be as intricate as a complicated machine. Evans' work was not a happy hunting ground for the exegetes. An Evans poem said what it had to say at first reading. It offered no temptation to the academic maggots.

The force of this life that had put together two such different impulses—the down-to-earth setting things in order of homely law work and the wild escape into free imagination, into a kind of intentional dis-ordering, of poetry—came across to MacDonald as he sat close to Evans, more or less silently studying him as the old man searched for and found his words. A frail but electric little man who all his life had had command of words, could summon them instantly to his use, and now, like the nightmare of a runner who cannot move his legs in his bad dream, a very nasty joke of fate, had to fight

to bring them from his brain to his tongue. Mac-
Donald could see how this injustice hurt Evans' pride.
The poet became silent and began to look at his hands,
rubbing one with the other. The hands were the only
part of him which really betrayed his age. They were
mottled with dark spots of brown and some of the
veins stood up like blue vines on the skin.

"I've been rubbing Helen's neck for her," he said.
"She still gets those bad stiff necks and they can't
seem to do anything about it. So I give her . . . I
give her . . ." and the word that he wanted simply
wouldn't come.

"Massages," said MacDonald. You had to help
him, you had to. At first you didn't want to show
in any way that you took notice of his problem. But
then you had to answer the appeal that came in the
eyes that turned to you as the tongue searched for
the word.

"I give her a little massage sometimes," said Evans,
going over it as if to show that he could do it.

Then he laughed. And that was another thing that
people always remembered about Evans, the way he
laughed. It was a soft, musical bark which carried
his voice into a range where it had a special timbre.
It made MacDonald think back to the sound of a
gong he had once heard in a Burmese temple. He
had given a coin in alms to an old man sitting cross-
legged on the stair landing of a hill pagoda in Mandalay and the man had struck a small bronze gong
with a little hammer as a prayer for him . . . and
MacDonald had recognized Evans' laughter. A laugh
and a prayer.

"It's tough, Marsh, it's tough. And it makes you
mad. I don't try to go over to the city anymore. I
still want to see people, I want to find out what's
going on over there, what the painters are doing now,

but I can't handle it. I try to talk to people and it wears me out. I have to let Helen do most of my talking for me now."

MacDonald couldn't find much to say. He just kept smiling at Evans, looking into his face and smiling. Somehow it seemed indecent to make useless conversation, even if he could have, when Evans had to fight so for every sentence. And if he only had half an hour with him it didn't seem right that he himself should take even a minute of it.

"She reads to me, too. The kids all send me their books and she reads them aloud to me. Some of them are good, too. That girl that you published what's her name . . ."

"Campbell . . . Daphne Campbell."

"That's the one. She's all right. I think she's got it. A lot of them have got it. They've figured it out. It's taken thirty years but they've caught on. It's American now. It really sounds the way we sound. It isn't just warmed-over England anymore. You know what I mean, we've talked about this before. There was Whitman, and then . . . the Chicago fellow, cats' feet . . ."

"Sandburg," said MacDonald.

"Yes, Sandburg, and then the rest of us. But Pound never looked for it . . . all that Greek and Italian . . . and his crazy Chinese, singing Chinese to himself down there in the bughouse. He's the end of the other thing. And Eliot just going backwards as fast as he could pedal—let them have him over there if they want him."

"You were the one, Hank, you really broke it loose. You know that."

"Well, I tried all right—God damn it, I tried. It took me ten years to find out what I wanted to do, to get out from under all that load of crap they piled on me in college . . ." Evans laughed again. "No, it's not crap, it's beautiful. I still read it. Helen reads it to me. We were reading Marlowe the other day, it was marvelous—it gave me the gooseflesh. But that wasn't for us you see, it couldn't do anything for us with what we were up against. We had to find out some way to do it for ourselves, some way so that it would sound like us. Ezra just dug in the backyard. The best ear, but he didn't want to listen to people talking over here. It was always music to him, hearing the music in all those old languages he boned up on. I don't think he knows yet what I was up to—the arrogant bastard! But you've got to hand it to him . . ." Evans shook his head. He was still rubbing one hand with the other.

"But these kids know what they've got to do and they're going on with it. I don't want them to copy me you understand. I give them hell when they're just doing what I did. They've got to go further with it. I don't know if I ever really made it a metric. But what is metric anyway? I read all the books about it once and I still don't know. But I know you've got to have it, it has to be there. It has to be speech and something else, too. It's nothing to do with scansion or tum-tee-tum but there has to be a base under the way the lines fall. I thought I had it the way I wanted it in 'Long Night,' I thought that was as far as I could go with it, but I'm not sure. I've still got more to do . . . and how am I going to do it now?"

"That was a great poem you had in *Poetry* last month," MacDonald said, "you never wrote anything better than that, Hank. That's a great poem."

"Well, I keep after it. I'm still pretty good with my left." Evans held up his hands in front of him and looked at them, as if they belonged to somebody else. "This one is pretty well shot—the fingers won't do what I want them to anymore. But I can still type with my left. I peck it out—without the capitals, it's too slow to hunt for that shift—and then Helen fixes it up for me. It still wants to come out. You'd think it would quit when everything else is going but it's still there. Some mornings it even wakes me up. I can't wait to get dressed or eat my breakfast. But it takes so long now to work it out. It's there and I know the words I want for it but I don't have them. I just have to sit till they come out of that fog in there. She can't help me on that. Sometimes it take the whole morning to work it out, just ten or twenty lines in a whole morning—or I have to go back to it the next day."

It was almost more than MacDonald could bear. There wasn't a shred of self-pity in it—Evans wasn't asking for sympathy, he was just telling it like facts— but it made a pain come in the back of MacDonald's throat as if he were going to cry.

"Does it bother you if I smoke, Hank?" He had to break it up.

"No, go ahead. Say, would you like a drink of something? We've got some bourbon around. They still let me have that, thank God."

"No, thanks, Hank, I've got to drive back to town." MacDonald took out his pipe and filled and lit it. This business helped him over the hump and he got ahold of himself. But Evans had more that he wanted to say.

"It's a funny thing that I can't quit. I sit here and take it . . . and you know I've never been able to write about death. I never had anything to say about it. All those poems and almost nothing about death in any of them. I don't like it, Marsh. I'm afraid of it. I have to rest a lot now but I don't sleep much. I just have to lie there and face up to it—that pretty soon now I'm not going to be around. That's just a lot of shit about people being ready to die. And you know I've never been able to get anywhere with the idea of anything coming after. You go out like a light and you're out. I believe that. I don't expect anything else. But this thing won't stop. It's as strong now as it ever was, maybe stronger. And I don't think it's just habit. Maybe it is, but I don't think so. It's like there was somebody else in there. Look at me. I can't talk, this is more than I've talked in six months. I'm ready to fall apart, but this thing is at me just as hard as ever."

MacDonald couldn't take any more. It was outside him, it wasn't happening to him, but he couldn't deal with it. He got up and looked at his watch.

"I guess I'd better get moving, Hank. I have to be back in town for dinner."

"Wait a minute now. I know Helen wants to see you."

Evans got up, hobbled into the hall and called up the stairs to his wife. She must have been waiting for his signal as she came right down. She shook hands with MacDonald, rather formally but with warmth in her greeting, and they sat down again in the living room. She was wearing a red silk dress with little black figures in it—a young woman's dress, MacDonald thought, but it suited her.

Helen Evans was nearly the same age as her husband but she too had kept herself young looking. As a girl—MacDonald had seen pictures of her then—she had been trim and slender, and she still was. You would have called the young woman in the pictures pretty; now she was something more than that—not beautiful perhaps but very close to it. In the past MacDonald had thought her a little prim. Compared to her husband who talked easily, almost intimately, to anyone, she had always been reserved, seeming to hold herself back, whether from shyness or because her mother had trained her in oldfashioned ladylike dignity MacDonald didn't know. But now she appeared much more relaxed, smiling and talking to him as if to a close friend. He wondered whether she might always have been a little in awe of her husband, easygoing as he was, deferring to his genius, or rather to her conception of it, for certainly modest, self-critical Evans would never have wanted to be put on a pedestal. Now that his illness had made him so dependent on her in his writing she was growing more self-confident, more sure of her right to be the wife of a man in whom she had always seen so much more greatness than the world had at first recognized.

There was really no reason, MacDonald thought, for her ever having had any feeling of insufficiency except, probably, the very great love, the devotion, that had made Helen Evans the good wife that she had been. Evans had never made much money and she had worked hard for him, cooking meals, keeping house, raising their two girls. The servant who had answered the door was something new in the household. A small-town lawyer does not earn large fees, even if he collects them all, which Evans could never force himself to do. And he was always taking on legal problems for indigent writer and artist friends without any fee at all. Nor does a poet, even a Pulitzer Prize winning poet, take in from his writing in a year, or three years, what a writer of popular fiction will get for one story in the *Saturday Evening Post*. What there was of extra money after living expenses and the annuity premiums were paid went to the girls, putting them through Barnard and Bryn Mawr and helping them get settled in their own homes as they married solid young men, but with small starting salaries, one a professor and one a lawyer, and began having children. It hadn't been a hard life— they had had many friends and never been in debt after the house mortgage was paid off—but it had been a life of hard work and little leisure. And now, when literary recognition had finally come and at the same time retirement from the law, there had been Evans' sudden loss of his health, completely unexpected as he had never been seriously ill before. Yet she seemed to MacDonald to have blossomed under this pressure. A happy woman was talking to him and the thing that made her beautiful, as she now was, was the radiance of her fulfillment.

They talked about her children and grandchildren and about MacDonald's children while Evans listened in silence, resting. MacDonald had a daughter who was reaching the age to be interested in boys— a phase which he was anticipating with some alarm— and Mrs. Evans had some good (and humorous) advice to give him on the problem. Evans did not add to the conversation but a few of his wife's reminiscences about their daughters brought out his laughter. Fearful of tiring him, MacDonald soon took his leave. Evans got up from the sofa to see him off. Then they both stood out on the stoop, saying their goodbyes, as MacDonald went down the steps and crossed to his car.

The indicator of the parking meter showed red— he had stayed longer than he planned to or should have—but there was no ticket. He felt cheerful again as he pulled into the traffic of Elm Street and headed back toward New York. The talk about death had made him grieve for Evans, but now the glow of the man's wonderful spirit had driven the pain away. Driving along, MacDonald found himself fitting together bits of what Evans had told him with lines that came back to him from the poetry. Particularly he remembered passages in the one attempt which Evans had made at a novel. This book came along fairly early in Evans' career, and had been billed as a novel but was really more a long series of lyrical reflections and descriptions, largely autobiographical, something in the nature of an interior travelogue. What plot it had concerned a young man's struggle to reconcile an overwhelming urge to write with the practical demands of conventional life. There was a girl whom the writer loved, though not with the same intensity that he gave to his writing. In the book the girl had left him—and the man in the book had not much cared. MacDonald thought about that (when he had first read the book this exit of the girl had seemed very unconvincing) and about the scene he had just witnessed—a love scene indeed, if you weren't afraid of being sentimental: a pair of lovers who had really come through together, who had really "made it."

MacDonald was well outside Hampton when it suddenly came to him that he had entirely forgotten the main purpose of his mission. It had completely slipped his mind—though he had thought about it long and seriously before coming. He had wanted to tell Evans that he was sorry.

There had been trouble in their relationship of author and publisher, rather bad trouble. MacDonald, as a young man starting in business for himself, had taken on Evans at a time when the poet's career, or at least his acceptance by the public, was in the doldrums. It was soon after the Depression and no one of Evans' early publishers wanted to continue with him. His name was well known in highbrow literary circles but poetry was not selling. For three or four years Evans had published no new books and most of his older ones had gone out of print. MacDonald had seen the opportunity to start his list with a writer who could give it literary prestige, who could set a standard for what he hoped would follow. He brought out Evans' backed-up books and re-issued some of the best that were out of print. He put Evans back into active circulation, for which the poet had been very grateful, the gratitude taking the forms of a kindly and generous friendship. They grew very close, with Evans assuming for MacDonald the role of a literary father.

This was at first a wonderfully exciting experience for MacDonald, but as time went along, without being aware of it, he began to take Evans too much for granted. As his business grew he became interested in other writers and, perhaps only because they were demanding, while Evans never made any demands—it just wasn't his way—he had worked harder at promoting these other writers' books than he had ever done for Evans. He went on publishing Evans, but, without intending to, and always thinking of him as a dear friend whose work he venerated, he neglected him. It came to the point, during the war, when paper for books was rationed along with most other commodities, that he put Evans off when a new book was ready, pleading the paper shortage, although it was obvious that he had paper enough for books by S. and B. (whose work happened to be easier to sell).

At the time MacDonald had had no understanding of what he was doing to Evans, so it came to him as a brutal shock when Evans, as tactfully as he could, suggested that he might best accept an offer that came to him "out of the blue" (he had not gone to look for it) from another firm. MacDonald took it hard. He had come to feel that Evans was almost a personal possession, something to which his merit in publishing him when others were not eager had given him title. MacDonald was a great believer in his own virtue and fully expected his just rewards for it. He had illusions about gratitude and had always expected that Evans' gratitude would go on forever.

MacDonald imagined that Evans had betrayed him

and wrote some bitter letters in which the word "knife" was prominent. Evans had replied with restraint but MacDonald's tone confirmed his decision and he went his way. MacDonald assumed a posture of injured benevolence, complaining very caustically to his intimates of the bad treatment he had received. His correspondence with Evans dropped off to a trickle of business letters. If they met at some gathering MacDonald was formally cordial; Evans was good-humored but at a loss for much to say to him. MacDonald could usually put up a good front of equanimity but inside he was a brooder. In certain moods his thoughts would focus, as if magnetized, on someone he supposed had wronged him and he would indulge himself in fantasies of revenge— nothing violent, but complicated strategems for humiliating the offender. And he would snap at his wife if she happened, quite innocently, so much as to mention one of these occupants of his doghouse.

Things went along thus for several years—no drastic rupture, but their old friendship in abeyance. Then one morning there arrived on MacDonald's desk a large manila envelope addressed in the familiar Evans hand. Inside it was the typescript of a new manuscript, the sequel to an earlier poetic narrative which MacDonald had published, with a note inquiring if he would not like to undertake it since he had already on his list the earlier volumes in the sequence. MacDonald read it through without opening the rest of the day's mail. It was a beautiful poem which brought all his true love for Evans' work, and for Evans himself, flooding back. Within the hour he had Evans on the telephone and it was as if nothing had ever come between them—all the hurt, and the resentment, disappeared as if it had never existed.

Sometimes, in the following years, MacDonald would remember what had happened, but it did not cause him pain. It was like remembering his automobile accident—something unpleasant that had occurred, leaving no recollection in the flesh of the actual pain. And nothing was ever said, or written, between them about it. They saw each other now and then, wrote to each other frequently about all manner of things, but were careful to skirt the subject of the break. Yet MacDonald had begun to feel that something should be said about it. He felt no need that Evans should bring it up but it grew on him that he wanted Evans to know that he, who had been in the wrong, had finally realized where the fault had lain. He wanted to tell Evans that he was sorry he had been so blind, and so ugly.

That was his real purpose in going to Hampton that day. Somehow in his absorption as Evans had talked to him he had forgotten all about it. But the need to go through with it was all the stronger now because Evans had been so affectionate with him, had confided so much. As quickly as he could MacDonald swung his car off the highway and turned around. It was late, but he had to go back.

Mrs. Evans answered the bell at the door. "Oh, Marshall, it's you. Did you forget something?"

"No, not exactly. Excuse me for bothering you, Helen, it's just that there was something quite important I meant to say to Hank and I didn't. It won't take a minute. I know he's tired, but I won't stay a minute."

Mrs. Evans seemed a little more than surprised, almost annoyed, but she let him come in. "Well he's gone up to rest before supper. I hate to get him down again. The stairs are so hard for him now. Couldn't I give him the message?"

MacDonald was stumped for a moment, then came out with: "Please, Helen, let me go up to him. Just a second. It's something sort of just between us."

She must have read what was in his mind because her manner changed. She gave him a smile and told him to go upstairs. "You remember where his room is, don't you, Marshall? To the right of the stairs." MacDonald raced up the stairs without taking off his coat. The bedroom door was ajar. He gave a light tap and took a step inside. The room was half dark but he could make out Evans lying on the bed, on his back, with a blanket over him. Was he asleep? If he were, he couldn't wake him. But Evans heard him and asked, "Supper ready?"

"It's not Helen, Hank. It's me, Marshall. May I bother you?"

"What's that . . . Marshall? I thought . . ."

Evans raised himself on his pillows and snapped on the bedside table lamp. He was in his shirtsleeves with his tie off. He fumbled for his glasses on the table. MacDonald put them in his hand and sat down on the bed beside him. His words came tumbling out.

"I'm sorry to disturb you, Hank, but I forgot to tell you the most important thing, what I really came to see you for. You see I . . . I don't know just how to . . . well I have to make sure that you knew that I was sorry."

"Sorry? I don't see what . . ."

"About what happened between us. Only really it was what I did to you. I can understand that now and I wanted to tell you I was sorry I wrote those letters . . . and all the rest of it."

Evans had been startled at first—he had been lying in the gloom with his eyes closed thinking about something that happened a long, long time ago, something that happened in Venice when he was only . . . how old had he been, twenty-four? twenty-three? . . . it was the summer after law school that he took that trip . . . they had been sitting at evening at a café table in St. Mark's square, with the flocks of pigeons wheeling through the dusk—he was startled, but then he took it in and he began to laugh. It wasn't the big laugh this time, but a little, soft prolonged chuckle, and his head nodded from side to side as he pulled the good left hand out from beneath the blanket, felt for MacDonald's hand and covered it with his.

"Why, Marsh," he said, "you didn't have to come back here to tell me that. I knew that. I knew it when it happened. I knew you didn't mean all that stuff you wrote me."

"I guess I did mean it then. But I shouldn't have. And I don't now." He gave Evans' hand a squeeze and got up. "I'll get out of here now. I'm sorry I woke you up."

"You didn't," said Evans, "I was just lying here . . . thinking of . . . of . . . Venice, of all things." And as MacDonald left him, "But I'm glad you came back."

INDEX